Shock Wave

Burton Seavey

Treasure House

An Imprint of

Destiny Image₍ᵣ₎ Publishers, Inc.
P.O. Box 310
Shippensburg, PA 17257-0310

"For where your treasure is,
there will your heart be also." Matthew 6:21

ISBN 1-56043-283-7

For Worldwide Distribution
Printed in the U.S.A.

This book and all other Destiny Image, Revival Press,
and Treasure House books are available
at Christian bookstores and distributors worldwide.

For a U.S. bookstore nearest you, call **1-800-722-6774**.
For more information on foreign distributors, call **717-532-3040**.
Or reach us on the Internet: **http://www.reapernet.com**

Dedication

My son Eric was four years old when we wakened in the morning to find that a heavy blanket of snow had fallen. With shovel in hand I set about the task of removing it. Not knowing that my young adventurer had hurriedly dressed and followed me to the task, I took my usual strides through the heavy white stuff. Then, in the stillness that only new-fallen snow can produce, I heard a familiar voice behind me saying, "Daddy, take smaller steps, 'cause I'm following in your footsteps." Those words would prove to be prophetic.

Eric is not four years old anymore and his stride is as long as my own. Because his heart has caught the vision of a matured and supernaturally empowered Church, he works untiringly with me in ministry. I humbly dedicate this book to my son, my *friend*, Eric.

Contents

Foreword

In these highly crucial moments that humanity now faces, we are all in urgent need of having a true orientation of what Christianity is all about. We also need to know what is happening around the world, especially in the subject of spiritual warfare.

Readers will find in Rev. Burton Seavey's book, Shock Wave, deep Christian convictions and inspiring, dynamic, and forthright teachings on every page that will give them practical and workable solutions to achieving their maximum potential in God's Kingdom.

I have known Rev. Burton Seavey for almost 25 years. I was exposed to his powerful ministry, and I count it a blessing to recommend this book.

Dr. Omar Cabrera

Introduction

Listen! The *shock wave* is coming! It's a sound from heaven of a rushing mighty wind that will impact the remotest parts of the globe; it will mature and equip the saints, and sweep vast multitudes into the Kingdom of God. The Holy Spirit has begun to stir. And we, His Church of this generation, are privileged to be not only *witnesses*, but *participants* in the drama that is about to unfold. Throughout the centuries revivals have come and gone with predictable regularity—approximately every 50 years. Some have been regional in scope, others more far-reaching, influencing whole nations; and periodically, powerful moves of the Holy Spirit have even impacted the entire world.

I hesitate to refer to the next great shock wave of the Holy Spirit simply as a *revival* because it will encompass far more than that. The word *revival* means the rekindling of something that has existed before. By that definition then, that which is about to transpire in the Church cannot be called a revival, because it has never been achieved before. For the Church to become what God intended, of necessity it must first be revived. But it will then move beyond to a position of greatness never attained in any prior generation.

The perception of *what could be* runs as a thread throughout the Word of God, with each of the writers adding his own particular insights and reflections. Can we sense, along with them, the excitement that must have permeated every fiber of their beings as they anticipated the possibility that *their* generation might be the one to experience the fullness of God's Presence? There can be no doubt that the early Church lived with the expectation that it would mature to a level of greatness transcending anything and everything until it fully exemplified the very life of Christ Himself!

Many generations have since faded from the scene, yet none has been the embodiment of the *glorious* Church as pictured in Ephesians 5:27; the *supernatural* Church of John 14:12; the *mature* Church as referred to in Ephesians 4:13-16; nor even the Church which is the *wisdom of God* as seen in Ephesians 3:9-10. It should be evident to even the most casual Christian observer that the Church has not even approximated all that God envisions it to be. Why? You will discover the answer to that question is far more complex than one might imagine. We are about to embark on a quest for truth: "And you shall know the truth, and the truth shall make you free"—JESUS (Jn. 8:32).

Chapter One

Search for Truth

Most of my life has been spent in a quest for truth. My earliest recollections are ones of insatiable curiosity and relentless desire to understand what made everything work. My dear mother spent many frustrated hours reassembling things that my inquisitiveness had caused me to disassemble in order to find out what made them tick. Speaking of "tick," there was this old mantle clock...but even *I* don't want to remember that incident. As I recall (and I *do* recall only too vividly), following that experiment my mother passionately applied the board of education to my seat of learning. I have a feeling that clock is *still* not reassembled. Some memories are literally too painful to dwell on, so let's move on. Fortunately (for me), with the passage of time came the knowledge that enabled me to reconstruct those things I had taken apart. Eventually I became my mother's favorite (the price was right) repairman.

The formative years of my life were spent without any true knowledge of God or His plan of redemption. Though our family was an admixture of Protestantism and Roman Catholicism, neither *ism* informed me that a Savior had been provided for my sins. My earliest religious memories are of a big old Methodist church I attended at the age of four. It was an impressive building with stained-glass windows, a well-educated minister, and a Sunday school to which I was *sent.* Occasionally the family would all attend together, usually on holidays, and at those times I would visit the adult church.

By the age of seven I had acquired a strong dislike for church because of hurtful experiences in Sunday school. My stern Sunday

1

school teacher had obviously never been informed that he could smile and still be religious. Though I was probably not the easiest student he had ever taught, he lacked the insight and motivation to meet my challenging behavior with *love*. Instead he would extend his huge hand (it looked huge to me), grab my ear, and twist it painfully. After this punishment, it took a long time for the feeling to return to my ear; but the feeling *never* returned to my heart. In retrospect I realize that my acting up in Sunday school was most likely a childish bid to gain from my male teacher the attention and love I did not receive from my father, a cruel man who showed neither love for me, nor interest in me. Sadly, I never received it! I eventually begged my mother not to send me to Sunday school again. Since the adults in my family only attended church on holidays, that's when I went also, and hated every moment of it!

My Aunt Kay lived with us. She was a devout Roman Catholic and I occasionally accompanied her to church. Because the services were conducted in Latin, I didn't understand what was being said (after 58 years I'm still trying to master English), yet was warmed inside. Somehow in my own primitive way I was reaching out and touching God for the first time, and it felt good! However, my aunt eventually moved away, and I was churchless again. Though denied that weekly religious exposure, I still possessed a desire to know something, *anything* about God. Although I was unaware of it, I had a divine appointment and God was busily arranging and rearranging the pieces of my life, thus drawing me ever closer to my heavenly destiny. I was fast approaching my first memorable encounter with Truth!

Baby, It's Cold Outside!

I was ten years old during the severe winter of 1947-48. We were subjected to sub-zero weather and frequent blizzards. Then the unthinkable happened. The fuel carriers went on strike!

In desperation, we all went to live with my Aunt Millie for the winter. While it was no easier finding kerosene where she lived, we all pulled together and managed to survive. I can still recall the nights when my aunt and I walked the snow-covered streets for hours. I pulled the fuel cans on a sled as we went from vendor to vendor looking for whatever dregs of kerosene might be left over. What we lacked in physical warmth that winter was well made up for by the warmth of the love we all shared.

You Can Starve on a Diet of Religion

In the spring of that year my aunt purchased a two-family house. She and two other aunts moved into the upstairs apartment and our family lived downstairs. Life had begun to look somewhat rosier and Mom felt that it would be good for my older sister, younger brother, and me to go to church. Since we had no strong denominational ties, Mom sent us to a nearby Lutheran church. Once again, my spirit went hungry. No one at that church ever pointed me to the cross, or told me of a loving Savior who had died to forgive my sins. We were simply fed the same old diet of religion, religion, and more religion!

After approximately two years on that starvation diet of religion, my sister Elaine began to attend a Baptist church a few blocks from our home. While at camp that summer, she committed her life to Christ. Needless to say, she arrived home a different person. When I visited her new church, I liked the friendly, outgoing young people who made us feel so welcome. I discovered that church could be enjoyable rather than just endurable. I knew that something (actually *Someone*) had led me there because, for the very first time in my life, I heard about the love of God in Christ that compelled Him to go to Calvary for me.

Shortly thereafter I accepted God's love for me and committed my life to Christ. Weeping tears of joy, I walked all the way home on cloud number nine. My childhood search for God had begun to bear fruit—little could I know then the broad scope this quest for truth would encompass, or to what great depths of the Word of God I would be drawn, or yet how voracious my appetite for truth would become.

Upon receiving Christ into my heart I discovered an intense desire to read and comprehend His Word and found myself spending long hours exploring its depths. I read the Word with an innocence born of the Spirit and with utter delight because of the vast promises of God, promises made to *me*! The following quotations from my teenage diary reveal the intensity of this initial encounter with God. They are so personal that until now I've only shared them with my wife.

April 3—"My faith has grown so that I can no longer contain my feelings within me. How true it is that faith *can* move mountains."

April 4—"We had a wonderful Bible study time tonight; God was present and His Spirit was felt. *He* has given me a yearning such as I've never had before, to want to learn and read the Bible. I know that God is leading me on to greater things for His name's sake."

April 6—"The Bible has become as much a part of my daily life as eating and drinking and sleeping."

April 12—"Today I spent a large part of the day reading the Bible. It really was a blessing to search the Scriptures. I find that in God's Word I find all that I need for my soul's sustenance."

April 13—"I read 38 chapters of the Bible today, and in them found verses which blessed my heart."

April 14—"The Scriptures were opened anew in my mind again tonight. A friend of mine named John came over to the house to help me study in God's Word. The Bible is becoming more of an open book to me, rather than a closed mystery which I'll never be able to fathom for myself. Praise God!"

April 25—"We had Bible study tonight. I can't learn enough about the Word of God."

Though the foregoing excerpts cover a span of less than one month, they reveal the *deep* hunger for the Word of God that was resident in my young heart. "How sweet are Thy words to my taste! Yes, sweeter than honey to my mouth!" (Ps. 119:103)

Feasting on the Word of God

I have never lost that earnest hunger for the Word of God. In fact, some years ago, in my search for truth, I determined to read the New Testament through every 26 days. I recently celebrated my 337th reading. At a later juncture, I decided to read the Old Testament through twice a year. To date I've completed 20 readings. I have not written this to boast. Anyone can accomplish this by reading ten New Testament chapters and five Old Testament chapters daily. All that is required is discipline, plus a deep and abiding passion for the Word of God!

Let's return to the narrative of my personal journey. During the days of my active involvement in the Baptist church, I was well sheltered by my pastor. I had never even heard of Pentecostals or their doctrines, so no one could accuse me of having been tainted by them. But I *had* been reading the Word of God, and the Holy Spirit had begun to birth in my spirit a desire for much more of God in my life and witness. I didn't know what I needed, or even where to look for it. I probably wouldn't have recognized it if I had stumbled onto it, but I knew it had to do with more of God. The more I prayed about it, the more convinced I became that I needed more. Everyone in the New Testament obviously had possessed more than I had obtained, so I set about to discover what it was they had and how I could get it.

Where would a teenager turn for that kind of direction? To his pastor, right? That's exactly where I went. I turned to the man I trusted most in life, the man whom I felt had all the answers concerning the Word of God. It was a Saturday afternoon in the fall of the year and the young people were having a party in the church. At some point I slipped away and sat on the church steps, alone and deep in thought. My hunger for more of God exceeded my desire for party fare. After awhile my pastor came and sat beside me, said he had missed me at the party, and wondered if anything was wrong. I poured my young heart out to him. I just knew he would understand about this aching in my spirit for more of God. Surely he would be able to direct me to the fullness I cried for. I don't know how long I spoke to him of my desires, longings, burnings, hungers—needs that I felt God Himself had planted inside me, but which remained unsatisfied. There had to be more, but where could I find it? Warm tears coursed down my cheeks as he reassuringly placed his arm around my shoulder. He spoke softly, but his voice resounded with such authority that I felt certain the answer for which I had yearned was forthcoming. My young mind hung on his every word as he said, "Burt, I used to feel exactly the way you do today—so I understand." (At last, my moment of discovery! My pastor was going to tell me what he had done, and therefore what I could do to satisfy these unrequited desires!)

"But there is no more," he said. "This is it! You must be satisfied with what you have. *There is no more!*" His words exploded inside me. "There is no more! *There is no more! THERE IS NO MORE!*" (I'm weeping even as I write this narrative.) A fountain of hopelessness erupted within me and enveloped me. I lowered my face to my knees and felt something within me die.

Words fail me to express the combination of feelings that flooded my being that afternoon as my hopes crashed down around me. There was a numbness all over, an intense hurt deep inside, a sense of being adrift; and, for the very first time in my life, I experienced anger toward God! To my young mind it didn't seem fair for Him to allow me to have such intense desires if there was no way for them to be fulfilled. I felt as though I were the subject of some divine prank. I wondered how I could continue living for God while such passionate desires for more of Him remained unfulfilled. The continual frustration would be more than I could endure. So, I turned my back on God and walked away.

The Prodigal Returns

As I would eventually discover, God's timing is perfect. Two years after my heart was broken, I began to sense deep within myself the drawing power of the Holy Spirit urging me to return to Christ and recommit my life to Him. When I did, I found that He had been waiting patiently for His prodigal son to come home. Our reunion was sweet and I repented tearfully for ever doubting Him.

Within a month, a new person became part of our church. Her name was Angie, and she was an absolute delight. She was so full of life and joy (which she expressed at every opportunity), and a magnetism seemed to radiate from her. My mother had since become a Christian and was warmly attracted to Angie, as was everyone. We didn't know what made her different, but Mom sensed that Angie possessed something we didn't have. When her new friend explained that she had been baptized in the Holy Spirit, Mom immediately wanted to know all about "this baptism in the Holy Spirit business."

I thoroughly liked Angie; I just didn't like her doctrines, especially when Mom and Aunt Millie began attending Sunday evening services at her home church. (Angie began attending morning services at the Baptist church because it was nearer to her home and her ill husband.) Both Mom and Aunt Millie displayed definite signs of being swayed toward Angie's strange way of worship. You see, I had become resigned to the idea that Christianity contained no more than the basic tenets of faith that I had already been taught. There was absolutely no room in my rigid belief structure for any dangerous new doctrines. After all, my pastor had said there was "no more," so there was no more. Period. End of discussion!

No Happy Camper

Before long Mom invited the pastor of the Pentecostal church to conduct weekly Bible studies in our house. She informed me that my attendance was not only requested, it was required. I was not a happy camper. Though I endured each session, my somber countenance was intended to make the pastor feel as uncomfortable as possible. Soon Mom and Aunt Millie received the truth and began to attend the Full Gospel church full-time. Had I not been convinced by my pastor that there was no more, I might have joyfully accepted these new truths also. Instead, I continued to resist the overtures of the Holy Spirit. Yet God faithfully drew me toward His fullness in various (and sometimes amusing) ways.

With undaunted enthusiasm, my mother continued to invite me to attend her new church. Believing that she would never relent until I agreed to go, I made a deal with her. "If I attend one church service with you, will you promise to never ask me again—ever?" Armed with her promise, I marched off to church one Sunday evening, certain that I would never have to endure another invitation or attend another service.

We arrived early, yet the people were already singing. Shortly thereafter the pastor and worship leader arrived and the service officially began. *O, did it begin!* Lively singing such as I'd never heard before was accompanied by enthusiastic hand clapping. Shouts of "Hallelujah" and "Praise the Lord" were liberally interspersed throughout. Although I enjoyed the music, I considered all the rest to be unnecessary fanaticism. The thought that my mother had become involved in all this excess was almost too alarming to comprehend.

Spooky Stuff Happening Here!

In the midst of these strange happenings, the pastor declared, "I believe the Holy Spirit just spoke to me and wants everyone to raise their hands and praise the Lord." I thought, "Not me—I'm Baptist!" Not wanting to be disrespectful, I stood with the congregation, closed my eyes, folded my hands, and thought, "I'll just silently pray a quiet

7

Baptist prayer." Suddenly I felt someone grasp my left wrist and elbow and raise my arm in the air. "Who would have the audacity to do such a thing?" I thought. "Don't they know I'm Baptist?" Pulling my arm down, I quickly turned to my left (my seat was on the aisle) to confront this presumptuous person—but there was no one there! Everyone was joyfully praising the Lord. In retrospect, I'm certain no one else even knew or cared that I was there.

I refolded my hands, closed my eyes, and once again proceeded to pray my sedate little prayer, determined to not be taken off guard this time. If he tried it again, I would catch him in the act! Sure enough, once again I felt the pressure of two hands, one on my left wrist the other on my elbow, raising my arm in the air. This time I turned immediately, certain I would come face to face with the one who possessed such unmitigated gall. But again *there was no one there!* This time I left my hand high in the air. My mother whispered to my Aunt Millie, "Look! Burton's becoming Pentecostal!" However, the absolute truth of the matter was that I was simply too scared to put my hand down!

Supernatural Stuff Happening There!

The following Sunday evening I began to dress for church considerably earlier than I would ordinarily have begun to prepare for my service. Mom smiled and asked, "How come you're getting ready so early?" Grinning sheepishly I replied, "I'm going to church with you, if that's okay." The hook had been set! What had actually transpired the Sunday before? The Holy Spirit had involved me in something miraculous, in such a way that even I couldn't deny it. And I wanted more!

Of course, that one incident didn't cause me to embrace every Full Gospel doctrine. But it did convince me that there was something *supernatural* happening there, and it drew me back again. Having once been exposed to the manifestation of the Holy Spirit, my appetite for the supernatural had been whetted. I would never again be the same. That *something* within me that had once died on the steps of the Baptist church had begun to experience resurrection power. The "something more" I had so earnestly sought a few years earlier was about to descend on my life like "a rushing mighty wind."

Chapter Two

But You Shall
Receive Power When...

With the advent of the baptism in the Holy Spirit, my life would never be the same again. Having finally received the "more" for which I had sought with tears some years earlier, I now discovered that the inner hunger pangs of my spirit were not permanently satisfied. How could that be? Since I now had more, shouldn't I be fulfilled, complete, satisfied, contented, and peaceful at all times? One would certainly think so (I know *I* did) but that was *not* the case at all. What I had received was an intensification of the hunger for more! The difference was that now, with the knowledge that accompanied the baptism in the Holy Spirit, I knew where to look. Never again would I have to believe those words, "There is no more!"

"Puzzled" is probably the best word to describe my attitude toward those who receive the baptism in the Holy Spirit and then live out the rest of their lives as though *their* pastor had also informed them that "there is no more!" How can anyone come into such intimate contact with the dynamic Person of the Holy Spirit and remain the same? Possibly this is one reason why non-Spirit-filled believers make light of the experience. They observe those who claim to be Spirit-filled and witness the powerless lives that contradict what they proclaim.

Put Your Money Where Your Mouth Is

As a young man growing up in Brooklyn, New York, I heard that expression often. It was always said to people after they had bragged about something they could accomplish or about something they were able to do. "Put your *money* where your *mouth* is!" was almost always said as a jeer, a taunt to the braggart to do what he said he could. In other words, it was time to stop talking and start performing! More often than not the challenge went unmet and, amidst laughter, the one challenged would slink away in embarrassment. Had he learned his lesson? Hardly! You could almost be certain that the next opportunity to boast would find his mouth promising what his body couldn't perform. From experience gleaned over more than 38 years of ministry, I've discovered that some Christians likewise never learn from the past. George Santayana is quoted as having wisely said, "Those who cannot remember the past, are condemned to repeat it."

"What has this to do with the Church, and me in particular?" you ask. In order for that question to be answered one must have a clear-cut picture in mind of what God's Word envisions the Church to be. Without that representation there can be no honest standard by which comparison or evaluation can be made.

Awakening the Sleeping Giant

"Tora! Tora! Tora!" (Japanese for *tiger*) radioed from the lead attack pilot to the waiting Japanese fleet was to be the code word signaling that the sneak attack on Pearl Harbor was successfully underway. Sunday, December 7, 1941, referred to by President Franklin Delano Roosevelt as "a day which will live in infamy," swept the United States into World War II. Japanese Zeros had come out of nowhere, unleashing fiery destruction on our Pacific fleet anchored at Pearl Harbor. Hours later the *USS Arizona* (along with other ships) lay on the bottom of the harbor. Acrid, billowing, black smoke filled the air—a silent reminder that the United States was at war!

Loaded with cargoes of doom, the Zeros had been dispatched from their aircraft carriers. Isoroku Yamamoto, admiral of the Japanese fleet, stood tense watch from the bridge of the battleship *Nagato*, awaiting the words "Tora! Tora! Tora!"—words that would forever change the course of world history. When the radioman carried the fateful message to the bridge and handed it to Admiral Yamamoto, the admiral's response was brief and to the point. "I'm afraid we have only awakened a sleeping giant, *and his reaction will be terrible!*" The outcome of World War II would prove those words to be prophetic!

(An aside: The *Nagato* was the only Japanese battleship to survive WWII. Captured by the Americans, it was later used as a target at an atomic test site.)

Satan's greatest fear is that the sleeping giant, the Church, will awaken to her God-ordained potential. Why else do you suppose (and I will prove this later in this book) that Satan has worked overtime for millennia to lull the Church to sleep, keeping her blinded to her divine possibilities? Could he possibly know something the Church ought to know, but doesn't? What did he have in mind when, for centuries, he kept the common people from reading the Word of God? Was there something contained within it that, if read and understood, would seriously threaten his evil kingdom? A thousand times, yes! The Word of God paints a clear portrait of the Church as the Bride of Christ, "without spot or wrinkle" (see Eph. 5:27), resplendent in all her majesty, triumphant, glorious, victorious, overcoming, powerful! She is not portrayed as *a* church, but *the* Church—not as some second-rate, broken-down has-been or some wishful want-to-be, but as the rod of God in this world, boldly declaring His righteous rule.

The sleeping giant is about to awaken to her commission and power, and this old world, Satan's kingdom, will never be the same again! God has a battle plan, and He has provided the anointing (the continuing "something more") needed to enable the Church to break down the gates and walls of fortresses behind which Satan has been hiding. The Church has been called and commissioned to wage unrelenting warfare against the forces of evil. Anything less than this is not God's program!

Wimpy, Wimpy, Wimpy

Those are the words of a TV commercial pitting one trash bag against another. One bag gets the job done, the other doesn't. Can you guess which one gets called "wimpy, wimpy, wimpy"? Right! We all recognize wimpy when we see it, don't we? Or do we? "Wimpy" also means more than a character in a Popeye comic strip. It typifies the general condition of today's Church. Since the Scriptures teach that we have not been called to anything less than total victory (let alone defeat), why do we see such abject poverty of Holy Spirit power among God's people? Why do they struggle simply to exist from day to day? Why does the devil have an unrestrained field day, causing sickness in their bodies as well as their emotions? Why is Satan the most faithful church attender, wreaking havoc in the Body of Christ and causing every kind of faction and dissention imaginable? Why? There can only be one answer to those questions. The Church is *wimpy*!

The Church is not wimpy by design. God never intended for her to be that way. Thus we are left with only two alternatives as to how she arrived at that ineffectual destination: (1) By desire—that is, church leaders simply didn't want people to know the truth. For centuries that was the scenario. (2) By ignorance of the truth. Since the Church labored for centuries under an oppressive regime, she still staggers today under an enormous load of scriptural ignorance; some is self-imposed and some is encouraged by equally ignorant, tradition-bound clergy. Ignorance is not a four-letter word. It doesn't imply wickedness or dishonor or even stupidity as many interpret it. It simply means to be "without knowledge or understanding." The apostle Paul used the same expression in First Corinthians 12:1: "Now concerning spiritual gifts, brethren, I do not want you to be unaware." The Greek word that we interpret as "unaware" is *agnoeo*, which means, "not to know (through lack of information or intelligence); by implication to ignore (through disinclination): not know, not understand, unknown."[1]

I saw an interesting bumper sticker whose succinct message said it all—"EDUCATION EXPENSIVE? *TRY IGNORANCE!*" The moral implied is, "If you think education is expensive, just wait until you discover how costly the antithesis (ignorance) can be." No matter what the price, the Church must not remain in ignorance. We must experience the fullness of Pentecost—at any cost! Not to do so is unthinkable! The major purpose of this book is to call attention to concepts, scriptural principles, or themes of which you may have been unaware. Of course, once so informed, you become responsible for those truths (see Lk. 12:47-48).

"I Was a 97-Pound Weakling..."

Thus began one of the most well-known ads ever read by the American public. It was displayed on the back cover of probably

---

1. James Strong, *The Comprehensive Concordance to the Bible*, (Iowa Falls, IA: World Bible Publisher, n.d.), Gr. # 50.

every comic book in America. Perhaps you remember it—the picture of an underweight young man on the beach with his girlfriend, having sand kicked in his face by some bully. The ad spelled out the intense embarrassment suffered by that scrawny young man as a result of this encounter, and what he determined to do so that it would never happen to him again. What developed out of that ugly, humiliating confrontation was the world-famous Charles Atlas Body Building Course subscribed to by millions.

I recall having heard Charles Atlas recount this personal incident on television. In stirring tones he recounted the milestone that changed not only his life, but the lives of countless others also. He and his girlfriend had been enjoying a day at the beach when a bully began tormenting him, kicking sand in his face, and otherwise humiliating him. This was certainly not the first time something of this nature had happened to this "97-pound weakling," but this time became the turning point for him. At that defining moment he determined that nothing like that would ever happen to him again! He began bodybuilding in earnest and the rest is history. "I can't imagine *anyone* being foolish enough to want to kick sand in his face *now*," I thought, as I listened to him tell his story. I wonder how many young men in similar circumstances read the Charles Atlas ad and repeated his promise, "This will *never* happen to me again"—and revolutionized their lives?

By now the analogy must be clear. Many in the Church are like that 97-pound weakling; they are pushed around by every bully in the spirit realm. An ever-present humiliation accompanies these assaults but, since we have been too afraid to strike back, we have endured the shame in painful silence. Sometimes (like Charles Atlas) we have to reach a point of crisis in our lives before we become motivated to extreme action. My desire is to inspire some who read this book to reach that place—and beyond. When God called me to the ministry, He gave me a twofold commission: He said to me, "I want you to *comfort* the troubled—and *trouble* the comforted!" I have attempted to obey both mandates with equal vigor.

A Law Is a Law

One of my favorite subjects in high school was science. I could hardly wait to get to class. (Remember, I have always had a desire to know what makes things tick.) My science teacher, Mr. Silver, had a way of making his subject come alive. In class he often spoke of theories, those aspects of science that were not yet proven. He also discussed certain laws, those facets of science that were set in stone, the *absolutes*. One such law states that "an object in motion tends to remain in motion, while an object at rest tends to remain at rest." That law is simple enough for anyone (even someone who doesn't like science) to understand.

At some time or another you've probably used the expression, "going like a snowball downhill." What you were likely attempting to convey is that when something as small and innocuous as a snowball becomes an object in motion, at some point in its unrestrained journey downhill, it becomes an extremely impressive power, with awesome potential. There is no way I would stand in front of it as it neared the bottom of the hill—would you? Conversely, the snowball *at rest* is no threat to anyone.

Too many Christians sit lethargically by, doing little or nothing to upset the devil's apple cart. "After all, if I don't do it, someone else will—right?" Dead wrong! Since most other church members parrot the same thing, the Church's enemy (and your enemy), enjoys a nearly unrestricted field of activity. The voice of the Holy Spirit is calling throughout the camp, "Who is on the Lord's side...?" Can you hear it?

It is evident that the Church must cease being the object *at rest* and become the object *in motion* as the Word of God describes it to be. Let us rise to the challenge to become that for which science has vainly searched: the irresistible force of the universe.

Chapter Three

An Eye for an Eye, and a Truth for a Truth[1]

There was a time when man truly knew his Creator in a singularly personal relationship that drew him into the very heart of God. Through this union of spirits Adam enjoyed perfect, unbroken fellowship. Because man was created in the image of God, he was endowed with the capacity to experience the most intimate communion with Him in his spirit. When sin entered upon the scene, the image of God in man was defaced, thus preventing mankind from drinking from the well of that exquisite awareness of God's Presence that Adam had known earlier. Man then became "from the earth, earthy" (1 Cor. 15:47). Adam, who once had been able to say, "I know God," thereafter could only claim to know *about* God.

Immediately after man fell, God began laying the building blocks of revelation through which we could know Him in His fullness once more. In every book from Genesis to Revelation, you will find that there is a continual unveiling of God's nature and attributes in order for mankind to rediscover Him.

Revelation Stops *Here*!

To really *know* God has never been an easy assignment in any age; persecutions have always plagued those who have had a determination

---

1. This chapter is an adapted excerpt from my book, *Christian Meditation: Doorway to the Spirit*, written in 1988. Copies are available from the author: 10350 Royal Oak Court, Osceola, IN 46561 ($8 plus $3 shipping and handling).

to experience a personal relationship with Him. This has been true from the time of Adam until the present and will continue through succeeding generations.

After Adam and Eve were driven from the Garden of Eden, they were faced with the problem of survival in a difficult new world where they existed by "the sweat of their brow." But God was there to guide the prodigals back to Himself. The first of many glimpses into the redemptive nature of the Father God was revealed when He wrapped them in the skin of a newly slain animal, an early revelation of the only acceptable sacrifice for sin—blood.

Abel, a man with a tender heart toward spiritual things, fully recognized the veiled meaning behind God's act of providing a blood sacrifice in order to clothe his parents' nakedness. Thus, when he came to present his offering before the Lord it was "of the firstlings of his flock" (Gen. 4:4), a *blood* sacrifice. His brother Cain, however, "brought an offering to the Lord of the fruit of the ground" (Gen. 4:3) which was not acceptable to God. In a sense, Cain's offering was the first *religious* act performed by man—an act of the flesh. Abel's offering sprang from revelation knowledge. Cain possessed certain truth: God required a sacrifice. Abel had further truth: God required a sacrifice of *blood.*

The First Religious Spirit

Realizing that his offering was unacceptable to God, Cain rose up in a jealous rage and murdered his brother. This religious spirit has continued throughout the ages, spawning an attitude whose slogan could well be: "Revelation Stops *Here!*"

Searching hearts have always discovered new truths (really they are old truths *re*discovered), then have proceeded to erect their denominational barriers, all the while proudly proclaiming, "Revelation stops *here!*"

Discoverers of new truth tend to follow a pattern: first comes the joy of discovery; followed by familiarity and regimentation; then a religious spirit of elitism and pride declares, "We have *all* truth—no one could possibly uncover more than our mainstream denomination has." In the face of that attitude, pity the person who dares to challenge the fortified positions of the ecclesiasticals, or who dares to venture beyond the arbitrarily established doctrinal perimeters of his denomination! To do so would be to subject oneself to the fear of excommunication, ridicule, harassment, and in past ages, to the pain of torture and death. As history bears witness, some of the most horrendous battles ever recorded have been religious wars, fought in the name of the Prince of Peace for causes thought to be lofty and noble.

Can you name even one religious group that did not persecute its successors? I can't! You see, the religious spirit always assumes command with the attitude, "Who could possibly have any more truth than *we* do?" Strangely enough, the very ones who made that statement were themselves swift to proudly and loudly proclaim *their* newly discovered tenet of faith perhaps a generation before, for which *they* were initially misunderstood and persecuted. How soon we forget!

The religious leaders of Jesus' day believed they possessed *all* the revelation of God that man would ever have. Then, along came a young upstart rabbi who upset their ecclesiastical apple cart. The major accusation made against Jesus at His mockery of a trial was that He was a blasphemer "...because He made Himself out to be the Son of God" (Jn. 19:7). He not only claimed to know *about* God but that He *knew* God intimately as His Father. And for that He was crucified.

That Jesus knew how much evil the religious spirit was capable of causing men to do is evident in His scathing rebuke of the religious leaders of His day: "Woe to you! For you build the tombs of the prophets, and it was your fathers who killed them. Consequently, you are witnesses and approve the deeds of your fathers; because *it was they who killed them, and you build their tombs*" (Lk. 11:47-48).

The Pharisees remarked that had they lived in the days of their forefathers they would not have put the prophets to death; yet there was no place found in their cold, stony, indifferent hearts to hear the voices of the two greatest prophets, John and Jesus! Both prophets met untimely deaths at the hands of their own people because of the religious spirit that declared, "Revelation stops *here!*"

Persecution of heretics has always been a part of the Christian(?) Church from its earliest days, and has been enthusiastically endorsed as a weapon against any encroachment of new truth upon the old. When Martin Luther received the divine revelation, "The just shall live by faith" (Rom. 1:17b KJV), the Reformation began as people realized they were delivered from religious enslavement to forms, rituals, and indulgences, and were free to live their lives by faith! There was nothing new about this truth. "The just shall live by faith" had been a foundational doctrine of the apostle Paul and was as old as the Epistle to Rome. Over the centuries this truth had become misplaced and forgotten, until it was revived through the prophetic ministry of Martin Luther. As might have been expected, the ecclesiastical fathers unleashed the full fury of the Roman Catholic church upon all who believed such heresy. "After all," the religious spirit declared, "Revelation stops here!"

More Than Salvation?

Out of the Reformation, which spread like a wildfire throughout Europe, came newer and more far-reaching revelations from the Word of God concerning His nature and His relationship with man. "Faith is not enough!" That was the cry of John and Charles Wesley as the Holy Spirit's light gave new revelation concerning the doctrine of "...holiness, without which no man shall see the Lord" (Heb. 12:14b KJV). Again, this was not new doctrine—simply a new revelation of age-old truth from the Word of God. These prophets championed the message throughout every village and hamlet as well as the largest cities of England, Scotland, and Ireland and soon were branded the "Holy Club, Bible Moths, and Methodists." Cruel treatment was heaped upon all who dared to believe this strange new doctrinal heresy.

It should come as no surprise that much of this disfavor and open hostility came from (of all people) the Lutherans! It was inconceivable to them that there could be any further unfolding of God's revelation than that which they had. Certainly such a powerful leader as Luther couldn't possibly have missed so great a doctrinal revelation as holiness, could he? The Lutherans forgot that they had once been the persecuted ones, and how greatly they had suffered at the hands of the ecclesiasticals. They in turn became the ecclesiastical persecutors of the new truth. The religious spirit had again declared, "Revelation stops here!"

You're All Wet!

The present-day Church is deeply indebted to the teachings of Roger Williams and the Baptists for the Holy Spirit's revelation concerning water baptism by immersion. This doctrine was opposed by all the ecclesiasticals of that era, since infant baptism was the only acceptable mode at that time. Controversy was the order of the day between the ecclesiasticals, the Massachusetts Bay Court, and Roger Williams, culminating in the banishment of God's prophet from the colony.

Nearly every generation thereafter experienced a spiritual awakening wherein God showed His prophets some old yet new revelations. With these truths burning in their hearts they forged onward—though the very forces of hell were unleashed against them by the established churches. Yet, each new group allowed their revelation to degenerate into dogma and musty doctrine with nothing left of its initial life which had heralded revival in their generation. Subsequently, when the "Revelation stops here!" spirit caused revealed truth to become regimented and stale, numerous reform movements arose, seeking to recapture the freshness of spiritual renewal and revelation.

From Dying Embers—A Worldwide Blaze

The dawning of the twentieth century saw the emergence of an age of science and learning with strong emphasis placed upon intellectual pursuit; anything that could not be measured in a test tube or analyzed in the laboratory was dismissed as insignificant and worthless.

This attitude was felt in the churches also. The shouting of the Methodists was a thing of the past, and spontaneous praise, which had been so much a part of Baptist meetings, was now only a memory they were struggling to forget. By this time large numbers of Lutherans had defected from "the just shall live by faith" message and had regressed into empty and meaningless forms. People worshiped the god of knowledge, while sacrificing their spiritual heritage on the cold altar of intellect. Those truths, for which their forefathers had paid such a heavy toll, were often laid to rest along with their forefathers' bones, in the cemeteries surrounding many of their churches.

The age was ripe for a sweeping move of the Holy Spirit. But when He came it would not be to vaulted cathedrals with imposing stained-glass windows and impressive pipe organs, nor to the ecclesiasticals who headed these august institutions. His advent would be to a few humble, but devout, seekers gathered in an unpretentious location in Los Angeles, California. There, in 1906 in the Azusa Street

19

Mission (a converted stable), a handful of believers gathered with the expressed purpose of spiritual renewal. The fires of revival, which had burned as beacons in years gone by, had dwindled until only sparks could be found. On those few smoldering embers God poured out the oil of the Holy Spirit and from the nearly extinguished sparks He ignited a sheet of flame that was to spread around the world more rapidly than any prairie fire fanned by heavy winds!

Word spread rapidly concerning inexplicable happenings among this new breed of believers. Those who visited the little mission came away with incredible tales of people who spoke in strange tongues they had never learned; while others told of witnessing miraculous healings of incurable ailments. Stranger still were the accounts of spiritual ecstasies—trances during which some related they had been caught up in the Spirit where they experienced visions of Heaven, Jesus, or future events. The nine gifts of the Holy Spirit as recorded by the apostle Paul in First Corinthians, chapters 12 and 14, were claimed to have reappeared as a sign to this age that Jesus was soon to return for His Church.

The little band at Azusa Street had grown weary of institutionalized religion laden with forms and rituals that led down dead-end streets. They had been instructed by the ecclesiasticals that much of the New Testament was no longer valid; miracles, signs and wonders, they had been told, were only for the Apostolic Age and should not be expected in their generation. Thus, the new movement swung heavily to the right when adopting a doctrinal position. They affirmed that the Bible, God's holy and unchangeable Word, would serve as their only guidepost. Anything that could not be substantiated in Scripture was to be discarded, while everything within Sacred Writ was to be tenaciously adhered to! This position taken, there was no turning back.

Whatever affection they might have enjoyed before leaving the mainstream denominations quickly vanished, and was rapidly replaced by open hostilities. Antagonism became the weapon of the various mainstream denominations, and names such as "Holy Rollers," "Holy Pump-Jumpers," and "Pentecostals" (to list just a few printable ones) were ascribed to anyone who became a part of their movement. Countless services were disturbed or broken up by hecklers; church windows were broken; and occasionally, the origin of suspicious fires that destroyed "holy roller" churches went largely uninvestigated and nearly always unaccounted for. The devout were often waylaid and beaten while preachers were prime targets for local bullies.

Those who had been baptized in the Holy Spirit and had spoken in tongues who sought to remain in their own churches soon found themselves ostracized. Old friends looked the other way or crossed to the other side of the street to avoid exchanging some kind of greeting. They were almost always dropped from church membership (excommunicated) if they were unwilling to change their views and disavow that New Testament miracles were for their day. As late as 1955, my own and my family's membership in a fundamentalist Baptist church was revoked, and many Charismatics report that this is the case with them even today. The renowned theologian Karl Barth gave this definition of a fundamentalist: "One who knows a bit of Scripture and thinks he has arrived. If you don't agree with him, you're lost. If you go ahead of him, you've gone astray!" Barth went on to say, "I don't ever expect to 'arrive' because Jesus is the Way...and there is no terminal!"

Who were the ones conducting these persecutions? Outsiders, sinners, the nonreligious? Yes, to some extent they were, but for the most part the worst persecutions came from church people—brothers and sisters in Christ. Lutherans, Methodists, Baptists, Presbyterians, Church of Christ, Quakers, Brethren, and people from every other denomination all joined in the attacks! The very ones who had suffered persecution for their faith (which had been established upon some new revelation) had now become the persecutors. Persecuted by those who had gone before, they now persecuted those who followed after. Thus it has always been, and always will be, to the everlasting shame of those who do not remain sensitive to the Spirit's flow!

Proponents of this new revelation were labeled *heretics*, while those who refused to have anything to do with them were titled *defenders of the faith*. The obvious attitude and the religious spirit that pervaded (and perverted) these denominations was and still is, "Revelation stops here!" No one may dare to claim any further light on the Scripture than *we* have. "No one may step outside the perimeters that we have drawn." These have been and still are the attitudes of ecclesiastical hierarchies in days gone by and up to this present age.

It is evident that each group, having received further revelation from the Word of God than their predecessors, has suffered greatly to maintain that truth. They in turn have committed the same hostile acts of aggression toward the recipients of the next new revelation.

Space fails me to comprehensively trace the unfolding history of the Church with its unending persecutions in each age: of inquisitions; of papal armies that marched against the Albigenses, slaying 30,000 in a single massacre; of John Wycliffe whose bones were exhumed from his grave and burned by dissenters, angry with him for having translated the Bible into the common language; of John Huss who was burned at the stake for preaching church reform; of Jerome of Prague, burned at the stake for being a heretic (a term fitting anyone who disagreed with the pronouncements of the ecclesiastical hierarchy); Felix Manz (Anabaptist), martyred; William Tyndale, martyred; Thomas Hawkes, martyred...these are but a few! The pages of Church history are stained with the blood of martyrs who have laid down their lives for new revelation. Multiple volumes would not be sufficient to record all the heroes of faith who made the supreme sacrifice for what they believed to be the truth and paid the price demanded by the religious spirit which declared, "Revelation stops here!"

Let Us Not Forget!

We loudly applaud those pioneers of faith who have gone before where no one else had dared to tread. But may we be constantly reminded that they have always been the followers of previously revealed truth (and often the leaders themselves) who have led the persecution against proponents of any new revelation from God's Word that did not originate in their mold. Bear in mind that Luther, Calvin, and Zwingli all advocated the death penalty for heresy.

Underlying the attitude perpetrated by the religious spirit of "Revelation stops here!" is the most damning heresy of all. By its very design it is a self-limiting error which, if adhered to, automatically negates any opportunity for the Spirit of God to elevate your spiritual horizon above its current level. Analyze what the ecclesiasticals are really saying when they state, "Revelation stops here!" Affirming their supreme and ultimate knowledge of God's Word, they make the declaration, "There will never again be any further truth revealed from the Bible. We are the last group to receive new revelation." *Nonsense!* First Peter 1:23b refers to the Bible as "the *living...*word of God." That is exactly what it is: alive, a living book, the truths of which will be unfolding throughout the aeons of eternity. No denomination can rightly claim to possess *all* truth, only that they have embraced all the truth that the Spirit of God has revealed up to the present time.

Repeating a quotation from an earlier chapter: "Those who cannot remember the past are condemned to *repeat* it!"

Chapter Four

A Time to Possess the Land

Egypt and its Pharaohs had oppressed the Israelites, keeping them in the cruel bondage of slavery for 430 years. Having endured ten generations of slavery, their faith was almost destroyed, and even hope was little more than a dying ember. Perhaps there were vague recollections among the elders concerning distant promises of a deliverer who would one day come and set their captive nation free, but even this was not enough to lift their sagging spirits. Promises without fulfillment were not enough to soothe their aching bodies and tormented minds during the long days spent building Pharaoh's super cities and massive tombs.

Generation after generation had fruitlessly cried out to God for deliverance, but none seemed forthcoming. Perhaps God had forgotten them, or worse yet, maybe He had deserted them. With the dawning of each new day, these and many other thoughts of like kind flooded the minds of these oppressed people. Every sunset brought reports of more who had died under the relentless whips of the taskmasters who cared nothing for the lives of worthless slaves. This was not living—it was existing! But what could they do?

Burning Bush "University"

In the wildest imagination who could ever have conceived the plan that God was about to unfold! Even while hopelessness mocked their every waking moment, God was convening a meeting with a man named Moses at, of all places, a burning bush. Moses received more revelation of God during those few minutes at the burning bush than many theologians possess after spending years at some of our leading seminaries! The President of Burning Bush University had this message for His people:

> *And the Lord said, "I have surely seen the affliction of My people who are in Egypt, and have given heed to their cry because of their taskmasters, for I am aware of their sufferings. So I have come down to deliver them from the power of the Egyptians, and to bring them up from that land to a good and spacious land, to a land flowing with milk and honey…. And now, behold, the cry of the sons of Israel has come to Me; furthermore, I have seen the oppression with which the Egyptians are oppressing them. Therefore, come now, and I will send you to Pharaoh, so that you may bring My people, the sons of Israel, out of Egypt. Go and gather the elders of Israel together, and say to them, 'The Lord, the God of your fathers, the God of Abraham, Isaac and Jacob, has appeared to me, saying, "I am indeed concerned about you and what has been done to you in Egypt. So I said, I will bring you up out of the affliction of Egypt to…a land flowing with milk and honey" ' "* (Exodus 3:7-10, 16-17).

Even though Israel was unaware of it at that moment, God had bigger and better things planned for them and was unveiling His program to Moses at the burning bush. At long last, a deliverer was on his way to Egypt. Surely now the rigors of slavery would begin to abate, the taskmasters would ease the Israelites' burdens, and life would take on new meaning. Since God had prophesied many wonderful and encouraging words concerning Israel's future to Moses, everything would be better now. Not necessarily so! As they were soon to discover, quite the opposite was true; the burdens of slavery were heaped even higher upon them as Pharaoh increased their workload and *decreased* their provisions (see Ex. 5:1-19).

The situation worsened with the passing of every new day, as Satan worked overtime in an attempt to prevent the promises of God from materializing for His people. (There seems to be a law in the Kingdom of God that says, "Things will always get worse before they get better!" That certainly was true for Israel. Perhaps we can all relate to that.) Fortunately, God was not finished with Pharaoh. When He said, "Let My people go!" He meant it, and brought the ten plagues to prove it! After the last plague, God finally led Israel forth. The journey toward Canaan had begun at last.

What a grand day that must have been, when two to three million slaves began to savor the taste of freedom. No fairy-tale writer could have conceived a better rags-to-riches ending! Slaves left as free men, the poor left rich, and the sick and infirm left in perfect health. Who could ask for better times?

The most direct route to Canaan was northeast to the southernmost border of the land, a brief journey by any standard. But that was not the path by which God would lead them. You see, if they had traveled by that course, upon entering Canaan they would have immediately met the Philistines who were known as extremely fierce warriors (see Ex. 13:17-18). God understood that after 430 years in servitude Israel was ill-prepared to face such an awesome army so soon after leaving Egypt. They still carried the stench of oppression. They were *slaves*, not *soldiers*! But in the years to come God would turn a nation of serfs into a fearsome army.

Two years had passed since the Exodus, and now this vast nation stood on the banks of the Jordan River, with God's promised land clearly in sight. They would soon enter and take possession of this rich land "flowing with milk and honey"—after all, that was God's plan for them. Twelve men (one from each of the 12 tribes) were selected to spy out the land and bring back a report (see Num. 13:1-3). They found the land to be everything God had said it was, and more, much more! In fact, so much more that it took two men to carry a single cluster of grapes, some figs, and some pomegranates. After having spent 40 days in the heart of the land, the spies returned to report their observations.

It's difficult to conceive how anyone who had seen Canaan firsthand could have returned with anything less than an ecstatic report. They should have been elated, filled with the anticipation of conquest, and eager to go up and possess the land—but that was not the case at all. All 12 spies had witnessed the fruitfulness of the land, yet 10 of the 12 allowed their own fears and anxieties to cloud their testimony and cause them to become liars. How quickly their witness changed and lies spewed forth. They gave out an evil report: "The land...is a land that devours its inhabitants; and all the people whom we saw in it are men of great size" (Num. 13:32b).

Time for an Attitude Check

Fear does strange things to people. It turns some into heroes and reduces others to paralyzed, quivering cowards. Unfortunately, most of the spies in the above story fell into the latter category. They trembled at the prospect of having to face the inhabitants of the land in battle, and they communicated this spirit of fear to the entire nation, no small task in itself. Grumbling and rebellion reverberated throughout the camp all that night and by morning light they were ready to replace Moses and return to Egypt! Return to Egypt—the land of tyranny, oppression, slavery, deprivation, pain, and death? Why would anyone choose to resubmit to that evil regime that had drained everyone's dignity and self-respect? We will discover the answer to this question in Chapter Seven.

Chapter Five

Type? What's a *Type?*

Canaan's significance lies not in the fact that the people wanted to possess it, but rather that God considered its conquest to be vital. Exactly why was it of such importance to Him? That question has multiple answers.

Why Us, Lord?

God's dealings with Israel had to do with more than simply making them a nation. Why did He select them? He chose them primarily to display His redemptive nature and to show Himself strong through them. The sins of the nations had mounted up before God and the cup of His wrath was about to spill over, and Israel would become His physical rod of judgment on the earth.

Referring to Israel, Stephen said, "This is the one who was in *the congregation* [or church, Gr. *ekklesia*; NASB marginal note] in the wilderness..." (Acts 7:38). It was God's plan for Israel to serve as an archetype of the Church, thus illustrating divine truths that were to be fulfilled in the New Testament Age. This is borne out by the apostle Paul, "Now these things happened *as examples for us...*" (1 Cor. 10:6); and again, "Now these things happened to them *as an example,*[1] and they were written for our instruction, upon whom the ends of the ages have come."

---

1. "From the Greek *tupos*; primarily denoted a blow; to strike, hence, an impression, the mark of a blow (John 20:25); the 'impress' of a seal, the stamp made by a die, a figure, image, form or mold; 'an example,' pattern; in a doctrinal sense, a type (Rom. 5:14) [*The fulfillment of the "type" is referred to as the anti-type. Author's note.*] The basic idea of *anti* is 'facing.' There is no instance of the uncompounded preposition signifying 'against.' " *Vine's Expository Dictionary,* 222.

Everything that God instructed Israel to do was to serve as a pattern of things to come. Since they were to be the model for the Church, it was imperative that they minutely fulfill every command and direction of God. Thus, thousands of years later when the negative of the "Church in the wilderness" was developed, the picture would reveal the true nature and plan of God for His Church.

The fact that God often uses symbolism is nowhere more evident than in the books of Ezekiel, Daniel, and Revelation. After careful examination of some of the metaphors contained in these books, we are left with two impressions: that God utilizes particular metaphors often; and that these symbols contain the hidden seed of deeper truths yet to be revealed. The study of these metaphors is called *typology*. One of my college professors said, concerning the Old and New Testaments, "The New is in the Old contained; the Old is in the New explained." So, journey with me now as we closely examine several Old Testament allegories and symbols (hereafter referred to as *types*).

Since large volumes have already been dedicated to the subject, it is not my intent to attempt duplication of these works.[2] Time and space limitations allow no more than a cursory examination of each type considered here. The purpose of this chapter is to simply lay a foundation of proof that types are scripturally valid for examination and doctrine.

Passover

Jehovah God was about to unleash the fury of His final plague upon Egypt. At midnight He would dispatch the death angel with the terrifying mandate to visit every home in Egypt and kill the firstborn in any household that refused to place blood upon the doorpost and lintel. The blood was applied as a perfect example (type) of God's Passover. The destroying angel spared those houses where the blood was in place (see Ex. 12). Israel was then instructed to observe this ritual slaying of the lamb throughout all generations as the Feast of Passover.

When John the Baptist first saw Jesus he said, "Behold, the Lamb of God who takes away the sin of the world!" (Jn. 1:29b), publicly

---

2. For example, the book *Preaching From the Types and Metaphors of the Bible*, by Benjamin Keach, is 1,007 pages.

alluding to Jesus as the Paschal Lamb who would become the supreme sacrifice for sin.

It was clearly the Father's plan for Jesus, the Paschal Lamb, to be sacrificed at Passover (see Mt. 26:17-19). At the Last Supper Jesus took bread and wine and gave it to His disciples. Using the analogy of the bread being His body and the wine being His blood, He clearly referred to the elements of the Passover (see Mt. 26:26-28).

The apostle Paul added, "Clean out the old leaven, that you may be a new lump, just as you are in fact unleavened. For *Christ our Passover* also has been sacrificed" (1 Cor. 5:7; see also 5:8; Ex.12:15).

Water Baptism

Knowing that Pharaoh and his army were following closely behind, God could have led Israel out of Egypt by another route that wouldn't have dead-ended at the Red Sea. Fortunately, hindsight usually reveals what God was up to while we were busily worrying about the outcome. So it was with the Israelites as they watched the Red Sea roll back to reveal a highway of dry land.

Having two to three million people pass through the Red Sea was God's way of establishing a type of water baptism. The apostle Paul shed additional light on this: "For I do not want you to be unaware, brethren, that our fathers were all under the cloud, and all passed through the sea; and all were baptized into Moses in the cloud and in the sea" (1 Cor. 10:1-2). Paul also elaborated on this in Romans: "Or do you not know that all of us who have been baptized into Christ Jesus have been baptized into His death? Therefore we have been buried with Him through baptism into death" (Rom. 6:3-4a). Paul carried this theme even further in First Corinthians 12:13: "For by one Spirit we were all baptized into one body, whether Jews or Greeks, whether slaves or free, and we were all made to drink of one Spirit."

Manna and the Bread of Life

When the children of Israel became hungry, God supernaturally supplied food for them which they called *manna*, literally "bread from heaven" (Ex. 16:15). Jesus stated that He was the fulfillment of manna—the type for God's provision in the wilderness:

Jesus therefore said to them, "Truly, truly, I say to you, it is not Moses who has given you the bread out of heaven, but it is My Father who gives you the true bread out of heaven. For the bread of God is that which comes down out of heaven, and gives life to the world." They said therefore to Him, "Lord, evermore give us this bread." Jesus said to them, "I am the bread of life; he who comes to Me shall not hunger, and he who believes in Me shall never thirst" (John 6:32-35).

Sacrificial Lamb

The earliest scriptural reference to an animal being slain as a covering for sin is found in Genesis 3:21: "And the Lord God made garments of skin for Adam and his wife, and clothed them." We see a similar incident in Genesis 22:1-14 where Abraham, as a type of God the Father, was willing to sacrifice His only son. The type is repeated in Exodus 12:1-11,14 where the Passover was instituted and a lamb had to be slain.

The apostle Peter continued this theme: "Knowing that you were not redeemed with perishable things like silver or gold from your futile way of life inherited from your forefathers, but with precious blood, as of a lamb unblemished and spotless, the blood of Christ" (1 Pet. 1:18-19).

Brazen Altar

It was this altar in the tabernacle upon which the sacrificial animals were offered for the sins of the people. References to the sacrificial altar are too numerous to list here (see Leviticus, chapter one). Naturally, the antitype (fulfillment) of the sacrificial altar is the cross where *our* Paschal Lamb, Jesus, was offered as a sacrifice for our sins. The writer of the Book of Hebrews explicitly identified the Old Testament sacrifices as the types which found their fulfillment in Christ's sacrifice on Calvary.

After saying above, "Sacrifices and offerings and whole burnt offerings and sacrifices for sin Thou hast not desired, nor hast Thou taken pleasure in them" (which are offered according to the Law), then He said, "Behold, I have come to do Thy will." He takes away the first in order to establish the second. By this will we have been sanctified through the offering of the body of Jesus Christ once for all. And every priest stands daily ministering and offering time after time the same sacrifices, which can never take away sins; but He, having offered one sacrifice for sins for all time, sat down at the right hand of God (Hebrews 10:8-12).[3]

Brazen Serpent

In Numbers chapter 21 we find that as a result of Israel's sin, God had sent a plague of fiery serpents into their camp, and the people were dying in large numbers. Obeying God's instructions, Moses made a brazen serpent, placed it upon a pole, and announced God's promise that whoever looked upon the serpent would not die, but live.

This is indeed a strange type (a serpent) used here to represent Christ—that is, until we view it in its full context. Jesus Himself mentioned it in John 3:14-15: "And as Moses lifted up the serpent in the wilderness, even so [in the same way] must the Son of Man be lifted up; that whoever believes may in Him have eternal life." Throughout Scripture a serpent is used as a metaphor for Satan, from the Garden of Eden narrative in Genesis to Revelation 12:9 where it says, "...the serpent of old who is called the devil and Satan...." Why, then, would God choose such a strange analogy for Jesus who is the very antithesis of evil? We must look to Scripture for our answer.

In Scripture we discover that:

1. The serpent is a type of sin (Satan).

2. Death is a type of the penalty for sin.

3. Brass is a type of judgment.

4. Looking is a type of obedience and faith.

5. The cure is a type of salvation.

Second Corinthians 5:21 records: "He made Him [Jesus] who knew no sin *to be sin* on our behalf, that we might become the righteousness of God in Him." On the cross, God made Jesus into sin—our sin! At that moment He became the personification of all that was evil—the ugliness, sin, sickness, and death—so that God could judge it all at the cross. Since Calvary, people of every generation have only had to look and live—just look to the cross in simple faith and be saved (see Jn. 3:14-15).

---

3. See also Hebrews, chapters 7-10 in their entirety. These chapters are replete with types and antitypes.

Water of Life

Deep in the wilderness, Israel's water supplies had been exhausted. All around was barren desert and the scorching heat of the day. Again, God supplied! He spoke to Moses, saying: " 'Behold, I will stand before you there on the rock at Horeb; and you shall strike the rock, and water will come out of it, that the people may drink.' And Moses did so in the sight of the elders of Israel" (Ex. 17:6).

The apostle Paul used the above incident as a metaphor for Christ, our smitten rock, out of which the water of life flows freely: "And all drank the same spiritual drink, for they were drinking from a spiritual rock which followed them; *and the rock was Christ*" (1 Cor. 10:4).

While speaking with the woman at the well in Samaria, Jesus offered her living water: "Jesus answered and said to her, 'Everyone who drinks of this water shall thirst again; but whoever drinks of the water that I shall give him shall never thirst; but the water that I shall give him shall become in him a well of water springing up to eternal life' " (Jn. 4:13-14).

The Bible is replete with word pictures, which would lead to the obvious conclusion that God frequently uses symbolism to portray His hidden agenda.[4] Because types reflect God's plans for the future, they can be viewed as God's prophetic paintings of what is yet to come. Because God's foreknowledge is perfect, His prophetic paintings reflect that flawlessness—absolutely *nothing* must be allowed to mar them. Because types were precursors of future doctrines that would reveal the nature of God, He looked upon types and their fulfillment very seriously. You can understand then, why He levied such severe punishment when they were violated. The following example illustrates this clearly.

In Exodus 17:6 God instructed Moses to strike the rock, which produced a flow of water sufficient to satisfy the thirst of the multitude. This was evidently a type of Christ, our Rock, smitten *once* for all! Concerning this, the New Testament is unmistakably clear: Christ was to be wounded for mankind *once*—and *only* once! "For the death that He died, He died to sin, *once for all*" (Rom. 6:10a); "For

---

4.   For a more comprehensive study of this topic see my book: *Christian Meditation: Doorway to the Spirit*, chapter 21, "A Picture Is Worth a Thousand Words."

Christ also died for sins *once* for all, the just for the unjust" (1 Pet. 3:18a). (See also Hebrews 9:7,12,26,28.)

Christ's sacrifice at Calvary (the antitype) was the fulfillment of the type established when Moses struck the rock at Horeb. He would not die repeatedly. His sacrifice would be perfect and *"once* for all." With that in mind, let's turn to the Book of Numbers, chapter 20. The scene was similar to that at Horeb—there was no water. God gave explicit directions to Moses for how to remedy the situation:

> *"Take the rod…assemble the congregation and* **speak** *to the rock before their eyes, that it may yield its water. You shall thus* [by speaking] *bring forth water for them out of the rock and let the congregation and their beasts drink."* … *Then Moses lifted up his hand and* **struck the rock twice** *with his rod; and water came forth abundantly, and the congregation and their beasts drank* (Numbers 20:8,11).

Moses and his brother Aaron blatantly disobeyed the command of God to "speak to the rock." Because they chose to *strike* the rock for the second time, they forever marred the prophetic image contained in the type—that Messiah would only be smitten once! They disregarded God's command. He didn't consider their disobedience a light thing! "But the Lord said to Moses and Aaron, 'Because you have not believed Me, to treat Me as holy in the sight of the sons of Israel, *therefore you shall not bring this assembly into the land which I have given them'* " (Num. 20:12).

That seems a heavy toll to pay for such a minor infraction. But *was* it minor? Types, as prophetic pictures, are one of the means by which God speaks to us of events to come. Thus, when God reveals a type He is not simply showing us pretty pictures. He is communicating His prophetic Word that cannot fail! Moses failed to execute the command of God and defiantly substituted his own actions. God was not amused! By disobedience Moses had treated Him as unholy (profane, or common) in the eyes of the congregation. Moses had treated the word of Jehovah with contempt before the people, for which he paid the ultimate price: He would not enter Canaan. The sentence was absolute and irrevocable!

Chapter Six

The Big Lie—*Exposed*

Having believed the evil report of the lying spies, the Israelites refused to act on God's command to go up and possess the land. Forty long, arduous years passed, during which an entire generation of people died in the wilderness. Now a whole new generation stood on the banks of the muddy Jordan and were given the same instructions as the prior generation: "Go up and possess the land!" The passage of 40 years had not changed God's plan concerning Israel.

There before them lay a beautiful, rich, lush, and fruitful land. Just as God had promised, it was truly a land "flowing with milk and honey." At sunrise the people of God would rise up and move forward. Signs, wonders, and miracles would be the order of the day as God prepared to show Himself strong on behalf of His people. In obedience to its Creator, the Jordan River (the greatest barrier to their entering Canaan) would roll back before the people of God. Nothing and no one would be able to stand as an obstacle before the onslaught of this people poised on the verge of fulfilling their divine destiny.

Israel and the Church are inextricably linked together in typology. Thus, we must carefully examine Israel's history to discover precisely what their God-ordained destiny was, and how it pertains to the Church. In order to begin unraveling this mystery, we must look back to Egypt. When we follow the natural, chronological order of the various types, God's intended plan crystallizes. What also becomes clear is how deftly Satan has manipulated the thinking and the doctrine of the Church, thus influencing her actions (or lack thereof).

Since the meanings of the following types are evident, only a cursory examination will be afforded them. The one exception will be that we will confront in detail the true meaning behind the crossing of Jordan and God's command to "go up and possess the land."

1. **Pharaoh**: a type of Satan, destroyer and cruel taskmaster, relentlessly reigning over the people.

2. **Egypt**: a type of sin and the world with all its attractions.

3. **Israel in Egypt**: a type of mankind helplessly enslaved to sin and without hope.

4. **Moses**: a type of Jesus (the deliverer, Savior) who rescued lost mankind.

5. **Passover**: a type of salvation and deliverance.

6. **Passover lamb**: a type of "the Lamb of God" (Jn. 1:29).

7. **The Exodus**: a type of the redeemed as they forsake the world and sin.

8. **Passing through the Red Sea**: a type of water baptism; circumcision of the heart.

9. **Israel in the wilderness**: a type of the Church in the wilderness; boot camp; in preparation to possess Canaan.

At this juncture we are confronted with two major types, both of which have been misinterpreted by the Church. (As we delve into their true meanings, it will become evident how and why Satan has blinded the minds of believers to their actual representation.) I will first list the types and the typical meanings given for them, and then demonstrate why these are not acceptable in the light of Scripture:

1. **The Jordan River** is wrongly interpreted to be a type of death.

2. **Canaan** is wrongly interpreted to be a type of Heaven.

As far back as I can remember (in evangelical circles) the Jordan River has always been alluded to as a type of death. Having passed through the river (death), Canaan (Heaven) awaited you. There was one major problem: This interpretation wasn't, by any stretch of the imagination, scriptural. Canaan doesn't even remotely fit the type, and can no more represent Heaven than Disney World. The land certainly "flowed with milk and honey" as God had promised, but there were also many giants there who were determined to thwart Israel's takeover. Canaan was a land full of walled cities that would have to be conquered in battle—large cities, inhabited by enemies intent on preventing their overthrow. Somehow that doesn't seem to fit the scriptural descriptions of Heaven. Heaven is our final destination after all our battles have ended—the place where we lay our armor down, and hang our shield of faith and our sword of the Spirit over the mantel. There will be no giants to be contended with in that land, and warfare will be forgotten. There will be no more battle scars to heal or tears to wipe dry. Sickness will be a thing of the past and death will have lost its power as we enter into His joy forevermore! That is how the Bible describes Heaven.

Since Canaan isn't a type of Heaven, then crossing over Jordan cannot be a type of death, thus presenting a basic problem with commonly accepted evangelical typology. It then becomes obvious that something major is missing in the chronology of the types.

The Father of All Lies

This title, which Jesus attributed to Satan (see Jn. 8:44b), tells us a lot about his methods. (On the lighter side, I figure that the devil has told *almost* enough lies to run for public office.) Since it is the very nature of Satan to lie and deceive, let's not be deluded into believing that he has changed his tactics in our generation. One of the methods Satan delights to use against believers is to allow them a spoonful of truth (enough to satisfy them), while delivering a shovelful of lies and deception (enough to destroy them). That is exactly what he's done through the erroneous interpretation of the types under discussion.

Notice how subtly Satan has perpetrated his lies on the Church with his shovelful of deception. Then observe how gullibly she has swallowed it, shovel and all. According to Satan's version of typology, Israel was *saved* out of Egypt (sin and the world); *baptized* into Moses as they went through the Red Sea; *wandered in the wilderness* for 40 years; *crossed Jordan* (died); and *entered Canaan* (Heaven). That's the shovelful Satan wants the Church to swallow—and she has! Is the picture clear to you yet? Here's the program as Satan presents it: (1) Be saved; (2) be baptized in water; (3) wander aimlessly in the wilderness throughout your lifetime, doing nothing to intrude on Satan's turf while waiting patiently for death or the rapture, whichever comes first; (4) die or be raptured; and (5) go to Heaven.

Please don't misunderstand what I'm attempting to convey. It's not my contention that Satan wants people to get saved, water baptized, and finally go to Heaven. He certainly does not! His ultimate desire is that all mankind would be lost and go to hell. Fortunately, that will never happen, and he knows it. Even though he may act it at times, Satan is not stupid. He recognizes that there are certain things he cannot prevent, no matter how diligently he may try. Multitudes have already accepted Christ as their Savior and are happily on their way to Heaven despite his best efforts to the contrary. However, Satan is also not a quitter. His motto could be, "If at first you don't succeed, try, try again!" He's had aeons to perfect his methodology, so he reaches into his arsenal for...

The Big Lie

Clearly, Satan's primary plan is for all mankind to be lost, and he strives diligently toward that end. When that goal is frustrated and people do get saved, he immediately turns his attention to preventing them from discerning God's scriptural program for them as members of the Church. This accomplished, they are precluded from becoming a threat to him. If he can't deter them from attending church, he will attempt to guide them to a nominal place of worship where his influence is not overly threatened. Unfortunately, churches of that ilk are not hard to find, even within the Charismatic movement; so Satan has quite a selection from which to choose.

The big lie that he foists upon Christians is: "Once you're saved, sit back and do nothing; be nothing and expect nothing. Pose no threat to Satan's diabolical kingdom. Be content with the status quo. Don't rock the ecclesiastical boat. Live mediocre lives and believe that this is the most you are called to be or do. Don't study the Scriptures; but if you do, don't believe *all* of what you read. Wander aimlessly, uselessly, and ineffectually in the wilderness for a lifetime. Look forward to nothing on earth, while awaiting death (or rapture) and Heaven."

Undoubtedly Satan knows better than any of us what crossing the Jordan River and possessing the land represent. He is terrified that the Church will discover this truth and claim it, and he is totally dedicated to doing his utmost to prevent you from seeing it for your-self. If someone presents the revelation to you, Satan will attempt to either blind you to the truth or, failing that, endeavor to steal the seed of the Word of God from your mind (see 2 Cor. 4:3-4; Mt. 13:4,18-19).

The True Types Revealed

Have you ever seen something so simple that it was profound; or looked for something, and not found it, only to discover later that all the while it was under your nose? This was my own experience when the Holy Spirit began to reveal the true meanings behind the Jordan and Canaan types. Although I will explain the true types of both in two simple sentences, it will take the rest of this book to fully deline-ate all that Scripture has to say concerning them.

1. **Crossing over Jordan**: a type of the *baptism in the Holy Spirit*!

2. **Possessing the land**: a type of the *Spirit-filled life*; moving in the sign-gifts of the Holy Spirit; maturing into "the meas-ure of the stature which belongs to the fulness of Christ" (Eph. 4:13b); continually overcoming the enemy; possessing our possessions; and becoming the rod of God on earth!

Why does Satan take tranquilizers when you finally see this truth? Because when you understand this concept, your ministry will cause a powerful *shock wave* throughout the kingdom of darkness!

If Satan possesses no legal rights to anything in the Christian realm (and he doesn't), then how does he wreak havoc in the Church? What can believers do to reverse the situation? The Church must first cease to believe a wilderness-followed-by-death-or-rapture doctrine. Secondly, the Church must awaken to her scriptural, God-ordained power and potential. Then the gates of hell will literally tremble as demons bow at our feet and irreversible damage is done to the king-dom of darkness.

Chapter Seven

Possess the Land? I'm *Afraid* Not!

It is apparent in scriptural record that God had only one program for Israel, clearly stated in Deuteronomy 6:22-23: "Moreover, the Lord showed great and distressing signs and wonders before our eyes against Egypt, Pharaoh and all his household; and He brought us *out* from there in order to bring us *in*, to give us the land which He had sworn to our fathers."

Jehovah had brought them *out*, in order to bring them *in*! Evidence indicates that God had no contingency plan, no hidden agenda, and no alternate purpose for Israel. His exclusive intent was to bring them into, and cause them to possess, the land He had promised them. Initiating His plan, God brought ten devastating plagues on the land of Egypt, culminating in the death of the firstborn of every household that didn't have the sign of blood displayed upon it. Shortly thereafter He parted the Red Sea. For the next two years Israel witnessed miracles of provision as they trained for battle in preparation to possess the land.

Fear—The Great Destroyer of Faith

Since Israel had occupied front-row seats for God's spectacular display of signs, wonders, and miracles connected with the Exodus, what could possibly have deterred them from fulfilling their divine destiny? Surely some overwhelming force must have raised a barrier between them and their possession of Canaan—but what? Would you believe—*fear*? That insidious destroyer of faith reared its ugly head and fulfilled its assignment well. As a consequence, the adult population (20 years of age and older) of an entire nation (excluding Joshua and Caleb) perished in the wilderness, their destiny unfulfilled. Let this scriptural record speak to us lest we discover ourselves falling into the same pitfalls.

Fear rarely attacks alone. It is almost always accompanied by other debilitating spirits, as evidenced in the following Scriptures: "And so we see that they were not able to enter because of *unbelief*" (Heb. 3:19). "...And those who formerly had good news preached to them failed to enter because of *disobedience*" (Heb. 4:6). Someone has well said, "The highway of fear is the shortest route to defeat." Numbers 13:28–14:3 records proof positive that fear was a major contributing factor in Israel's failure to enter into and possess the land. While the whole context depicts a narrative of fear that paralyzed a nation, verse 33 sums it all up succinctly: "There also we saw the Nephilim [*Nephilim* is the Hebrew word for "giants."] (the sons of Anak are part of the Nephilim); and we became like grasshoppers in our own sight, and so we were in their sight."

The spies observed strong people living in great walled cities. They noticed all the *ites*—Hittites, Jebusites, Amorites, Canaanites, and Termites (*smile*)—but mostly, they saw the giants. (Satan will always diligently call attention to the many obstacles standing between us and the fulfillment of our divine destinies. He not only points out the obstacles, he greatly magnifies them, and simultaneously amplifies our many deficiencies, shortcomings, and past failures.)

If the spies had harbored any reservations before entering the land, they emerged from their explorations immobilized by fear. It is important to note that their fears were based on facts. There really *were* notable giants there, as well as vast numbers of people who inhabited impregnable cities with high walls—formidable deterrents to their conquest. To the casual observer these facts might well add up to a no-go situation. They certainly did to 10 of the 12 spies, who said, "We are not able to go up against the people, for they are too strong for us" (Num. 13:31b). The fact is, God had instructed them to bring back reports, not opinions! The factual report stated that all the aforementioned obstacles were in place. It was man's *opinion* that they were insurmountable. A major fact (obviously overlooked by ten of the spies) was that God knew all those barriers existed when He promised to deliver the land into their hands. For that generation, the price they paid for a brief moment of hesitation was a lifetime in the wilderness—*until every doubter was dead.* Someone has well said, "On the plains of hesitation bleach the bones of countless thousands who, upon the dawn of victory, sat down to rest—and resting died!"[1]

Seeing Is Believing (Not Necessarily)

With little effort, Satan succeeded in diverting Israel's attention from the promise and provision of God by causing them to focus on the obstacles and their own obvious inadequacies. All of this was guaranteed to generate fear of the highest magnitude—and it did! The people of Israel observed fleshly barriers through fleshly eyes and, with fleshly minds, arrived at a fleshly conclusion. That's how the flesh works. Our flesh (mind) has nothing else on which to base its conclusions except physical evidence, evidence that will never allow us to launch out on the promises of God. God's Word is explicit regarding this: "A natural man does not accept the things of the Spirit of God; for they are foolishness to him, and *he cannot understand them,* because they are spiritually appraised" (1 Cor. 2:14). The phrase "natural man" does not refer to the unsaved, but to saved individuals who live their lives after the senses! The Greek word for "natural" is *psuchikos,* which means:

> "Belonging to the *psuche,* soul (as the lower part of the immaterial in man), 'natural, physical,' describes the man in Adam and what pertains to him (set in contrast to *pneumatikos,* 'spiritual'), 1 Cor. 2:14; 15:44 (twice), 46 (in the latter used as a noun); James 3:15, 'Sensual' (RV margin, 'natural' or 'animal'), here relating more especially to the mind, a wisdom in accordance with, or springing from, the corrupt desires and affections; so in Jude 19."[2]

The human soul (mind) knows only what it receives through sensory input—that which is perceived through our five senses: taste, touch, smell, hearing, and sight. These five wonderful senses are God's gifts, which enable us to experience the physical world.

---

1. Author unknown.
2. *Vine's,* 426-427.

Every day, throughout every waking hour, the mind receives physical (sensory) input. Thus, all the knowledge it contains is of a physical (sensory) nature. Because of this, it is not qualified to make *spiritual* appraisals. First Corinthians 2:14 states quite clearly that the "natural man" doesn't accept spiritual things, and explains that spiritual things are "foolishness to him." The Bible says he cannot grasp them because they are only understood in the Spirit. That single verse entirely disqualifies unspiritual, carnal, fleshly minded individuals from understanding anything in the realm of the Spirit.

If he cannot prevent Christians from receiving the baptism in the Holy Spirit, Satan will do his utmost to convince them that this experience is an end unto itself. Sad to say, he's deceived the majority of those who claim to be Spirit-filled. Though *in type* they have crossed the Jordan River, they now sit just inside Canaan, complacently taking up space, but never *taking* space for the Kingdom of God. They have been born from above by the Holy Spirit and baptized in the Holy Spirit, but have never learned how to listen to and be led by the Holy Spirit.

Ask yourself the question, "What percentage of Spirit-filled believers in my church manifest a spiritual gift, and what percentage of them do so on a consistent basis?" For many of us, the answers are saddening. If your answer indicated a low or nonexistent number of people exercising gifts, ask yourself the following questions: (1) Does my pastor actively promote spiritual giftedness among the flock? (2) Does he or she allow the flow of the Holy Spirit to control the services, rather than always following a predetermined program? (3) Are manifestations of spiritual gifts allowed in public meetings or, for that matter, in any meetings? The responses generated by the above questions may well explain the dearth of supernatural activity in most Pentecostal, Full Gospel, and Charismatic churches today. It's a sad commentary.

Nothing to Fear but Fear Itself

Over half a century ago President Franklin Delano Roosevelt coined the phrase, "We have nothing to fear but fear itself." He was right. Some Christians fear so many things it's a wonder they ever accomplish *anything*! The children of Israel had their own collection of fear generators, one of which acted as a prime hindrance and prevented them from acting upon God's command to possess the land.

During their first two years of wandering in the wilderness, Israel encountered the enemy in battle on only a few minor occasions. They knew that upon entering Canaan they would see continued warfare until the entire land was conquered. Up until their arrival at Jordan all the miracles of power, deliverance, and provision had been provided by the leadership, Moses. But upon entering the land the people themselves would play an integral part in fulfilling the plan and purpose of God. The change would be noteworthy. God would require that they no longer be inactive spectators in the unfolding drama. They were to become active *participants* in the development of their national destiny!

Upon entering Canaan, God planned to work through all the people, not just through the leadership. This is clearly reflected in scriptural typology. When the Red Sea stood as an obstacle before Israel, God used Moses (leadership) to bring about deliverance. But when the Jordan River posed an equally insurmountable obstacle 40 years later, God involved the people in the resultant miracle (see Josh. 4:1-7). Notice that the manna (God's provision) ceased to fall the day after they entered the land (see Josh. 5:12); now it became their responsibility to make the land provide for them. God never intended that His people would continue to be spoon-fed by their leaders. It was always His plan for all the people to mature in faith and work closely with Him to extend His kingdom!

Chapters 12 and 14 of First Corinthians clearly reflect that this is also God's plan under the New Covenant—that every member of the Church be an active participant. The apostle Paul sums up these chapters on the manifestations of the Holy Spirit by saying: "What is the outcome then, brethren? When you assemble, *each one* has a psalm, has a teaching, has a revelation, has a tongue, has an interpretation. Let all things be done for edification" (1 Cor. 14:26).

Ephesians 4:11-12a lends us yet another insight into God's desires for the Church: "And He [Jesus] gave some as apostles, and some as prophets, and some as evangelists, and some as pastors and teachers, *for the equipping of the saints for the work of service.*" God's emphasis is obviously on the phrase "for the equipping of the *saints* for the work of service." This is the purpose for which God set apostles, prophets, evangelists, pastors, and teachers in the Church—to equip individual saints (you) for the work of service! Every believer is supposed to be involved in the work of extending the Kingdom of God, not simply warming a pew and listening to a sermon. For this "work of service" God has called us to, He has provided a supply of supernatural power.

The Book of Acts encourages us through examples of *ordinary* individuals who performed *extraordinary* miracles (see Acts 8:5-40). Others manifested various gifts through the power of the Holy Spirit. Even deacons worked miracles (see Acts 6:8). This remained the norm into the third and fourth centuries when a cataclysmic event caused radical changes in Church infrastructure.

The Roman emperor Constantine converted to Christianity and soon thereafter proclaimed Christianity the state religion. It immediately became popular to be a Christian (at least in name) and pagans filled the churches. These people had no concept of truly serving Christ. (To be *Christian* became politically correct.) Pagan temples, which now stood empty, were converted for use as church buildings. (Before this period believers met in homes.) Temple idols were destroyed, only to be replaced with statues of the saints. The clergy was composed (in large part) of men who had never had a genuine power encounter with Jesus Christ, but who were powerfully connected politically. During this upheaval (much to the detriment of the true Church), the Roman Catholic church became the leading voice for Christianity. Drastic measures were implemented to bring the common people into submission to the powerful clergy.

Perhaps the greatest crime perpetrated on the people was the clear-cut division of clergy and laity, which conveyed the clear (though unspoken) message: The clergy stand up *here* at the altar (symbolizing holy things, access to God and ministry) while the laity sits out *there* (removed from holy things, denied personal access to God and ministry). All functions of the ministry were performed for the people and no meaningful participation by the laity was permitted. The clear intent was to keep the people in spiritual darkness. It's no wonder this led to the "Dark Ages." In later centuries, when the advent of the printing press made the Bible available to everyone, the religious hierarchy forbade the common people to read it. Spiritual ignorance remained the norm for all but the clergy.

Nicolaitans? Has Anyone Seen the Nicolaitans?

In the Book of Revelation the apostle John vigorously denounced a certain group and their teachings:

> *Yet this you do have, that you hate the deeds of the Nicolaitans, which I also hate. He who has an ear, let him hear what the Spirit says to the churches. ... Thus you also have some who in the same way hold the teaching of the Nicolaitans. Repent therefore; or else I am coming to you quickly, and I will make war against them with the sword of My mouth* (Revelation 2:6-7a,15-16).

The apostle John referred to the "deeds" and "teachings" of the Nicolaitans, and stated emphatically that God not only hated them, but He *"will make war against them* with the sword of My mouth" (literally, the Word of God). The Nicolaitans were obviously proponents of a belief structure that was making insidious inroads into the Church.

If God is vehemently opposed to something, it is imperative that the Church has an understanding of what that something is, in order to diligently avoid it. However, aside from this brief mention in the Book of Revelation, I found only one other reference to the Nicolaitans in Church history. During the ante-Nicene period (A.D. 100-325), it was believed by some that the Nicolaitans had been a sect that followed Nicolas, one of the first deacons (see Acts 6:5). There seems to be no credible evidence for this assumption. Also, some of the deeds attributed to Nicolas are, according to one historian, "extremely improbable."[3] Confronted with this conundrum, I began searching the Greek language for a possible explanation. I found not only what I believe to be the answer, but a startling revelation—one that many church leaders would probably rather not talk (or have me write) about.

I discovered that the word "Nicolaitan" is a composite of two Greek words, *nikao* and *laos*:

> *Nikao*—"To overcome (its usual meaning) is translated 'conquering' and 'to conquer.'"[4]

---

3. Philip Schaff, "Ante-Nicene Christianity," *History of the Christian Church II* (Grand Rapids, MI: Wm. B. Eerdmans Pub. Co., July 1980): 464.
4. *Vine's.*

Laos—"Is used of the people at large, especially of people assembled."[5]

From this clarification, the message the Lord Jesus was attempting to convey when condemning the deeds and teachings of the Nicolaitans becomes obvious. The combination of the two words intimates that there had been a conquering (suppression) of "people assembled" (an expression used of the Church). The Nicolaitans then were members of the clergy who had subjugated the people of God.

We often associate such actions only with cults that keep their people under tight restraints physically, emotionally, and spiritually. But, please, let us not be so naive. The domination of people often takes a more subtle, though no less repressive, approach in today's Church. The fact is, because the manipulation is so subtle, most Christians don't even realize they are dominated. They attend church faithfully week after week and never suspect that something is wrong in their sheepfold. (Sheep are some of the dumbest animals in God's creation.) The Scriptures are clear that the Body (the Church) is supposed to minister to the Body (see 1 Cor. 14:26); yet, in most instances that simply does not happen. When the evangelical denominations took a strong stand against any and all manifestations of the Holy Spirit in the early years of the twentieth century, Full Gospel churches were raised up to allow the people to have a forum where the gifts of the Holy Spirit could function unhindered. For some time that was the norm, but today many of the Full Gospel churches and denominations that were born in that fire now exist only in the smoke of past glory!

During my extensive travels, which have taken me (as of this writing) to 35 countries of the world, I have witnessed the rise of mega-churches and the simultaneous decline of individual ministries among the people. More and more pastors tell me they will not permit any supernatural manifestations in some public meetings, while others refuse to allow them at all. These are not evangelicals, but Full Gospel pastors, who should know better. Among the minority who still permit the laity to manifest spiritual gifts there is a subtle, growing trend to exercise increasing control rather than oversight. Here is

---

5. *Vine's.*

the scenario: you feel that the Holy Spirit has impressed you with a word to share. Instead of simply giving the word, you are directed to first explain it to a deacon, who must "pass" on it before it is spoken to the congregation. If he does not pass on it—sorry! What's wrong with that picture? The problem is that in many cases the very one designated to "pass" on the word has never personally exercised any gift of the Holy Spirit. Thus, he has absolutely no concept of right or wrong in that realm. The decision to allow or disallow a spiritual word is based on carnal intellect—hardly the criteria for discerning spiritual gifts (see 1 Cor. 2:14-15). This form of subtle control assures that the congregation hears only what the leaders want them to, and nothing else!

One of the fears that led to Israel's failure to possess the land was the fear that they would have to participate in what God was planning to do. We still see that same fear among the people of God. Another prevalent fear today, which leads to a Nicolaitan spirit, must also be dealt with. This fear often invades the clergy when the Holy Spirit begins to manifest Himself through the people. Simply put, it's the fear of losing control. Pastors have confided in me that they will not allow any manifestations because "they may get out of control." When defending the people's right to be used of God in the gifts, I have been grieved to hear men of God respond by saying, "I won't allow it—because I can't control it!" What a sad commentary! It's my understanding that the Holy Spirit is supposed to be in control, not only of our lives, but our worship services as well.[6] Why should we fear that the Holy Spirit would somehow conduct our services in a manner inferior to any program we mere mortals could possibly orchestrate? We would do well to heed the injunction given, almost without exception, whenever an angel appeared in the Bible to herald some supernatural work: "Fear not!"

---

6.   I heartily recommend *The Open Church* by James H. Rutz. It's available from your local Christian bookstore or: The Seed Sowers, P.O. Box #3368, Auburn, ME 04212-3368. I also encourage you to purchase another copy for your pastor, who will probably thank you for it!

Chapter Eight

Where Has All the Power Gone?

That was the question Gideon asked of the visiting angel. (See Judges 6:13.) Unfortunately, several thousand years later, the issue remains the same. If we claim that God is with us, then where are all the miracles the first-century Church and our early Full Gospel forefathers experienced? Sadly enough, the Full Gospel denominations have strayed so far from their heritage of signs, wonders, and miracles that hardly anyone bothers to ask that question anymore.

We claim so much, but possess so little. The blind come into our churches and leave still blind; the lame and crippled come and leave still lame and crippled; the deaf come and leave still deaf! We live in sin-tortured cities where murder rates soar to new heights every year. The plagues of drug addiction, alcoholism, and prostitution run rampant. The murder of unborn babies is not only allowed, but sanctioned by our local and national governments, yet the Church has had a negligible impact on these conditions. Where in heaven's name is the Church, the Spirit-filled Church, the Full Gospel Church, while all this is happening? Some Christians are actively participating in protest rallies and anti-abortion marches, sending petitions to our elected representatives, etc. I'm not questioning the methods, the effectiveness, or even the sincerity of those involved in these actions. What I am asking is: In all of this, *where is the power of God*? If we have traded the power for protest then something is radically wrong. If the gospel we present to the world is powerless to deliver meaningful results, why should anyone want what we have?

God is raising up a prophetic voice in the world that is asking, "Where has all the power gone?" The religious establishment has closed its ears hoping that few will hear the question, and it certainly isn't holding them responsible for answering. But God's prophetic question will not go away!

God is finished "winking at sin" (see Acts 17:30). He is calling Full Gospel leaders to account, holding them responsible for their attitudes and actions. The Holy Spirit has been given the mission of preparing a glorious Church. If some choose not to be a part of that great Body because of lukewarm desire, so be it. He will then seek out those whose hearts *burn* for Him. These will be mightily anointed by the Holy Spirit, and their ministries will be accompanied by signs, wonders, and miracles. How can you make sure you are included among them?

If we don't know where we are, we can never get to where we need to be! Until believers face the fact of how spiritually anemic the Church truly is, they will never cry out to the Holy Spirit for help. Tragically, most Christians (even Spirit-filled ones) have never had a power encounter with the Holy Spirit. Living ordinary, instead of *extraordinary* lives, they know nothing of the Scripture, "But the people *that do know their God* shall be strong, and *do exploits*" (Dan. 11:32b KJV). Exploits? The average church member (the operative word is *average*) has never even volunteered to work in any facet of church ministry, let alone done exploits!

A national survey of church members reports the following: 10% can't be found anywhere; 20% never attend a church service; 25% admit they never pray; 35% admit they never read the Bible; 40% never contribute to the church; 60% never read or study their Sunday school lesson; 70% never attend the Sunday evening service; 75% never assume any responsibility in the church; 85% never invite anyone to church; and 95% never win even one soul to Christ.[1] *Yet, 100% of them expect to go to Heaven!* These statistics force us to confront the diminished, backslidden state of the Church. If doing so causes us to feel anguish, what must the heart of God feel? The condition of the Church is far more than disturbing; it's absolutely frightening! How

---

1. *Radiant Life*, Volume #63, #4, Part #2, June-August Sunday School Publication for 1990.

did it get that way? Perhaps for the moment we should forget about doing exploits—and just get back to basics!

The World's Largest Entertainment Center

No, it's not Disney World—it's the Church. Despite the startling figures quoted above, we're faced with the seeming contradiction implicit in the rising numbers of mega-churches. It would appear that today's Church is not only alive and well, but thriving. Please understand that what I'm about to say does not apply to every large church; neither do I discount the various music ministries, etc., nor the pageantry that often brings glory to God. However, like Cinderella, if the shoe fits, we must wear it.

Sometimes when evaluating vocalists, we often misidentify a high note that is held forever as a result of the anointing, when in reality it is no more than a good set of lungs mixed with a large dose of human talent. When evaluating churches, we likewise often mistake fatness for growth; but God has no such mistaken illusions. Prophet Paul Cain says that the church is "dying of terminal boredom," which may be why so many churches have felt the need to become large entertainment centers in order to attract people. ("Are they really interested in the people and their needs, or do they just like crowds?")[2] Once this entertainment syndrome is entered into, it becomes necessary to continually schedule the latest well-known personality with a big name (while ignoring Him who has a "name above *all* names") in order to keep drawing ever-increasing crowds. "It has been too easy to substitute froth for fullness, emotion for enduement, hype for holiness."[3] Please remember that there is a vast difference between having a crowd and being the Church!

The following illustration will stand alone, followed only by scriptural commentary:

> A leading Chinese minister toured the United States, visiting many large churches along the way. Just before his return to China he was asked, "What is your view concerning the American Church?" He replied, "I am absolutely amazed at

---

2. Richard G. Champion, "Pentecostal Pretenders," *Pentecostal Evangel* (Dec. 29, 1991), 3.
3. Champion, "Pentecostal Pretenders," 3.

how much the American Church has accomplished—*without God!*"

Unless the Lord builds the house, they labor in vain who build it (Psalm 127:1a).

*'Not by might nor by power, **but by My Spirit**,' says the Lord of hosts* (Zechariah 4:6b).

Following the Spirit

Some years ago the Holy Spirit led my wife and me to relocate to Chicago. After our arrival we began attending a small church of approximately 50 people, who met in a building that would seat 700. The pastor confided to me that they were on the verge of financial bankruptcy.

My pastor offered his church building for rent and I began conducting Friday night miracle services. Attendance soon reached 200-300 people. Bill Cromie, a nationally syndicated columnist who wrote for the *Chicago Daily News*, heard about what God was doing, so he attended one miracle service to see for himself what was happening. That night, along with many other miracles, God healed five people who had large goiters. Impressed by what he saw, Mr. Cromie asked if he could bring a cameraman the following week, do a photo shoot during the service, and interview me afterward for a column.

The following week proved to be a repetition of the one before. The Holy Spirit performed many miracles, the most notable of which was the immediate restoration of sight to a man who had been totally blind in both eyes for 40 years.

After the article was featured in the *Chicago Daily News*, people came from all over the Chicago area to see the wonders of God—and they were never disappointed. The crowds were so large that the church quickly reached capacity. Every seat was occupied; the foyer and cloak room were filled with chairs; chairs lined each aisle and across the front; and the last of the latecomers found themselves seated in the choir section.

As many as 100 people accepted Christ as their Savior in a single service. Some of these converts had no church home, so I encouraged them to attend that church. Within nine short months the little 50-member church on the verge of bankruptcy had grown to 280 people.

The increased attendance brought an expected increase in cash flow along with the need for additional church staff. An associate pastor was hired who "knew" how things should be done. The new order of the day for church growth became gags, gimmicks, clowns, give-aways, busing, and any other promotional hype he could dream up. Oh yes, I must not forget the Yogi Bear outfit the new associate pastor loved to wear!

It wasn't too long before I received a letter from the senior pastor informing me that I could no longer rent the church facilities for miracle services; and the church that had once enjoyed the continual visitation of the Holy Spirit became simply an entertainment center. My wife and I continued to attend the church and watched with sadness as the people gradually began to go elsewhere. (Programs are sorry substitutes for power, and people who were born in the *fire* will not be content to live in the *smoke*.) As the attendance diminished (and the finances plummeted), one of the first cutbacks was the position of the associate pastor, "Reverend Gags and Gimmicks." The attendance ultimately fell back down to 50 people; the Yogi Bear suit was packed away; and the senior pastor left with a broken heart.

Years later I developed a warm relationship with a subsequent pastor of that church. One morning upon entering his office, I found him red-faced with laughter. He explained that the former associate pastor, "Reverend Gags and Gimmicks," had just called him to ask a favor. The conversation had gone something like this: "Hello, Pastor! This is 'Reverend Gags and Gimmicks,' the ex-associate pastor of your church. I was wondering if you still have the Yogi Bear suit in storage. If so, I'd love to borrow it. We always had such a wonderful anointing of the Holy Spirit when I wore that Yogi Bear suit!"

I wish there was a happier ending to this story, but this is the real world, not a Hollywood script. Unfortunately, some people never learn to depend upon the power of the Holy Spirit. "Reverend Gags and Gimmicks" was assured that the suit was somewhere in storage. It would indeed be sent to him promptly—and he could feel free to keep it. Yogi is probably still out there, and is possibly the only *anointing* the "Reverend Gags and Gimmicks" will ever know. (Although we are commanded to possess our Promised Land, many settle for the land of make-believe.)

Jesus needed no celebrity singers or entertainers, no acrobats or trapeze artists, to travel with Him to attract the masses. Huge crowds thronged Jesus everywhere because of the authority with which He spoke and the miracles He performed (see Jn. 6:2). But many tell us that it's different today. Many say He no longer performs miracles. If that were true, the Church *would* be left to its own devices to draw crowds—but it is not! "Jesus Christ is the same yesterday and today, yes and forever" (Heb. 13:8).

Full Gospel denominations still retain a statement on miraculous healing among their tenets of faith, yet when was the last time anything miraculous took place in many of their churches? If Full Gospel pastors and church members were ever indicted for being Full Gospel, for many of them there wouldn't be enough evidence to convict them!

On the day of Pentecost, 120 believers received the baptism in the Holy Spirit, and they turned the world upside down. Today we could have 120 Full Gospel *churches* in a city and no one would even know they were there! Something is wrong, *desperately* wrong!

Pharisees Are Alive and Well

In Scripture there were two major factions of Jewish religious leaders—the Pharisees and the Sadducees—and they were about as far apart doctrinally as was possible. The Pharisees believed in (or at least gave lip service to) the supernatural, whereas the Sadducees denied everything supernatural. (Aside: the Sadducees didn't believe in the supernatural, so they were sad-you-see.)

The Pharisees were purists. They maintained purity of doctrine but they had difficulty translating doctrine into action. They vehemently fought anyone who debated the existence of the supernatural, yet they crucified Jesus who performed more miracles than they had ever seen. You see, it's one thing to maintain written tenets of faith in the supernatural, but it's another thing altogether to practice and experience them regularly! Sadly, down through the centuries the Church has not heeded the admonition of Jesus to, "Watch out and beware of the leaven [teachings] of the Pharisees and Sadducees" (Mt. 16:6). Because of the destructive nature of these doctrines, Jesus' dire warning to His disciples was that they must have nothing to do with the insidious teachings of the Pharisees and Sadducees. (Unfortunately the Pharisees and Sadducees are alive and well in today's

Church—along with the "Don't-want-to-sees," "Cannot-sees," "Refuse-to-sees," and "Will-not-sees.")

Sometimes I Just Wonder...

The new breed of Full Gospel ministers has in large part shifted the emphasis from the Holy Spirit's control (which is scriptural) to the carnal control of self and flesh, which is against everything Scripture teaches. In some church bylaws the pastor is even listed as the C.E.O. (Chief Executive Officer) or, more plainly stated, head of the Church! It's no wonder, then, that pastors actually begin to believe that they are in control. Mere mortals in control of the Church?! I think not! That is the absolute antithesis of scriptural teaching: "And He put *all* things in subjection under His feet, *and gave Him as head over all things to the church*" (Eph. 1:22; also Eph. 4:15b; 5:23; Col. 1:18; 2:10).

Jesus Christ (not any man or woman) is head over *all* things to the Church—head of the Church, head of the body, and head *over all rule and authority*. May we conclude that "over all rule and authority" (see Col. 2:10) includes every pastor—even those who claim C.E.O. status? Jesus Himself, through the Holy Spirit, demands His rightful position as C.E.O. of the Church. *He* wants to be in charge. Have these pastor/C.E.O.'s forgotten Zechariah 4:6: " 'Not by might nor by power, *but by My Spirit*,' says the Lord of hosts." If leaders would lay aside their desperate desire to be in charge, it would be one giant step forward toward a powerful shock wave of the Holy Spirit. We will experience that shock wave, with or without those leaders. The Holy Spirit is in the process of raising up an army of leaders who will not be "company men" to their backslidden denominations, who will not only allow, but *welcome* the Holy Spirit's control of their lives, their churches, and their ministries!

The Church Has Some Brass!

Unquestionably, the Full Gospel church has lost its former glory. What used to be, for the most part, is no more. Where the Holy Spirit once reigned, oftentimes man is now in control. Where the glory of God once filled our churches and the praises of God resounded in every service, we often hear only hollow echoes of what once was.

Most people who attend Full Gospel churches today have little knowledge of their glorious heritage, when signs and wonders were the order of the day and miracles a common occurrence.

We see a foreshadowing of this same spirit in Scripture.[4] King Solomon had made 500 shields of gold, which hung in the temple. (In Scripture gold is always a type or symbol of God.) When King Rehoboam forsook the law of the Lord, God sent judgment upon him in the form of Shishak, king of Egypt (a type of Satan). Shishak came against Judah and Jerusalem, pillaged the house of the Lord, and removed all the golden shields. Rehoboam should have hotly pursued Shishak (Satan), battled with him, and retrieved the shields of gold (God). Of course, that thought probably never even entered the mind of the backslidden king. It was much simpler to create shields of brass that looked just like the genuine—shields that would fool most of the people. To the untrained eye they were no different from the shields that had adorned the house of God since Solomon's day. The people were led to believe that the rumors they had heard were false. After all, everyone could look and see for themselves that the golden shields were still in place. *Only they weren't!* Instead, convincing counterfeits filled the empty spaces where the genuine shields of gold had hung before. Of course, before long another generation arose who knew nothing of Shishak and his plunder of the house of the Lord. To those who had never known shields of gold, brass shields were not only acceptable, but proper!

All That Glitters Is *Not* Gold!

Today's Full Gospel churches have lost much of the anointing, and the former glory is no longer in place. Satan has pillaged the house of the Lord and the shields of gold were long ago removed. The Full Gospel leaders should have risen up in unity, pursued and waged war with the enemy, and restored the shields of gold (the type of God's Presence) to the house of the Lord. But, in most cases, they have not! Instead they have manufactured shields of brass and continued on with business as usual! When writing a warning to Timothy, the apostle Paul addressed these types of people: "Holding to a *form* of godliness,

---

4. Please read First Kings 10:16-17; 14:25-28 before proceeding.

although they have denied its power; and *avoid* such men as these" (2 Tim. 3:5).

In seeking to avoid the trouble associated with warfare, Full Gospel leaders have allowed Satan to walk off with whatever he pleased, and they have created look-alikes to fool the people. Worship services are often no more spiritually appealing than dry Pablum. In many churches, services are planned in advance by people who entertain, with no thought of the Holy Spirit's being in control. In fact, the mere concept that the Holy Spirit should do anything in the service is foreign to many of them. Their theme song could well be, "I Did It *MY* Way!"

In glaring contrast, it was recorded of the Azusa Street revival that began in 1906, "All who are in touch with God realize as soon as they enter the meeting that the Holy Ghost is the leader."[5] The account continues by saying, "Pride, self-assertion, self-importance, and self-esteem could not survive there."[6] To which I say, *Hallelujah!*

The Full Gospel Church Is in Good *Form*

In many Full Gospel churches people still clap their hands during the song service and many raise their hands in praise. Occasionally they mention the Holy Spirit. At the outset everything seems to be all right, but is it? They've maintained their Full Gospel form, but have no anointing and no power. Attending many of these churches is akin to visiting a Hollywood movie set where everything you see is just a facade behind which nothing is genuine! Everything appears just fine on the surface but when you search behind the set for the anointing, the supernatural power of the Holy Spirit, then you discover how vacant, shallow, and hollow everything really is. "We pride ourselves on the informality of our services. But if every service follows the same pattern, is it Pentecostal worship or Pentecostal ritual? Some services are, as one person described them, a mile wide and an inch deep. Neither noise nor quiet guarantees Pentecostal reality."[7]

---

5. Stanley H. Frodsham, *With Signs Following*. Revised Edition (Springfield, MO: Gospel Publishing House, 1946), 33.
6. Frodsham, *With Signs Following*, 36.
7. Champion, "Pentecostal Pretender," 13.

Many Full Gospel churches don't even attempt to fool anyone. They are far removed from the kingdom, the power, and the glory, and offer no excuses for it. They have deliberately left the old path with absolutely no intention of returning to it. For a long while the Full Gospel denominations craved acceptance by their evangelical brethren. But this acceptance carried a high price tag. In many quarters, churches have forsaken their heritage (the supernatural anointing of the Holy Spirit) and have become just like all the others.

God Himself intended to be Israel's King, their only leader. Israel's downfall began when they demanded a flesh-and-blood king, so they could become "like other nations." We are not called to be like the others. We are called to be unique—the standard-bearers! When the prophet Samuel despaired because of Israel's demand for a king, God replied:

*"Listen to the voice of the people in regard to all that they say to you, for they have not rejected you, but **they have rejected Me** from being king over them. Like all the deeds which they have done since the day that I brought them up from Egypt even to this day—in that **they have forsaken Me** and served other gods—so they are doing to you also."*

*... Nevertheless, the people refused to listen to the voice of Samuel, and they said, "No, but there **shall be a king over us, that we also may be like all the nations...**" (1 Samuel 8:7-8,19-20).*

In their mad rush toward acceptability and respectability among the evangelicals, Full Gospel churches lost their distinctiveness—the supernatural manifestations of the Holy Spirit, which were their hallmarks. When visiting a Full Gospel church in earlier times, it soon became clear to you that this church was *different*! The power and Presence of the Holy Spirit were unmistakably present.

Much of today's churchgoing generation likes things neat and in place; but when the Holy Spirit moves He isn't compelled to abide by our rules. In fact, He delights in overriding them. His manifestations aren't always pretty or acceptable to the world or the Church. On the day of Pentecost the crowds accused Spirit-filled believers of being drunk at nine o'clock in the morning saying, "They are full of sweet wine" (Acts 2:13b). When John Wesley preached, people began "falling out" under the power, and dignified (mummified) churchgoers thought that was disgraceful! At the turn of the twentieth century, believers began speaking in other tongues and were likewise disdained. Today there is a new breath of the Spirit in the land; it is accompanied by holy laughter and this is likewise raising the eyebrows of many Full Gospel/Charismatic leaders. When will we learn that *whatever* the Holy Spirit does is right and proper?

These Signs Shall Follow Them That Believe...

For many churches, the only "sign" to indicate that they are Full Gospel is the one in front of the church announcing that this particular church is affiliated with a denomination that used to be Full Gospel. They are now God's frozen people, of whom it could have been written, "many are cold, a few are frozen!" I suppose that would make them *the frozen chosen*.

If You Have the *Name*—Play the *Game!*

It's absurd to maintain the name "Full Gospel" (or any denominational name associated with being Full Gospel), if one is unwilling to play the game. It's not my intention to speak badly of our evangelical brethren. What I desire to convey is this: If I wanted to worship like a Baptist or a Lutheran, I would attend a Baptist or Lutheran church. Likewise, if I wish to be called Full Gospel, I should worship in the Spirit (see Jn. 4:23-24) and manifest Full Gospel power and anointing.

"A Rose by Any Other Name Would Smell as Sweet"

Thus said William Shakespeare many centuries ago. By the same token, a decomposing corpse by any other name would also carry the odor of decay. Judging by the stagnant smell emanating from many Full Gospel churches and denominations, it's time for change. It is time for the Full Gospel church to awaken from her *gravely* weakened spiritual condition. Only then will the cry for renewal and revival bring about needed change.

Where Do I Start Looking?

The world is rife with evil. Sin and sinfulness dominate the evening news and politicians and police promise changes that will never be forthcoming. Purveyors of drugs attach their vicious tentacles to younger children every year and hopelessness pervades our nation and the world. The blame for this deteriorating condition is not only

63

to be laid at the gates of hell, but also at the door of the powerless American Church!

In Second Kings 6:1-7, a building for the School of the Prophets was under construction when suddenly one of the workers saw his axe head fly off its handle and sink into the river. The axe head clearly represents power for service—lost! Running to the prophet Elisha, the worker explained his dilemma. His first move was the correct one. He admitted that he had lost something. A great many Christians today who have lost their power for service continue to swing the empty axe handle, producing a lot of noise but accomplishing nothing. They maintain the same motions, and the same form, but the power for service is no longer present. What a tragedy!

Elisha asked, "Where did it fall?" In other words, "Where did you lose it?" That's a legitimate question, yet many leaders today become incensed at the slightest hint that things may not be quite the *status quo* in their churches, ministries, etc. No one likes to be confronted with the fact that they have backslidden, yet we can never regain what is missing until we first admit that we have lost something.

Immediately the young man took the prophet to the spot where he had lost the axe head. This is the action that causes a problem for most Full Gospel churches and people. They adamantly refuse to return to the place in time or the experience in their lives where they lost the Holy Spirit's power for service. Yet this step is absolutely essential to the reclamation of the Holy Spirit's anointing upon our movements and our individual lives. Please notice that only when the young man: (1) *recognized* his loss, (2) realized the *extent* of his loss, and (3) was willing to *return* to the place of his loss, was he able to *regain* what was lost. Going somewhere else just won't work. You must return to the place where you lost it!

The story is told of a police officer who observed a drunken man on his knees at night under a streetlight, apparently looking for something. The policeman approached him and asked, "What are you doing down on your knees in the street?" To which the drunk replied, "I lost a quarter, and I'm looking for it." The policeman inquired, "Exactly where did you lose it?" "Way up the street," the man answered. The policeman, looking puzzled, asked, "Well then, why are you looking for it here?" With the profound wisdom that only a drunk can muster, he replied, "Because there's more light here, that's why!"

Sadly, in the entire annals of church history, no denomination, having lost its former glory, has ever been renewed. Please reflect once again upon my earlier quotation: "Those who cannot remember the past are condemned to *repeat* it."

Chapter Nine

Why Has All the Power Gone?

Backsliding is not a new phenomenon; it's as old as time itself. Israel's frequent backsliding (as recorded in First and Second Chronicles and First and Second Kings) is well-known. Pitifully, the tendency to stray from God didn't end with the Old Testament, and it is nowhere more evident than in the Book of Revelation. In the first chapter (v. 13), Jesus is portrayed as standing in the midst of the lampstands, which represent the Church. By chapter three (v. 20) we find Him standing outside the Church, knocking at its door while pleading for someone, anyone, to let Him in. He is apparently locked out of His own Church—and only someone on the inside can open the door and invite Him back in. What a heartrending scene.

All seven of the churches of Asia Minor were in various stages of backsliding when Jesus, through the apostle John, wrote to them.[1] Please note that without exception every discourse addressed to the seven churches began with God saying, "I *know*" (Rev. 2:2,9,13,19; 3:1,8,15). And He does! He knows where we have been, where we are, and where we are going. There is absolutely nothing hidden from His sight—*He knows*! " 'I am *He who knows*'...declares the Lord" (Jer. 29:23b). And again, "*All* things are open and laid bare to the eyes of Him with whom we have to do" (Heb. 4:13b).

---

1. Revelation 1:10-11; also Revelation, chapters 2 and 3. Please note especially chapter 2, verses 1-7.

It's urgent that the Church awaken from her self-induced trance and realize how far she has strayed from God's scriptural design. Because many of our churches are prominent and wealthy, many preach that things are better in the Church now than ever before (that's also what the Laodicean church said in Revelation 3:17). But *He knows!* Many even deny that the Church is backslidden. But *He knows!* One purpose for this book is because He wants *you* to know!

Keeping firmly in mind the fact that He knows all about us and the condition of the Church, let's turn our attention briefly to Christ's admonition to the Ephesian Church. By any standard it was one of the least backslidden of the seven churches, and was the first to be addressed by Jesus. He praised them for several things they had done correctly, but then quickly drew their attention to their major weakness: "But I have this against you, *that you have left your first love. Remember therefore from where you have fallen, and repent and do the deeds you did at first; or else I am coming to you, and will remove your lampstand out of its place—unless you repent*" (Rev. 2:4-5).

It is important that we recognize the true state of the Church in Ephesus. It was a church that was doing a whole lot of right things. As churches go, it had a great deal to commend it, yet it was in deep trouble with the Lord! His major indictment against the Ephesians was that they had left their first love—no small thing with the Lord.

First love! Isn't it grand! Nothing is quite like it when those wonderful feelings of attraction are awakened deep inside you, and you begin to know that "special someone" is fast becoming more than a casual acquaintance. Your heart races at the very thought of your new love, and your appetite for food and other company fades. Hours with that one person are not adequate—in fact, they seem like fleeting moments. Your every waking thought focuses on them. Others have to call your name twice to snap you out of your reverie, and just the mention of that special name makes your heart skip a beat, your face flush with warmth. Any excuse will suffice for you to hear that voice. In fact, several phone calls a day are not uncommon. You will go to any length to be together, and not even wild animals could keep you apart. That person is your constant topic of conversation. Ah, yes, first love! But how soon we forget!

> "Pastor/author Francis Frangipane once told me of the beginning of his little church in Cedar Rapids, Iowa. A spiritual idealist, Frangipane committed himself to spend every

morning—all morning—in prayer. Then his church grew. (Churches with praying pastors, it seems, always grow.)

"However, people with problems began showing up at Frangipane's church. Then, there just weren't enough hours in his day to minister to God and minister to people, too. So he cut his prayer time to three hours a day. Then two.

"One day, he said, a young friend who had just spent the morning with God stopped by his house. He had a message from God.

" 'What did God say?' Francis asked the friend.

" 'God said, "*Tell Francis I miss him.*" ' "[2]

Likewise, I believe that Jesus is saying to me, "Tell My people I miss them!" Perhaps we also need to be reminded of what our first love for Jesus was like. Can you recall how the mere mention of His name thrilled you and your heart yearned to spend long hours alone in His Presence? The church doors couldn't open soon enough or often enough to suit you. Your appetite for His Word exceeded that for earthly food; thus you spent long hours feasting on His Word. You longed to know everything about Him, so He became the center of almost every conversation. Prayer was not a chore. It was a privilege. Supernatural manifestations were like a magnet to you, drawing you wherever the Holy Spirit was moving. Jamie Buckingham writes, "Having tasted from the sweet spring of intimacy with God, we will never again be satisfied with lapping from earth's polluted puddles."[3] Ah, yes—*first* love! But how soon we forget! (Have *you* forgotten?) "How blessed are all those *who long for Him*" (Is. 30:18c).

The next item on Jesus' agenda for the Church in Ephesus was to command them to "remember therefore from where you have fallen" (Rev. 2:5a). It was urgent that they take a good hard look backward to see what they once had possessed, imperative that they review their first love. Doing so might rekindle that long-forgotten flame. Backslidden churches often refuse to consider their past, fearing to confront the glaring contrast between today's *brass* and yesterday's *gold*! Yet Jesus Himself commanded the Church at Ephesus to look backward in

---

2. Jamie Buckingham, "Dual Status," *Charisma Magazine* (Aug. 1993), 106.
3. Buckingham, "Dual Status," 106.

time as their first step forward toward spiritual renewal. We often treat the Lord's commands as mere suggestions (see Lk. 6:46). (Had Moses been Charismatic, he probably would have come down from Mount Sinai with the *Ten Suggestions!*)

Repent? Who, Me?

Jesus' next command to the Ephesian Church was that they *repent*, a word seldom heard in our churches anymore. In order for people to repent they must first be confronted with their sins. Since many churches have become entertainment centers for the saints(?), their leaders hesitate to say or do anything that might cause the least bit of discomfort. Talking about sin and repentance does just that!

The Greek word for "repentance," *metanoeo*, has to do with undergoing a change of mind:

> "*Metanoeo*: to perceive afterwards (*meta*, 'after,' implying 'change,' *noeo* 'to perceive'; *nous* the mind, the seat of moral reflection)...hence signifies, 'to change one's mind or purpose,' always for the better, an amendment, and *always*, except in Luke 17:3-4, *of repentance from sin.*"[4]

Paul said that godly sorrow (Greek = *lupe*: "*pain* of body or *mind*") produces repentance (see 2 Cor. 7:10), indicating that a contrite heart is necessary in order to repent. Repentance is more than simply changing your mind (as some would have you believe). True, repentance *is* a change of mind, but it's brought about because your heart is broken with grief over your sin! Another (Hebrew) rendering for the word *repentance* means to turn about-face and proceed in the other direction. To do so would place us back where we started, back to our first love. This was what Jesus instructed the Church in Ephesus to do: "change your mind, make an about-face, and head back toward your glorious beginning."

If It Ain't Broke—Don't Fix It!

Through the centuries the Church has continually tried to improve on perfection. What a silly thing to do. Jesus' plan for the first-century Church was uncomplicated. He was to be its Head! He would fill believers with the power of the Holy Spirit, and equipped with

---

4.   *Vine's,* 525; emph. mine.

that anointing, they would tear down Satan's strongholds. Simple enough, wasn't it? Yet, even in those formative years of the Church, there were those who sang, "I Did It *My* Way!" (That must be a very popular song, because it keeps cropping up throughout Church history.) Obviously there were quite a few in the Ephesian church who sang it. They had strayed far afield from their initial walk with Jesus and they were under strong indictment for having done so.

Jesus' last command to this Church was, "...do the deeds you did at first" (Rev. 2:5a). Simply put, "Stop doing whatever it is you're now doing and go back to what you used to do!" There is a desperate need for the Church of this century to read and heed those words.

The final words of Jesus to the Church in Ephesus were uncompromising: "or else I am coming to you, and will remove your lampstand out of its place—unless you repent" (Rev. 2:5b). This threatened visit, mentioned above, had ominous overtones! This would not be a social call. "If you do not do precisely as I have instructed you," said Jesus, "I will remove your lampstand out of its place!"[5] End of discussion!

John's vision was of the Ancient of Days, resplendent in all His glory, surrounded by His Church (the seven lampstands). The Churches were perfectly situated (surrounding Him) to continually behold His glory, always in His Presence! What more could any Church desire than His continuous Presence in their midst?

What then were the implications of Jesus' threat to remove their lampstand? Simply stated, they would cease to be His Church. Jesus would refuse to be in their midst, and they would no longer behold His glory or stand in His Presence. They had possessed it all—His kingdom, His power, and His glory—yet they turned a deaf ear to the Lord's entreaty. The twentieth-century Church has done much the same thing, and have become like the people to whom the prophet Jeremiah wrote: "For My people have committed two evils: *they have forsaken Me*, the fountain of living waters, *to hew for themselves cisterns*, broken cisterns, that can hold no water" (Jer. 2:13).

Jesus told the Ephesian Church where they were, reminded them of where they had been, and admonished them in no uncertain terms to

---

5. Before proceeding, please read Revelation 1:9-20, taking special note of verses 12, 13, and 20.

return to Him! Likewise, the Church of this generation must return to its origins in order to proceed to our Holy Spirit destination. Does that sound a wee bit confusing to you? If so, it's because we are part of...

God's Upside-Down, Inside-Out, Topsy-Turvy Kingdom

The Kingdom of God is a strange Kingdom in which nothing seems to be done according to logical or accepted standards. The rules by which it operates are foreign to the rational mind and won't be found in any how-to books on success and motivation. According to the Word of God: the first are really last, and the last are actually first; you have to die in order to live; to become great, you must become humble; to have money, you must give it away; to be a great leader, you must first be a servant; and in order to have life, you must lose it. If all that isn't confusing enough, God also multiplies by division, and that's just for starters![6]

What does the makeup of the Kingdom have to do with the subject of this book? Allow me to explain. There is a stirring among God's people (myself included) who believe that we are going to experience a mighty visitation of God in a worldwide shock wave, unparalleled since the day of Pentecost. This coming outpouring of the Holy Spirit will exceed the Azusa Street revival, which began in Los Angeles on April 9, 1906, and served as the foundation for the subsequent healing/miracle revival that began around 1946; this, in turn, led to the Charismatic Movement of the 1970's.

During the coming visitation, the Church will have far greater anointing and power than the first-century Church. Simple logic would dictate that we cannot have *greater than* until we have *at least as much as*! (For instance, you can't have more than a glassful of water, until you have at least a glassful!) So, there is little value in talking about having more than the early Church until we have received (and walk in) an anointing that is at least equal to what they had. We are operating far below the level of power and anointing resident in the early Church. It is essential that we go backward and obtain the same power and anointing for service that they had—then go forward into greater exploits for the Kingdom!

---

6.   Mt. 19:30; Jn. 12:24-25; Mt. 18:4; Lk. 22:24-27; Lk. 6:38; 12:22-34; Mt. 23:11-12; Mt. 10:39; 16:24-25; Acts 8:1-8.

Let's preview what the Holy Spirit intends to make of us. In order to understand where God is taking the Church, we must consider what she was like in her past glory.

Chapter Ten

What Was All the Power Like?

Since the Church has such a rich history of supernatural manifestations, the restraints of time and human language prevent an adequate representation of the awesome power and Presence manifested during past visitations of the Holy Spirit.

After having been caught up into the third heaven Paul said that he had seen things that mortal words could not adequately describe (see 2 Cor. 12:1-4). Everything in creation is the work of the Holy Spirit. Jesus spoke the words of creation, but the Holy Spirit was the agent by which His commands were accomplished.[1] Thus the entire universe is a reflection of the magnitude of the Holy Spirit's power, the very same power now at work in the Church.[2] Every revival has been ushered in by a sweeping shock wave of the Holy Spirit, and no genuine revival has ever occurred without His Presence.

In the Beginning God...

It was nine o'clock in the morning, just 50 days after the crucifixion of Jesus. His followers had questions concerning their future, and the words *what, when, where* and *how* clamored for answers. The frightened disciples felt weak and helpless now that He was no longer physically with them. Following Jesus' instructions to stay in the city of Jerusalem until they were "clothed with power from on high"

---

1. Gen. 1:1-2. Note in verse 2, "...and the *Spirit of God* was moving...."
2. 1 Cor. 12:4,11; Gal. 3:5, Col. 1:29.

(Lk. 24:49), they gathered together to pray. No one knew when that power would arrive, or for that matter, what it would be like—only that it would come. Jesus had assured them, "...You shall receive *power* when the Holy Spirit has come upon you" (Acts 1:8a). They were not to be disappointed!

On the day of Pentecost, *suddenly* and without warning, there came "...a noise like a violent, rushing wind, and it filled the whole house where they were sitting" (Acts 2:2). Tongues of fire descended on each believer, "And they were *all* filled with the Holy Spirit and began to speak with other tongues, as the Spirit was giving them utterance" (Acts 2:4). Visitors from 15 nations who were in Jerusalem for the feast witnessed the fiery display of supernatural power that accompanied the advent of the Holy Spirit. Confronted with this startling mélange of rushing wind, strange sounds, tongues of fire, and what appeared to be drunken babbling, observers noticed only the external manifestations. They missed the true purpose of the Holy Spirit's visitation—the inward transformation of believers into the image of Christ! The accompanying signs served only as God's "fireworks display" by which He captured the attention of sinners in order to speak to them.

Peter, the former foot-in-mouth Peter, was the first one to speak publicly—the one who almost always seemed to say the wrong thing, and who only shortly before had even denied ever having known Jesus![3] Not exactly the best track record for the keynote speaker of Pentecost Sunday, but he was the Holy Spirit's choice. Peter spoke fearlessly and with great authority (see Acts 2:22-24). After his sermon 3,000 sinners turned from sin to Christ that day, and that was just the beginning! Soon, the number of new believers swelled to 5,000 (see Acts 4:1-31).

What *really* happened to the 120 when the Holy Spirit arrived? Certainly there must have been more than strange sounds, rushing wind, and tongues of fire involved. The mighty Holy Spirit anointing of power did more than transform cowardly Peter into a courageous spokesman for Christ. This power also brought an anointing for signs, wonders, and miracles! That little band of believers would never be the same again, and neither would the world!

---

3.   Mt. 16:21-23; Mk. 9:2-8; Lk. 22:54-62; Jn. 21:15-17,20-22.

The Book of Acts must become our textbook and should serve as the pattern by which the Church measures herself. Even a cursory study of Acts proves that miracles were the order of the day for the early Church. Miracles began in Acts, chapter two, and continued throughout the book.[4] Luke opened the Book of Acts with these words, "The first account I composed [the Gospel of Luke], Theophilus, about all that Jesus *began* to do and teach" (Acts 1:1). While the Gospels contain accounts of all that Jesus began to do and to teach, the Book of Acts is an account of all that He *continued* (and continues) to do through His Body, the Church! The footnote references below should be sufficient proof to convince any thinking believer that Jesus Christ also expects His present-day Church to function as a supernatural Body, accompanied by signs, wonders, and miracles. However, in today's Church all too many Christians refuse to proceed beyond Acts 2:4 to Acts 3:1-8. They speak in tongues but manifest no power.

Somebody's Not Telling the Truth

Detractors of the supernatural maintain that all the miracle-working power ended with the close of the Apostolic Age. *Au contraire!* After reading the New Testament 337 times, I have yet to find even one reference to an Apostolic Age. The only *ages* mentioned are: "this present evil age" and "the ages to come" (see Gal. 1:4; Eph. 2:7). The facts of history refute the theory that miracles terminated at the close of an imaginary Apostolic Age and document clearly that miracles continued unabated in the Church for centuries. However, when there is a dearth of the power of the Holy Spirit in their churches, people will often create all kinds of theories to excuse this. Some even struggle with historical facts, when those facts don't support their non-scriptural theories. I once read a postcard that said, "My mind is made up—*Please don't confuse me with the facts!*"

A Person With an Experience Is Never at the Mercy of Someone With an Argument!

A wise man once said, "He who neglects to drink of the spring of experience is apt to die of thirst in the desert of ignorance." The

---

4. Acts 4:29-31; 5:1-19; 7:55-56; 8:4-13,26-40; 9:1-19,32-43; all of chapter 10; 11:4-5,27-30; 12:1-17,20-23; 13:1-12; 14:1-12; 15:12; 16:6-10,16-18,25-26; 17:6; 18:9-10; 19:6,11-20; 20:8-12; 21:4,10-11; 22:17; 28:1-9.

unsupported argument of the fundamentalists (that supernatural signs and wonders went out with a hypothetical Apostolic Age) is about as weak as the broth made from the shadow of a chicken that starved to death. Believers during the ante-Nicene Church period (before A.D. 325) experienced undiminished supernatural healings, signs, wonders, and miracles. One early Church father, Irenaeus (A.D. 130-200) wrote a book in defense of true Christianity. Even in his era many had already departed from the true faith of the Word of God and had espoused the heresy that supernatural signs were no longer required in the Church. Irenaeus responded to this heretical teaching thus:

> "Wherefore, also, *those who are in truth His disciples*, receiving grace from Him, *do in His name perform miracles*, so as to promote the welfare of other men, according to the gift which each has received from Him. For some do certainly and truly drive out devils, so that those who have thus been cleansed from evil spirits frequently believe in Christ, and join themselves to the Church. Others have foreknowledge of things to come: they see visions, and utter prophetic expressions. Others still, heal the sick by laying their hands upon them, and they are made whole. Yea, moreover, as I have said, the dead even have been raised up, and remained among us for many years. And what more shall I say? It is not possible to name the number of the gifts which the Church, scattered throughout the whole world, has received from God, in the name of Jesus Christ...calling upon the name of our Lord Jesus Christ, she [the Church] has been accustomed to work miracles for the advantage of mankind, and not to lead them into error."[5]

> "Irenaeus, who sprang from the Eastern church...holds a kind of mediating position between the two branches [Eastern and Western] of the church, and may be taken as, on the whole, the most moderate and sound representative of ecclesiastical orthodoxy in the ante-Nicene period."[6]

---

5. Irenaeus, *Against Heresies* (London, England: The Society for Promoting Christian Knowledge, 1916).
6. Schaff, "Ante-Nicene Christianity," 511.

Irenaeus was quite clear that miracles were performed by disciples—not only by apostles.

> "The major emphasis of Irenaeus is that one sign of a true heretic is his denial that supernatural signs are currently resident in the Church. Conversely, signs, wonders, and miracles are a (super)natural function in the lives of true believers. On this fact the Early Church fathers were in total agreement!"[7]

Breaking Through the Time Barrier

Since miracles happened in abundance as late as the ante-Nicene period, the arbitrary time barrier of an imaginary Apostolic Age has been dissolved and cannot form the basis of any reasonable argument. Regrettably, we have space to consider only a mere sampling of the miracles that have occurred in this present century.

The following accounts are taken from the book *With Signs Following*.[8] In this book, author Stanley Frodsham chronicled the Holy Spirit outpouring of the late 1800's and early 1900's. (This is must reading for every truly serious believer who desires to know his Full Gospel roots.) I wept as I read chapter after chapter—with joy over what the Holy Spirit accomplished in eras long past, and with sadness at the dearth of comparable supernatural happenings in the Full Gospel church of today.

From the Foreword:

> "The Gospel Publishing House in 1916 issued a book entitled *The Apostolic Faith Restored*, by B.F. Lawrence. In writing the introduction to this book, J.W. Welch said, 'If the Lord should tarry, it is hoped and expected that this book will be followed by another in which it will be possible to present a fuller and more accurate account *of the greatest revival the world has seen since the Early Church period.*' "[9]

D.L. Moody and Ira Sankey:

> "In the year 1873 Dwight L. Moody and Ira Sankey went to England.... The Lord began to send a gracious awakening....

---

7. Seavey, *Christian Meditation*, 49.
8. Frodsham, *With Signs Following*.
9. Frodsham, *With Signs Following*, from the Foreword; emph. mine.

When I got to the rooms of the Y.M.C.A. I found the meeting on fire. The young men were speaking in tongues and prophesying. What on earth did it all mean? Only that Moody had been addressing them that afternoon."[10]

Visitations of the Holy Spirit with Signs, Wonders, and Miracles Following:

"When they arrived, they saw a man who had had his limb broken...one from among them arose, laid hands on him, and in the name of Jesus bade him arise and walk. He did so.... Then, turning to the invalid sister that had the hunchback, he laid hands upon her, and bade her to be straight in the name of Jesus. She was instantly healed."[11]

"There were many remarkable healings, and very often as Pastor Thompson was preaching, the power of God would fall, (with) people dropping to the floor and speaking in other tongues as the Spirit gave them utterance."[12]

Speaking in Known Tongues:

"As we worshiped the Lord, I...prayed in tongues. A Bohemian, who was present, said I spoke his language.... Since then, others have understood...languages that I have spoken."[13]

"...The Holy Spirit was manifested in heavenly song. An interpretation came in English. Two nuns...heard the anthem that the Spirit gave. They said it was sung in the most perfect Latin and that it was translated into the most perfect English. They said the cathedral church choir had tried to learn that anthem for a month, but had finally given it up as too difficult."[14]

Throughout the book, accounts are given of similar happenings, where someone present at a meeting heard another speaking in his or

10. Frodsham, *With Signs Following*, 9-10.
11. Frodsham, *With Signs Following*, 11.
12. Frodsham, *With Signs Following*, 15.
13. Frodsham, *With Signs Following*, 20.
14. Frodsham, *With Signs Following*, 26.

her own language. Often the most personal sins of the individual were revealed through tongues.

Healings:

> "My right eye was virtually blind from birth.... She was prayed for and anointed according to James 5:14,15 and was perfectly healed.[15]...Two meetings were held each day...and all the city was moved. Large numbers from surrounding towns came, for God stretched forth His hand to heal the sick by the hundreds."[16]

> "...A woman...had been crippled for thirty-two years, unable to walk.... A six-year-old girl who had received the baptism [of the Holy Spirit] and speaks in other tongues, walked in and put her hands on the woman and said, 'Jesus wants to heal you. The Spirit has sent me to put my hands on you.' Instantly, the toes on the woman's feet straightened out and she arose and walked."[17]

London—Report from the *Daily Express*, Easter, 1933:

> "Of those who testified there were 72 guaranteed cures of cancer and malignant growths; 20 had been crippled; 17 had been blind; 70 had been afflicted with stiff muscles or useless limbs; and 18 had been deaf."[18]

Outward Signs:

> "The tent was filled with angels and these were seen even by sinners. Those who stood on the outside saw a white cloud come down and rest on the tent."[19]

> "Some have seen Jesus at our meetings, and tongues of fire have been seen over my head by an infidel, convincing him of the power of God. Many are seeking salvation...."[20]

---

15. Frodsham, *With Signs Following*, 25.
16. Frodsham, *With Signs Following*, 26.
17. Frodsham, *With Signs Following*, 40.
18. Frodsham, *With Signs Following*, 65.
19. Frodsham, *With Signs Following*, 26.
20. Frodsham, *With Signs Following*, 71.

"A few of us who met for prayer...will never forget the awe of God's holy Presence in the room when everything in it gently rocked. This occurred on two occasions."[21]

Accounts of Happenings During the Azusa Street Revival:

At the turn of the twentieth century the Holy Spirit laid His hand upon a black holiness preacher named William J. Seymour, calling him to Los Angeles where the greatest revival since the day of Pentecost was about to burst forth. At first he met with a little band of believers in a small house located at 214 North Bonnie Brae Street, where God began to pour out His Spirit. Let's join the narrative as written in *With Signs Following*.

> "People came from everywhere. By the next morning there was no getting near the house. As the people came they would fall under the power, and the whole city was stirred. The sick were healed and sinners were saved just as they came in.
>
> "People came from all over the country by the hundreds and thousands. *That meeting lasted for three years, day and night, without a break.*
>
> "In those days of that great outpouring, when they said God would heal, you were healed."[22]

The power of God manifested there was so great—and the conviction for sin even greater—that people thronged there to see what was happening. Immediately, a larger location was needed. Brother Seymour and his flock soon found themselves situated in what at one time had been a stable, located at 312 Azusa Street. The account continues:

> "All who are in touch with God realize as soon as they enter the meeting that the Holy Ghost is the leader."[23]
>
> "There is such power in the preaching of the Word in the Spirit that people are shaken in their benches."[24]

---

21. Frodsham, *With Signs Following*, 60.
22. Frodsham, *With Signs Following*, 32.
23. Frodsham, *With Signs Following*, 33.
24. Frodsham, *With Signs Following*, 34.

"The service ran almost continuously. Seeking souls could be found under the power almost any hour, day or night. People came to meet God. He was always there, hence the continuous meeting. Pride, self-assertion, self-importance, and self-esteem could not survive there."[25]

"After a while a Spirit-filled woman gave a mighty exhortation, an appeal for the sinner to turn to God. Suddenly she broke out in a language with which she was utterly unfamiliar. It was the native tongue of the…reporter…. She poured forth such a holy torrent of truth, exposing his sinful licentious life, that he was dumfounded…. He told her that she had given an entirely accurate statement of his wicked life…he fully believed her utterances were from God to lead him to true repentance…."[26]

One last (and perhaps the most profound) quote from the book:

"When I learned that the Holy Spirit was yet to be poured out in greater fullness, my heart became hungry. *At times I longed more for the Holy Spirit to come in than for my necessary food.*"[27]

Similar sentiments are echoed by others throughout the narrative. Could this imply a definite connection between such *intense* desire for the Holy Spirit's Presence and the resultant *shock wave*?

The Azusa Street revival spread over the United States, then rapidly around the world. People from every walk of life came and participated. The rich and the poor, the high and the lowly, and all the races blended together into a beautiful tapestry of God's grace. It is no wonder that the writer of Hebrews says, "Remember those who led you…*imitate their faith*" (Heb. 13:7).

Eyewitness to Miracles

I would love to recount here the testimonies of modern-day believers who (like Philip in Acts 8:39-40) were transported physically from one location to another by the Holy Spirit; or (like the apostle Paul in Second Corinthians 12:1-4) who have had out-of-the-body experiences; or those who have participated in creative miracles such as

---

25. Frodsham, *With Signs Following*, 36.
26. Frodsham, *With Signs Following*, 38.
27. Frodsham, *With Signs Following*, 20.

the multiplying of food; or the raising of the dead; or control of the weather; or of those who have witnessed angelic appearances.

Since the age of 19, my own life and ministry have been earmarked by signs, wonders, and miracles. The work of the ministry has taken me (as of this writing) to 35 countries of the world where I have witnessed innumerable miracles. Only Heaven's records contain the full accounting of the multitudes who have received their sight, the crippled who have walked, the myriad of deaf ears that have received their hearing, the deformed limbs that have been straightened, the cancers that have vanished, and if that were not enough, the two people who have been raised from the dead. I not only *believe* in the supernatural—I *practice* it and believe it is incumbent upon the entire Church to do so, also!

The lamentable truth is that many, if not most, older churches are living on memories. Sadder yet is the fact that an even greater number of newer Charismatic churches have never experienced a Holy Spirit visitation of a magnitude sufficient to generate any memories of the supernatural. Thus, they exist in a supernatural vacuum. Though this is true, it need not continue to be so, for God has glorious plans for His people. These plans include you, your church, and your pastor. Let us move on in faith!

Chapter Eleven

Don't Doubt, or You'll Stay Out

"God said it. I believe it. That settles it!" I was just a young man in college when I heard a visiting preacher make that statement, which had a lasting impact on my impressionable mind. For years, *I* too went about declaring that same grand statement of faith, until one day the truth dawned upon me. What I believed (or didn't believe) had absolutely nothing to do with the certainty of what God had spoken. The fact is, God said it, *that* settles it! "Forever, O Lord, Thy word is settled in heaven" (Ps. 119:89).

God's Word is true! Over many centuries critics and skeptics, within and without the Church, have waged their petty warfare against the citadel of God's Word. But when the dust of battle has settled, only the Word of God has stood firm. If we can learn anything from the past, let it be that it is useless to mount an assault against the Word of God. Perhaps that admonition seems completely out of place in this book and should be reserved for rebuffing atheistic opposition; but atheists will not attack the truth-liberating concepts contained here. It will be well-meaning Christians, some of them leaders in the Church, who will rise up in resistance to its message. Of these attackers, it can be said with certainty that, without exception, every one of them will be a doubter!

Doubt is a most dangerous attitude to entertain. According to Webster's Dictionary, *doubt* is: "To be uncertain in opinion about; hold questionable; hesitate to believe. *To distrust.*"[1] James addressed the subject of doubt:

---

1.   *Webster's Encyclopedic Unabridged Dictionary of the English Language* (Avenel, NJ: Gramercy Books), 1989.

*...Let him ask of God.... But **let him ask in faith without any doubting**, for the one who doubts is like the surf of the sea driven and tossed by the wind. For let not that man expect that he will receive **anything** from the Lord, being a double-minded man, unstable in **all** his ways* (James 1:5, 6-8).

Mission Impossible?

God's prophetic word to Israel was His promise to bring them *out* of Egypt's bondage in order to bring them *into* the Promised Land. In spite of God's promises, the miracles of deliverance from Egypt, and the supernatural provision in the wilderness, still the Israelites failed to enter and lay claim to the bountiful land. That generation died in the wilderness. God raised up a new generation, which He brought to the banks of Jordan with the same promises and commands as their parents before them.

They entered the land and began to fulfill the word of God; yet even after a sufficient period of time, 7 of the 12 tribes still had not fulfilled their mandate to claim their possessions. "So Joshua said to the sons of Israel, '*How long will you put off entering to take possession of the land* which the Lord, the God of your fathers, has given you?' " (Josh. 18:3).

The Holy Spirit is asking the Church in our generation that same question: "How long will you put off entering to take possession of the land which the Lord...has given you?" God has commissioned His Church to possess the land—to claim what is rightfully ours, and to live in the fullness of His Spirit and power. That was Israel's assignment also, when the nation was instructed to "Go up and take the land"; yet they failed miserably. In Chapter Seven we covered one of the three major reasons why the Israelites turned their backs on the task that God set before them—*fear*. Fear has evil accomplices—in this case, *unbelief*. Speaking of the nation of Israel, the writer of Hebrews said: "And so we see that they were not able to enter *because of unbelief*" (Heb. 3:19).

Satan is the architect, the master designer of unbelief, having had aeons during which to perfect his art. There are perhaps as many reasons for unbelief as there are people. One aspect of unbelief remains consistent; it is as though you looked God right in the face and called Him a liar! That's one reason why the apostle Paul brought the hammer of the Word of God down so strongly: "But he who *doubts* is condemned...and *whatever* is not from faith is *sin*" (Rom. 14:23).

The Church in All Her Gory

At first glance there seems to be an "L" missing in the subtitle above, but it wasn't an accident. For too long now the world has witnessed the Church in all her gory. Exposés of leading televangelists have rocked Christendom with shocking stories of sexual and financial misconduct, and the world has laughed us to scorn. Full Gospel denominations are for the most part backslidden and have little, if anything, to offer a sin- and sickness-weary world. The power and anointing that once rested upon them has vanished like a puff of smoke, yet they continue on with empty, meaningless form and formality. Unfortunately, we have learned the art of doubting! Doubt and miracles, like oil and water, simply do not mix. You cannot possess both at the same time.

The Full Gospel movement was once the standard-bearer of the supernatural. Because the beacon light of healing and deliverance that shone from our churches pierced through their despair, the sick and infirmed knew where to turn in their most desperate hours. Shouts of victory over sickness, disease, and infirmity were heard in service after service, in churches around the globe.

The world must receive a twenty-first century revelation of the Church in all her glory. But first, we must be simple enough to take the Word of God at face value, lay aside all doubt, believe everything He said, and act upon it in faith. The results will boggle your imagination: all hell will be in an uproar and Satanic entities will fear the anointing that rests upon the Church. Miracles will become commonplace (though not common), as the foundation of Satan's kingdom trembles to the core! Certainly, this is not happening on a large scale now—but it will! How? When? Where? By whom? If you desire to be numbered among the "who," then you need to discover the "how."

Chapter Twelve

Reflections in a Mirror

Mirrored reflections are sometimes disturbing, or at the least, unsettling. Perhaps this is because mirrors reflect, with no apologies, exactly what they see. Sometimes, first thing in the morning, it takes a great deal of courage just to stand in front of the mirror and come face to face with reality. For some men the physique they once had has become like a treasure—a sunken chest. We still have the strong barrel chest of our youth, only now it has settled down around our waistline. I'm always amused at men whose large bellies hang out over their blue jeans. They adamantly close their minds to the fact that they cannot wear the same size trousers as when they were younger, so they wear them lower. (They suffer from Dunlop's Disease— their bellies have *done lopped* over their belts!)

Then there are the balding men who stubbornly refuse to admit what Mother Nature has done to them; they comb their remaining hair into positions that would amaze a contortionist. A friend of mine wears one of the most artificial-looking toupees I've ever seen. (I think he bought it at Wigs 'R' Us.) The only thing it lacks is a chin strap. Yet he's convinced that no one knows it's not his real hair. Of course, the only person he's fooling is *himself*.

O, me! If we just didn't have to confront those telltale mirrors— but we do. God's Word has an interesting reflection on reflections:

> *But prove yourselves doers of the word, and not merely hearers who de-*
> *lude themselves. For if anyone is a hearer of the word and not a doer,*

*he is like a man who looks at his natural face in a mirror; for once he
has looked at himself and gone away, he has immediately forgotten
what kind of person he was* (James 1:22-24).

The Word of God is the mirror of the Holy Spirit, reflecting without partiality our true selves (which is how God views us). Throughout the first portion of this book I've attempted to hold up the mirror of the Word so the people of the Full Gospel movements can take a good hard look at themselves. What we've seen has been distressing. Some will refuse to believe the image, and will walk away from the mirror denying what they have seen. But we should thank God daily for the true reflection given by His mirror, for not all mirrors are truthful.

Years ago, while ministering in Portland, Oregon, for Pastor Joseph Dunets, I had the privilege of eating at Rose's Delicatessen—a culinary treat never to be forgotten. It would have been enough that the food was delicious, but the portions were also monstrous in size. A sandwich could easily be shared by two, with some left over. Our dessert was a piece of chocolate fudge cake. Not any ordinary slice of cake, mind you. It was three layers high. On the top, sides, and between each layer was an inch of genuine chocolate fudge laced with pecan halves. Just recalling it makes me feel stuffed. No one could leave Rose's Delicatessen with a clear conscience. Everyone left with a full stomach. (I believe that day at Rose's was when my own chest began settling down around my waistline.)

Strategically placed near the cash register at Rose's was an old carnival mirror—the kind with a curved glass that distorts the image of the person looking into it. Some carnival mirrors make you look tall or short, while others make you look wavy, fat, or thin. This particular mirror made the viewer look thin—very thin. I stood nearby, watching the reactions of people (all of whom had overeaten), as they stopped to pay their bills. Everyone paused to look in the mirror, and everyone smiled. I noticed one particularly large woman as she approached the cashier to pay her bill. She put her hand to her mouth, obviously in gastric distress, her face reflecting the discomfort of tarrying long at the table. She stopped to look in the mirror (the lying mirror that made everyone look slender) and her countenance changed immediately. As she threw her drooped shoulders back and calmed her labored breathing, the frown was quickly replaced by a smile. She obviously loved the reflection in the mirror. Perhaps she went away believing that what she saw was real—or at least *wanting* to believe. People are like that.

Mirror, Mirror, on the Wall…

In the world of illusion, mirrors can be constructed to reflect anything you want to see. This is not so with God's mirror. The mirror of the Word is absolutely truthful—sometimes painfully so—but it is the best friend you will ever have. Many churches today offer mirrors of one's own choosing. (After all, it would never do for the saints to leave a church service unhappy or under conviction.) Remember the fairy tale where the vile queen asked her magic mirror for its opinion? She asked, "Mirror, mirror, on the wall, who's the fairest of them all?" That mirror knew for certain which side its bread was buttered on! It lied like the devil and told her exactly what she wanted to hear: "You are, O Queen!" It must have choked on those words, but it would never do to upset Her Royal Wickedness.

Let's not delude ourselves like the wicked queen. Let's tear down all the distorted mirrors, including the mirrors on the walls in all our churches, and replace them with the only truly unbiased mirror—the Word of the living God! We probably won't like our reflection initially, but we'll be pleasantly surprised with what we can become after consistent exposure to the beautiful image of Christ!

Throughout this book we have been forced to look at unpleasant reflections of the Full Gospel movement, simply because they are there. In every instance the mirror has answered with truth, and truth often hurts. I apologize for the wounds, the discomfort, even the pain this may have caused many of you, but I cannot apologize for speaking the truth!

Though often painful, the truth is actually a liberating force. "And you shall know the *truth*, and the truth shall make you free" (Jn. 8:32). We must be confronted with the dearth of our spiritual experience and the ugliness it produces; for only then can God initiate our transformation into the glorious image of Christ. Jesus said: "Thy word is truth" (Jn. 17:17b); also "But when He, *the Spirit of truth*, comes, He will guide you into *all* the truth" (Jn. 16:13a); and "Everyone who is of the truth hears My voice" (Jn. 18:37c).

For too long now the Church has drunk freely from the polluted waters of the world and denominationalism, and has turned its back on the crystal-clear river of the Holy Spirit. "For My people have committed two evils: They have forsaken Me, the fountain of living waters, to hew for themselves cisterns, broken cisterns, that can hold no water" (Jer. 2:13). Why do the people of God fast when a feast is set before them? Why do they merely exist, eating meager scraps of the Word, while ignoring the spiritual banquet God has prepared for them? They starve in the midst of plenty because they simply don't know it is there, and that it is for them. The "undershepherds" (unlike the Good Shepherd) have not led them into green pastures!

What You Don't Know *Can* Hurt You

Many years ago a man decided to emigrate to the United States, having saved just enough money to pay for his passage on a steamship. During the entire voyage he existed on crackers and cheese that he had brought with him. Arriving in New York harbor, he came up on deck. A crew member asked him where he had been during the crossing. He replied that his paltry finances had caused him to remain in his room and exist on crackers and cheese. Imagine his sense of loss when the crew member explained that his fare included access to everything aboard the ship, including all the facilities and sumptuous meals!

Can you imagine barely existing on starvation fare while surrounded by more food than anyone could ever hope to eat? Yet the Church is in a similar situation, and God commented on their condition in Hosea 4:6a: "My people are destroyed *for lack of knowledge.*" They lack heart knowledge—not head knowledge! There has never been a time in the history of the Church when we have had so much intellectual knowledge that only fattens pride. Heart knowledge nourishes the spirit. To paraphrase then, "My people are destroyed for lack of *heart* knowledge."

My Prayer for You

Though I've taken the liberty of borrowing the apostle Paul's words, his prayer for the Ephesian believers is likewise my own sincere desire for you:

*That the God of our Lord Jesus Christ, the Father of glory, **may give to you a spirit of wisdom and of revelation** in the knowledge of Him. **I pray that the eyes of your heart may be enlightened,** so that you may know what is the hope of His calling, what are the riches of the glory of His inheritance in the saints, **and what is the surpassing greatness of His power toward us who believe.** These are in accordance with the working of the strength of His might which He brought about in Christ, when He raised Him from the dead, and seated Him at His right hand in the heavenly places, far above all rule and authority and power and dominion, and every name that is named, not only in this age, but also in the one to come. And He put **all things** in subjection under His feet, and gave Him as **head over all things to the church, which is His body, the fulness of Him who fills all in all*** (Ephesians 1:17-23).

Chapter Thirteen

Some of God's Word Is Hard to Swallow

The fact is, the Church of Jesus Christ has failed to grow up. The primary reason is because the people are starving to death. The writer of Hebrews has some interesting comments concerning this problem:

> *...You have become dull of hearing. For though by this time **you ought to be teachers**, you have need again for someone to teach **you** the elementary principles of the oracles of God, and you have come to need milk and not solid food. **For everyone who partakes only of milk is not accustomed to the word of righteousness, for he is a babe. But solid food** is for the **mature**, who because of practice have their senses trained to discern good and evil. Therefore **leaving the elementary teaching** about the Christ, let us press on to maturity, not laying again a foundation of repentance from dead works and of faith toward God, of instruction about washings [baptism], and laying on of hands, and the resurrection of the dead, and eternal judgment. And this we shall do, if God permits* (Hebrews 5:11–6:3).

There are four concepts proposed in the writer's statement:

1. They were not listening to the Holy Spirit (5:11).

2. Sufficient time had elapsed in their Christian experience for them to have matured to the level where they should be

teaching others. Not only had they not matured to this level, they had gone backward. They again craved milk instead of solid food (5:12).

3. Those who drink only milk are spiritual babies—infants who are not accustomed to the deeper truths of the Word of God (5:13). The apostle Peter reaffirms this: "Like *newborn babes,* long for the pure *milk* of the word, that by it you may *grow* in respect to salvation" (1 Pet. 2:2).

4. Solid food (the deeper truths of the Word) is for the mature (5:14), which is also borne out by Paul: "And I, brethren, *could not speak to you as to spiritual men,* but as to men of flesh, as to *babes* in Christ. I gave you *milk* to drink, *not solid food;* for you were not yet able to receive it. Indeed, even now you are not yet able, *for you are still fleshly*" (1 Cor. 3:1-3a).

Babies, Babies Everywhere

It's high time for the Church to grow up, take off her (spiritual) diapers, and put on the whole armor of God! It's time to trade the bottle for the battle, and the pacifier for the sword of the Spirit! When this book was in the planning stages, I entertained the thought of a cover design that would illustrate the Church's infantile state. My idea was to outfit several adults in baby costumes—complete with oversized baby bottles, rattles, pacifiers, etc.—and photograph them in a church setting. I was outvoted—my wife said "NO!" Of course, I wasn't really serious. (I say that *now.*) Yet, that's precisely how the writer of Hebrews portrayed the immature Church of his day.

After listing a host of evil powers with which the Church should be at war, the apostle Paul admonished the Ephesian believers to "take up the full armor of God" (Eph. 6:13a). If my understanding is correct, diapers are for babies and armor is for adults. The major thrust of the New Testament Epistles is to mature the saints and send them forth in the power of the Holy Spirit to destroy the works of the devil.

Paul had explained to the Ephesian believers that the primary function of the fivefold ministries was "for the equipping of the *saints* for the work of service" (Eph. 4:12a). It is clear then, that all the saints (not just the paid clergy) are expected to perform the work of service. For too long believers have held to a wrong concept that the church building is a place where we are ministered to, rather than a place where we are trained to minister to others. (Please don't lose sight of the fact that when we minister to others, we also are ministered to.)

Because children are immature, parents often refuse to allow them access to things that could be harmful to themselves or others. In the same way, God will not allow immature Christians to grasp deeper truths of the Word. To responsibly handle truth, you must first grow up. "To whom would He teach knowledge? And to whom would He interpret the message? Those just weaned from milk? Those just taken from the breast?" (Is. 28:9) The only answer to these rhetorical questions is, of course, a resounding *NO!*

In strongly admonishing his readers to grow up, the writer of Hebrews also revealed the process. They must gradually but steadily begin to consume the solid food of the Word of God.

Shhhhh! The Baby Is Starving!

When my wife and I were new parents, we visited some friends of ours who, after many years of childlessness, had finally become parents of a baby girl who was then nine months old. Upon entering the house, their first words were, "Shhhhh, the baby is sleeping." We thought perhaps they were just being overly cautious since they were new parents. But they explained that the baby slept fitfully all the time and cried often. My wife, herself a new mother, asked our friend what she was feeding the baby. She replied, "Milk and Pablum." Donna said, "That's your problem—your baby is starving. She needs solid food." The mother could have more literally said, "Shhhhh! The baby is *starving.*" The change to a more advanced diet soon brought about a much healthier, happier, quieter baby!

Unfortunately, this scenario is repeated week after week around the world in many Full Gospel churches. The people are continually fed the milk of the Word, and no one seems to know or care why they are crying. An improvement in diet might produce some healthier, happier, quieter saints!

When I forget to replenish my dog's food or water, she has her own unique way of reminding me. She picks her dish up in her mouth and bangs it on the floor; or sometimes she pushes it around, making noise she is sure I will respond to. This little creature isn't going out of her way to be annoying or obnoxious. She's simply indicating in the only manner she knows that she is hungry and thirsty—and that I have somehow forgotten her. Perhaps some restless saints are expressing similar feelings when they relate their unrelenting hunger and thirst to their pastors.

Be Quiet and Eat What I Give You!

Granted, some people really are troublemakers who go about fomenting dissatisfaction and unrest among believers, and nothing is ever to their liking. The churches I've pastored have had their share of these malcontents. (If Jesus Himself had been their pastor they would still have found fault with something He said or did, or something He didn't say or do!) Such people are seldom, if ever, pleased with anything.

I am not referring to these perpetual grumblers in this chapter. Rather, I wish to discuss the company of believers who have found the new birth and have drunk freely of the wonderful "pure milk of the word" (see 1 Pet. 2:2). Having experienced as much growth as that milk provides, they now crave the meat of the Word. They sincerely desire to grow, but are not being fed the scriptural diet necessary to mature them. These people are being systematically starved to death, yet when they cry for more spiritual food they are labeled "troublemakers" (or worse). The wording is often more subtle, but the bottom line is basically, "Get in step with the program of this church and with everyone else in it—or leave!" Then, if their hunger does force them to leave, they are branded as deserters. Sometimes you just can't win, no matter what you do.

How can you tell if your church is on a starvation diet? Analyze what the writer of Hebrews said in chapter 6:1-3. Chapter six begins with the word *therefore* (a conjunction that connects two thoughts). According to Webster's Dictionary, *therefore* means to: "agree in introducing a statement resulting from, or caused by, what immediately precedes...imply exactness of reasoning...especially used in logic."[1] Whenever you see the word *therefore*, ask yourself, "What is it *there for?*"

The beginning of chapter six is really a continuation of what was said at the end of chapter five and these passages should never have been separated from each other. In Hebrews 6:1 the word *therefore* is

---

1. *Webster's Encyclopedic Unabridged Dictionary.*

used in the sense "because of what I have just said...." What the writer had said in the last verses of chapter five (in a condensed form) was that they were spiritual babies who, though they should have grown up and become teachers, had retrogressed (backslidden) to the place where they needed milk and not meat. So we should read Hebrews 6:1 like this: "Therefore [because you have backslidden and need to grow up] leaving the *elementary teaching about the Christ....*"

It's obvious that these believers had become mired down in baby doctrines (primer doctrines for new believers), which the writer calls "elementary teaching about the Christ." Why would the writer admonish them to leave teachings about Christ? Because it was a basic (primary) truth, which had long ago been accepted and understood. The Greek word for *Christ* is equivalent to the Hebrew word for *Messiah* (the anointed One, Savior), which of course was Jesus. The Hebrew believers had become mired down in the most basic doctrines. They were certainly saved, but they hadn't gone beyond the milk of the Word to any deeper teachings.

I was saved in a church where our bland diet was the spiritual baby food of salvation and other basic doctrines. I thank God for salvation, just as I thank God that when I was an infant my mother fed me milk. But just as my mother had to gradually lead me to eat meat, pastors must see the need to do the same spiritually! It is a scientific fact that no one can exist on milk alone, and it is a spiritual fact that no one can exist on scriptural milk alone!

In verses one and two of chapter six, the writer's next instruction was, "...press on to maturity, *not laying again* a foundation of repentance from dead works and of faith toward God, of instruction about washings [baptism], and laying on of hands, and the resurrection of the dead, and eternal judgment." Every teaching in these first two verses is a basic, foundational doctrine! They can be compared to the training wheels on a bicycle—great for beginners. They are the primary doctrines taught in new converts' classes where baby Christians are instructed in the elementary tenets of faith. Yet, in myriad churches believers must continue to exist on this starvation diet of scriptural baby food.

There are two major (though not the only) reasons for such a meager fare. The first is obvious: Some shepherds simply do not feed the flock. "...Prophesy against the shepherds...and say to those shepherds, 'Thus says the Lord God, "Woe, shepherds...who have been feeding themselves! Should not the shepherds feed the flock?" ' " (Ezek. 34:2; please read verses 3-16 also.) (In Jesus' commission to Peter, He spoke to him twice as much about feeding the flock as He did about leading the flock! See John 21:15-17.) God's nature is clearly reflected in Ezekiel 34:15: " 'I will *feed* My flock and I will lead them to rest,' declares the Lord God." Where God leads—He feeds. The Good Shepherd of Psalm 23 leads His sheep into green pastures, beside quiet waters (v. 2), and prepares a table (v. 5). That illustrates the nourishing ministry of the Good Shepherd—and *all* good shepherds!

Ministers cannot give what they do not have, and there is a spiritual price to pay for the anointing of the Holy Spirit that leads us into all truth. During more than 38 years of ministry I've had the opportunity to know many pastors, most of whom have been sincere and dedicated people. The sad fact is that far too many pastors have become so busy working *for* God that they have little time left to spend *with* God. (So much time is spent in the *work* of God, but little time is spent with the *God* of the work.) That statement is not my own supposition. Many pastors have confided in me that they have become so burdened down with the *business* of the church that they never seem to have enough time to spend with the *Lord* of the Church. Revelation knowledge comes only by spending quality time in the Presence of Almighty God.

If You Can't Make Them Drink, Salt Their Oats

In my ministry I attempt to teach truths that will draw believers into a place where they will hunger and thirst after righteousness, and I encourage other ministers to do the same. Often, pastors will say, "My people aren't quite ready for such deep truth yet." My response is usually, "I understand." (I *do* understand—perhaps more than they think I do.) Sometimes I gently ask, "What is your timetable for bringing them to the place where they will be ready for deeper truth?" In response to that question I've heard a lot of silence and a lot of throat clearing, but never even one thoughtful answer! The reason is: you can't take someone else where *you* have never been. One of my favorite TV commercials shows a Boy Scout leader alone and, quite obviously, lost. His little scouts are nowhere to be found and he searches everywhere for them to no avail. He finally stops someone and asks, "Have you seen a group of Scouts anywhere around here? I'm their *leader!*"

Hey, Baby—You've Got It Made!

Let's discuss the second major reason for the existence of starvation diets in our churches. There are some Christians who *refuse* to grow up! They just adore their infancy with all its fringe benefits. Their every need is supplied. They are clothed, fed, changed, held, cuddled and coddled, pampered, indulged, spoiled, kootchy-kooed, and fussed over by everyone. They are carried from place to place; someone else always cleans up their mess; they don't have to be productive; and they are held responsible for nothing. All they have to do is look cute. So why grow up? Such intentional babies refuse even the slightest suggestion of anything but milk or Pablum in their diet. Just watch as they spit out anything that doesn't taste like the most basic doctrine and everything that even hints at deeper truth. The antithesis of babyhood is growth, which requires responsibility, work, and active participation in life. A productive, adult human being contributes to society.

My wife and I have parented five children. I've shared in tending to their needs as babies, doing whatever was needed to care for them (including getting up in the middle of the night to change diapers). So you see, I'm no stranger to babies. I write from firsthand experience. There came a time in each of our babies' lives when they had to experience progressively less-strained food, gradually moving on to solid (adult) food. I recall with amusement the first reaction of each baby to that somewhat less-refined food. They hated it! Well, aren't we surprised at that? (I don't think so.) They made the most terrible faces imaginable, and sometimes they cried, clearly registering their displeasure. They spit the food out. They wanted no part in this business of growing up.

When the babies repeatedly spit out the unwanted food, we repeatedly spooned it back in again. Granted, there were times when they seemed to spit it out faster than we were capable of spooning it back in, but we never yielded for a moment. Sometimes we had to take time out for breathers, but we never gave up feeding them what they needed in order to progress to the next stage of physical development. Did we enjoy causing such distress? I think not! We did what we did because we *loved* them. We understood what our babies didn't—that this brief, unpleasant moment was necessary for continued growth and maturity. And, with that in mind, we lovingly persevered. Needless to say, we now have five fully grown and healthy children, all of them much taller than average. (Would you like to see pictures? I have pictures! Are you *sure* you don't want to see my pictures?)

It is a fact of life that there will always be many babies in the Church—babies who have been saved for years, but who still refuse to grow up. Why then do so many pastors allow *them* to dictate the diet of others who *long* for the meat of the Word, but who are instead forced to exist on the milk of the Word? The truth is, if one begins to preach some deeper truth from the Word of God, some babies will be offended. They will spit it out, make awful faces, cry, pout, kick their heels, hold their breath, and (God forbid) withhold their tithes. Some may even leave to occupy another playpen.

The word *tithe* opens up yet another can of worms. I am firmly convinced that there would (should) be far more people offended by the truth in our churches, if pastors were not so afraid of losing the almighty dollar and simply told it like it is in the Word of God. The pastoral approach to most situations is not to offend anyone. But if the truth is to be conveyed, that simply isn't possible. Tough love works! Remember, it was Jesus Himself who said, "*Woe, to you when all men speak well of you, for in the same way their fathers used to treat the false prophets*" (Lk. 6:26).

People have always been delighted by having their ears tickled by false prophets who never say anything to upset the status quo. They show only what people want to see (there's that lying mirror again!), and tell them only what they want to hear. (Read the story in Second Chronicles 18:5-7,12-17. It's great.) Prophets like that are always welcome. They warm your heart, always make you feel good, and *never* offend you. Is it any wonder then that false prophets are so popular with the crowds?

I'm currently pastoring my fifth church, so I fully understand the pastor's position. Concerned about budgets, church payments, etc., many pastors feel they must walk a tightrope trying to please everyone—lest some leave the church and take precious, much-needed finances with them. But we who minister are called to preach the truth, and let the chips fall where they may. My approach has always been that *God* is my source, not people. If I can't meet a bank payment, I must answer to the bank. But if I don't preach the truth because I'm afraid to offend someone, *I must answer to God!* Since I fear (have awe-filled respect for) God more than the banker, I have always chosen to minister the truth. If the fact that I fed them something more substantial than Pablum offended some people in my church, there were always lots of other churches they could attend where they would not be compelled to grow up. When the truth chafed them, they usually pouted awhile, then took their toys with them to the playpen of their choosing where, undoubtedly, they were coddled, kootchy-kooed, and otherwise fussed over. Consequently, after 25-30 years, some of them are probably still in diapers. I can only hope and pray that somewhere down the road they find a pastor who is able to mature them to the full stature of Christ (see Eph. 4:13). Thankfully, over the years there have been those who have repented of their juvenile attitudes and risen to higher heights in God.

All's Quiet on the Western Front

Some pastors may argue, "No one in my church is dissatisfied. Everyone seems happy and content, so why should I rock the boat?" This argument introduces yet another group within the Church. You may have heard it said that there are three groups of people in the Church: (1) those who *make* things happen; (2) those who *watch* things happen; and (3) those who *don't know what's happening!* Unfortunately, many who don't rock the boat fit into the third category above. They aren't bad people. They don't reject deeper truth. They just don't know that there is more to be had! I believe that most churches are made up of sweet, sincere people who, if they knew the Holy Spirit had more for them, would readily accept it and grow. My prayer is that this book will find its way into the hands of these sincere seekers of truth.

Why am I so intent on prodding the babies in the Church to grow up? Because of what Paul wrote to the Church at Galatia:

Now I say, as long as the heir is a child, he does not differ at all from a slave although he is owner of everything, but he is under guardians and managers until the date set by the father. ... And because you are sons, God has sent forth the Spirit of His Son into our hearts, crying, "Abba! Father!" Therefore you are no longer a slave, but a son; and if a son, then an heir through God (Galatians 4:1-2,6-7).

The heartbreaking analogy drawn for us here is a word picture of those who have inherited everything—yet possess nothing. All the inheritance includes will be held in trust until they grow up. *Nothing may be claimed until they come of age!* My heartfelt desire is that in some small way this book may point many to their inheritance in Christ, and having been challenged to do so, they will "...grow up in *all* aspects into Him, who is the head, even Christ" (Eph. 4:15).

Chapter Fourteen

Life in the Spirit

"And they were all *filled* with the Holy Spirit..." (Acts 2:4). These words chronicle a shock wave of power and anointing as believers were filled with the Holy Spirit. Interestingly, there are four other references in the Book of Acts that clearly indicate that believers who had already been filled with the Holy Spirit, were being filled *again*.[1] Which makes me wonder—did they leak? Was the reservoir of the Holy Spirit within them somehow depleted? Something must have happened that exhausted their supply of the Holy Spirit, and if so, what? Or could it be that our understanding of the term *filled* is incorrect?

One day, while I was pondering this question, the Holy Spirit drew my attention to Ephesians 5:18, "And do not get *drunk with wine*, for that is dissipation, but be *filled* with the Spirit." I began to see past the surface meaning of that verse, and the revelation that unfolded revolutionized my life, my theology, and my ministry. Paul's first admonition was, "And do not get *drunk with wine*...." We've all observed people who have had too much to drink. They often do or say things they would never do or say under normal circumstances; and we comment, "That person is under the influence." We recognize that it's not the person speaking or acting a certain way; he is under the control of alcohol. So, Paul admonished the Ephesian believers not to

---

1. Acts 4:8; 4:31; 13:9; 13:52. (The Acts 13:9 reference is valid because Paul was initially filled with the Holy Spirit in Acts 9:17-18.)

come under the influence of alcohol, not to let it control them. He completed that thought with, "... but be *filled* with the Holy Spirit." The logical flow of thought then says, just as drunkards have given themselves over to the control of alcohol, even so believers should yield themselves totally to the control (or "come under the influence") of the Holy Spirit.

This concept is strongly supported in the Greek text. In the Book of Acts, two different words are used to denote *filled*. In Acts 2:2 we read: "And suddenly there came from heaven a noise like a violent, rushing wind, and it *filled* the whole house where they were sitting." Here, referring to an inanimate object (the house), the Greek word used is *pleroo*, which means "to make replete, i.e. *to cram*."[2] There was not a nook or cranny of the building that the Holy Spirit did not occupy. He was everywhere!

In every reference in the Book of Acts where it refers to people (animate objects) being filled, a different word is used. The word is always *pletho*, which means "to imbue, *influence*."[3] It's evident then that the Father longs for His children to live their lives under the absolute, supreme control of the Holy Spirit, precisely as Jesus did. Let us examine the scriptural path that will lead us there.

John 4:24 tells us that "God is spirit," so we understand that His substance, His essence, is *spirit*. Scripture is perfectly transparent on that subject. He *is* spirit. In Hebrews 12:9 we are given an insight into God's relationship to believers. He is referred to therein as "the Father of spirits." Throughout the entire creation, like begets like; each species reproduces after its own kind. Monkeys give birth to monkeys; humans give birth to humans (regardless of what *The National Enquirer* may tell you).

God would not and did not violate His own order of generation. How often I've heard someone excitedly say, "At our church last Sunday, seven *souls* were saved!" The truth is, *no souls* were saved in any church last Sunday! If there were conversions, *spirits* were saved, not *souls*! Although Nicodemus was confused (he didn't understand how a grown man could possibly enter into his mother's womb a second time and be reborn), Jesus promptly explained what is involved in the new

---

2.   *Vine's.*
3.   *Vine's.*

birth: "That which is born of the flesh is *flesh,* and that which is born of the Spirit is *spirit*" (Jn. 3:6). Flesh gives birth to *flesh,* and Spirit gives birth to *spirit*! Nothing could be clearer?[4]

Adam walked with God and experienced a wonderfully personal relationship with the Father. Communion and fellowship between these heavenly lovers were sweet beyond imagination. Who can even begin to comprehend how intimately joined they were, as God unveiled His heart and shared His innermost secrets with His beloved Adam? Thus, through revelation knowledge, Adam knew the Father in the same manner that the Father knew him.

The Garden of Eden was indeed a lush tropical paradise. All but one of the trees of the garden were Adam's to enjoy. Concerning the "tree of the knowledge of good and evil," God warned Adam, "...for in the day that you eat from it *you shall surely die*" (Gen. 2:17). The saddest fact of history is the record of Adam's disobedience of God's command not to eat fruit from the forbidden tree. Immediate death was the penalty God prescribed. Yet, Adam didn't die immediately; he lived to the ripe old age of 930 (see Gen. 5:5). How can we reconcile this apparent contradiction? What seems to be a contradiction is instead a misunderstanding of two scriptural truths: (1) Adam was not the physical body, but the *spirit* that owned and operated that body. (2) Death, as referred to in Scripture, is not cessation of life, but *separation from God.* Adam (the spirit) died (was separated from God) the moment he disobeyed God's warning—his body died later.

Majoring On Minors

The Church has majored on minors, preaching that men should be saved in order to avoid going to hell. That is not God's priority. (Since the cross has been presented solely as a divine fire escape from hell, why should we register surprise when many who are converted under such teaching never develop an in-depth relationship with God?) The primary purpose for Jesus' death on the cross was not to rescue men from hell. Being rescued from hell is a by-product of salvation, not its main purpose. The paramount reason for Jesus' sacrifice was to redeem fallen men from the hand of the enemy—*and bring*

---

4. For an in-depth treatment of this subject, see chapter 12, "Flesh Births Flesh— Spirit Births Spirit" in my book *Christian Meditation: Doorway to the Spirit.*

mankind back into an intimate, Edenic relationship with the Father! Since God's holiness precluded any relationship with sinners, it was imperative that fallen mankind be redeemed and be provided with a means by which they could approach God—thus, the true reason for the cross. It is a fact that redeemed people who now share an intimate relationship with the Father will not go to hell—but that becomes a secondary benefit of the cross.

The Path of Understanding

*I have many more things to say to you, but you cannot bear them now. But when He, **the Spirit of truth**, comes, He will guide you into all the truth; for He will not speak on His own initiative, but whatever He hears, He will speak; and He will disclose to you what is to come. He shall glorify Me; for He shall take of Mine, and shall disclose it to you. All things that the Father has are Mine; therefore I said, that He takes of Mine, and will disclose it to you* (John 16:12-15).

O blessed, inescapable, indisputable, undeniable fact—the Holy Spirit has come to reveal the hidden secrets of God's Word to believers! If we had no other incentive than this to motivate us to press toward the goal of life in the Spirit, it would be sufficient. The Holy Spirit longs to lead us into a deeper understanding of the Word of God, and unfold His mysteries before us. Mysteries? Yes, mysteries! Despite what human pride would tell us, we do not now have complete insight and understanding of everything in God's Word, for His word is a continually unfolding revelation.

"It is often preached that the Word of God is very simple and easily understood—thus anyone and everyone can easily comprehend it. I strongly disagree with this premise! Scripture (Isa. 35:8) bears out that the way of salvation is eminently clear, so much so that even a fool could not miss it—but what about the rest of the Word of God?

"Concerning the writings of the Apostle Paul, Apostle Peter wrote: 'As also in *all* his letters, speaking in them of these things, in which are some things *hard to understand*' (II Pet. 3:16). And hear Paul himself: 'But we speak God's wisdom in a *mystery*, the *hidden* wisdom' [1 Cor. 2:7].

"Everywhere we look in the New Testament, we discover evidence of those things which God Himself has concealed with a distinct purpose. The words 'mystery, mysteries, hid' and 'hidden' appear a total of thirty-eight times in the New Testament, which would be strange if it were true that the Bible is a completely open book and totally comprehensible to even the casual observer.

"Consider also the numerous parables spoken by Jesus. The words 'parable' or 'parables' occur no less than forty-six times in the Gospels. A parable is an illustrated story, often with a *hidden meaning concealed from the hearers* (Matt. 13:13,34,35). Fortunately, as Daniel wrote, 'However, there is a God in heaven who reveals mysteries' [Dan. 2:28a]."[5]

Will Somebody, *Anybody,* Please Turn the Light On?

If the Holy Spirit has come to shed so much light, why are so many Christians walking around in the dark? Blame must be laid at the doorstep of some of the undershepherds, pastors who for one reason or another cannot or will not feed their people the meat of the Word. Someday they will be required to render an account before God for their powerless ministries and careless tending of the flock (see Jer. 23:1-2).

The question of why so many Christians are living in the dark brings us full cycle to Ephesians 5:18: "And do not get drunk with wine, for that is dissipation, but *be filled with the Spirit.*" We already understand that Paul's admonition to believers was not to come under the controlling influence of wine, but to come under the controlling influence of the Holy Spirit.

Many Christians consider being filled with the Holy Spirit a one-time affair. Having yielded once to the Spirit and spoken in tongues, they are forever satisfied. How is it possible to be satisfied with a one-time taste of the Holy Spirit? The only thing that speaking in tongues proves is that you have yielded to the Holy Spirit at least once. If it *were* possible to leak the Holy Spirit, it could certainly be said that many Christians are running on *empty.*

---

5. Seavey, *Christian Meditation*, 59-60.

The scriptural concept of the infilling of the Holy Spirit is definitely not that of a once-for-all happening. Actually, the opposite is true. The original Greek text strongly supports the concept of an *ongoing* experience. In Ephesians 5:18 the word translated "be" should be more accurately translated in the continuing tense as "being"— "but *being* filled." In the Greek the word for "being" communicates a continuing action. Paul is encouraging believers to *continually come under the influence of the Holy Spirit*! That is the portal by which we enter into a spiritual relationship with the Holy Spirit, from whom springs the fullness of divine revelation. This principle is also apparent in Galatians 5:16, where Paul instructed believers to "*walk* by the Spirit." The Greek word for "walk" means *live*. The New International Version translates it this way: "*live* by the Spirit."

Many ministers will disagree with the concepts in this book. One Full Gospel pastor recently said, "All this preaching about the supernatural only hurts believers; because when they don't see the miraculous in their lives, they get discouraged." Poor babies! Since when has it been the Christian's mandate to seek a comfort zone? Should we then structure our preaching and teaching around the spiritually anemic lives of people who don't profess or possess anything of a supernatural nature? That would certainly keep all the pouters happy and solve the problem of frustration. On the other hand, perhaps a dose of spiritual frustration would drive some Christians to seek God in order to fill their emptiness.

I have been told that it is unrealistic to expect believers to "live their entire lives in the Spirit." How can it be unrealistic when God Himself commanded us to do so? God never instructs us to do anything for which He has not already supplied the enabling spiritual power and anointing that we need to accomplish it.

In an attempt to defend their lackadaisical lives, opponents of total commitment ask, "Have you ever seen even one Christian live his entire life—*every* moment of *every* day—in the Spirit?" The fact that no one yet has totally appropriated life in the Spirit does not negate the actuality or "factuality" of the commandment to do so. Many Christians fail even to attempt living in the Spirit because they enjoy existing (wallowing) in the flesh far too much. Others remain mired in a life of mediocrity because no one has ever directed them to higher ground. "Lead me to the rock that is higher than I" (Ps. 61:2b).

Chapter Fifteen

Metamorphosis

Life in the Spirit is eminently clear in the Word of God. Yet, for most Christians it remains an elusive will-o'-the-wisp. Some have even made a valiant attempt to live it out, but when it didn't work for them they joined the ranks of the disillusioned. But the Bible is still clear on the subject: Believers *can* and *should* live their entire lives in the Spirit. But if life in the Spirit really *is* in the Bible, then why hasn't someone already attained it? That's a valid question, for which there is a multifaceted answer.

Again we come back to the undershepherds (pastors) who have failed to feed the sheep anything more nourishing than milk and Pablum. If the saying that "an army travels on its stomach" is true, how far can the army of the Church march on spiritual mush? God's promise to Israel was, "Then I will give you shepherds after My own heart, *who will feed you* on knowledge and understanding" (Jer. 3:15). God declared that the shepherds who were "after My own heart" were those "who will *feed* you." Jesus' post-resurrection commission to Peter (see Jn. 21:15-17) had more to do with feeding than leading the sheep. Many pastors have been guilty of starving the flock through ignorance, while a few are simply uncaring. What kind of dynamic, overcoming, powerful army of believers can be developed if all we have are *preacherettes* preaching *sermonettes* to *Christianettes*? Remember, you cannot lead where you yourself have not gone! As someone once said, "You teach what you *know*—you reproduce what you *are*."

Thank God, there are pastors who have caught the revelation and are fervently and honestly preaching it to their people. They are leading, marching out ahead, blazing a path for the Church to follow. They faithfully wait on the Holy Spirit for their messages so that they can always deliver the mind of God to their flocks. Inevitably, despite the best efforts of these men and women of God, some of their people will refuse to follow; others will leave the church in search of greener pastures where they will be made to feel more comfortable. But Jesus never told us to make the flock comfortable; He said *"feed* My flock" and *"tend* My flock."

Some Christians have a distorted view of what a pastor is because their picture of Jesus is limited to a sweet, tender portrayal of the Good Shepherd gently carrying a lamb on His shoulders (see Lk. 15:3-5). But one must understand the background of that parable. If a lamb strayed from the flock, it immediately became vulnerable to attack from predators. If it wandered away more than once, the shepherd would, upon finding it again, break its leg! Then he would carry it on his shoulders until it was completely healed, thus making it dependent upon him *and curing its wandering spirit.* An archeological discovery from the first or second century depicts the Good Shepherd with the lamb across His shoulders, but with both the front and rear legs held very securely by the Shepherd.[1] That sheep wasn't going anywhere soon! Some sheep in the Church today need to have their legs of self-will broken. But that would demand tough love, and many ministers are not willing to travel that route for fear of offending someone.

Stinkin' Thinkin'

Stinkin' thinkin' is the seat of the problem for the vast majority of believers, and this will be the scope of our concern for the remainder of this chapter. Man's mind is what gives him the most trouble (in concert with desires of the flesh), yet the problem of the mind is seldom addressed from the pulpit. The Church at large seems reluctant to confront the subject of man's mind and avoids mentioning or

---

1. Graydon F. Snyder, *Ante Pacem, Archaeological Evidence of Church Life Before Constantine*, Plate 9, Sarcophagus of Sta. Maria Antigua (Mercer University Press, 1991), 23.

dealing with it at all costs. The major reason for this is ignorance, not understanding the difference between soul and spirit. Once the distinction is clearly defined, the way is opened to begin making necessary changes in the mind that will provide the genesis of life in the Spirit.

Satan, the archenemy of the Church, has dedicated himself to its overthrow, and over aeons has amassed an awesome arsenal of weapons that he uses in his relentless onslaught against believers. Obviously, certain weapons are more effective against some people than others, but there is one that surpasses all the others. Satan does his utmost to keep this one under wraps. The Holy Spirit has given me the pleasant task of unwrapping and exposing it before the Church.

(The following illustration was given to me by the Lord, and had been included in this book from the start. Yet, just before sending the manuscript to the publisher, I searched through it to reword the illustration. I found to my amazement that it had vanished from my computer's hard drive, from both backup disks, and even from the final printed manuscript. If its disappearance could be traced to a simple computer malfunction, why was this entire illustration the *only* part of the book's text to disappear? And what could have caused it to vanish from pages already printed? The obvious [and *only*] answer is that Satan does not want the Church to know the simple yet profound truth contained therein.)

Some years ago the Holy Spirit spoke clearly to me asking, "Would you like to know what Satan's greatest tool is?" Though I immediately answered, "Yes," His answer didn't come immediately. He allowed me several minutes in which to search my own mind for what I thought the answer might be. During those minutes my mind ran through the gamut of what I considered to be mankind's most besetting sins, but I was wrong on all counts. (On several occasions since, I have put this question before audiences ranging into the thousands and have never *once* received a correct answer! That alone convinced me just how subtle and cunning this choice tool of hell really is—and why it *must* be revealed.)

The Holy Spirit's answer was simple, yet extremely profound. He said, "Satan's greatest tool is *a closed mind!*" He further explained that as long as a person maintains a closed mind, he can never receive further revelation from God. A closed mind presupposes that it has already absorbed all truth and thus refuses all subsequent revelation.

In order to portray this truth, the Holy Spirit gave me an illustration for a lesson in deeper life. Following His instructions, I showed my class a flower seed and a container of rich potting soil and explained that this was a combination certain to bring forth life and beauty. I described the flower's potential constituent parts in detail—its form, height, vibrant colors, and fragrant aroma. All these were resident in that tiny, unimpressive seed. Before that flower could germinate, however, the seed and the soil would have to be joined together to begin the life process; this alone releases life. I covered the flower pot with a plastic wrap and secured it with a rubber band. I then placed the lonely seed on top, and passed it around for everyone to see. "That," said the Holy Spirit, "is what a closed mind is like. All the form, beauty, color, and fragrance of the flower are resident in that seed; but because of the plastic wrap barrier, no one will ever see its glory." The seed is the Word of God (see Lk. 8:10-11) full of mystery and wonder, and the soil is an *open mind*! Whenever we close our minds to new truth from God's Word, we preclude the seed from taking root and producing fruit.

In Mark 6:52 we read of the disciples, "...They had not gained any insight from the incident of the loaves, but *their heart was hardened*." The literal translation is, "They had not gained any insight from the incident of the loaves, for *their mind was closed*." Having personally witnessed the miraculous multiplication of loaves and fishes, the disciples should have gained spiritual insight and understanding, but they hadn't—because their minds were closed! The scenario is repeated in Mark 8:17 where Jesus chided them, "...Why do you discuss the fact that you have no bread? Do you not yet see or understand [understand, a *mental* function]? Do you have a hardened heart [a closed mind]?" Their lack of faith was caused by a lack of understanding, and Jesus said this was due to a closed mind—Satan's greatest tool! The word *hardened* is derived from the Greek word *poroo*, which means "a stone—to petrify, that is, to harden."[2] We know that when the Bible uses the word *heart*, it is metaphorically referring to the *mind*. A "hard heart" is really a *closed mind*. Thus, using today's jargon we might say, "Don't be so hardheaded!" The apostle

---

2.   *Strong's.*

Paul wrote concerning Israel, "But *their minds were hardened*; for until this very day at the reading of the old covenant the same veil remains unlifted, because it is removed in Christ" (2 Cor. 3:14). Paul described a closed mind as one covered with a veil, but went on to say that the veil is removed in Christ. Sadly, many Christians live out their lives with the veil firmly set in place—limited by closed minds.

There has never been a revival that has not to some extent been quenched by those in spiritual authority—leaders who closed their minds to the new thing the Holy Spirit was doing. Many revivals have never even gotten off the ground for much the same reason; religious leaders closed their minds to any new move of the Holy Spirit. "New" is the traditionalist's way of saying *unfamiliar*. (And what traditionalist would ever admit to being unfamiliar with anything?)

The Pharisees were firsthand observers as Jesus performed mighty miracles (see Mk. 3:1-6). They had the testimony of eyewitnesses that He had raised the dead (see Jn. 11:46-47). Yet they chose to close their minds to the fact that Jesus just might be their Messiah! (See John 11:48-53 and Acts 4:16-17.) As William DeArtega, in his book *Quenching the Spirit*, says, "Thus, although they believed themselves to be the protectors of orthodoxy, the Pharisees were really the *opponents* of the Holy Spirit."[3]

(In his outstanding book, William DeArtega outlines many significant revivals, beginning with those of the first-century Church and continuing to the present day. He relates how religious leaders, in the name of God, consistently quenched the Spirit. Every earnest Christian—from the highest ruling official of every denomination to every officeholder in the local church—every minister and member of the laity needs to read *Quenching the Spirit*. It will help them understand how the opposition of religious leaders is mounted against grassroots revivals that spring up among the people. It will also enlighten believers as to what they can do to maintain the fires of revival once the Holy Spirit has kindled them.)

Please understand that when I implore you to maintain an open mind I'm not asking you to be gullible or to swallow without investigation every new doctrine in its entirety. But the earnest cry of my

---

3. William DeArtega, *Quenching the Spirit* (Lake Mary, FL: Creation House Publishers, 1992), 23.

heart is that God will raise up Berean Christians in our day who will spend time *"...examining the Scriptures daily,* to see whether these things were so"* (Acts 17:11). Upon being exposed to the *new* doctrines that Paul and Silas had introduced, the Bereans didn't examine their denomination's "Position Paper"; they examined the Scriptures! They were open-minded enough that they were able to think for themselves instead of needing to be spoon-fed by their denominational leaders (Pharisees and Sadducees). And if we cannot have only Bereans, then at the very least, let the rest heed the advice of Gamaliel, "...For if this plan or action should be of men, it will be overthrown; but if it is of God, you will not be able to overthrow them; *or else you may even be found fighting against God"* (Acts 5:38-39; see also 5:33-37). If you are not scripturally certain whether or not a new move is born of the Holy Spirit, the best approach is to follow the wise counsel of Gamaliel and withhold judgment (see Acts 5:33-39; 2 Sam. 6:6-7). Then, follow the wisdom of the Bereans and search the Scriptures to see for yourself whether these things are true (see Acts 17:10-12). Jesus Himself revealed the formula for open-mindedness: *"If any man is willing to do His will,* he shall know of the teaching, whether it is of God, or whether I speak from Myself"* (Jn. 7:17).

Get a Checkup From the Neck Up!

Christians have no problem with their spirits; for their spirits were born from above, then reunited with Father God when they accepted Christ, and are in perfect unity with Him and His Word. First Corinthians 6:17 tells us, "But the one who joins himself to the Lord is *one* spirit with Him." His Spirit and ours have melded into one. Since that union occurred, your spirit has had no problem believing everything in the Word of God (see Rom. 7:22), no trouble appropriating it, no trouble living it! Your spirit is in total agreement and conformity with the Word of God! That raises the question, "If that's true, why do I live so far below my station and privileges in Christ, continually struggling to maintain my Christian walk?" The answer is simple: Your spirit is not the obstacle standing between you and all that God's Word declares is yours; your soul (which includes your heart and mind) is the big offender, and you need to know how to bring it into submission.

> "It is of primary importance to understand what *heart* means in Scripture. The word is *"kardia,"* from which we derive the

word "cardiac," meaning "having to do with the heart." It is absolutely certain that the physical, fleshly pump which we call a heart is *not* what is meant here. The physical heart, which circulates the blood, is the chief organ of physical life (Lev. 17:11) and occupies the most important place in the human body. By an easy transition, the word came to stand for man's entire mental and moral activity, both the rational and emotional elements. In other words, the heart is used *figuratively* for the hidden springs of man's personal life."[4]

The Bible describes sin as being "in the heart," because sin is a principle that has its origin in the center of man's inward life, and from there it defiles the whole circuit of his actions (see Mt. 15:19-20). On the other hand, Scripture regards the heart also as the sphere of divine influence (see Rom. 2:15; Mt. 15:19). The heart, lying deep within, contains "the hidden person" (1 Pet. 3:4), the real man. Its usage in the New Testament denotes:

1. The seat of physical life (Acts 14:17; Jas. 5:5).

2. The seat of moral nature and *spiritual life*—the seat of grief (Jn. 14:1; Rom. 9:2; 2 Cor. 2:4).

3. Joy (Jn. 16:22; Eph. 5:19).

4. The *desires* (Mt. 5:28; 2 Pet. 2:14).

5. The affections (Lk. 24:32; Acts 21:13).

6. The *perceptions* (Jn. 12:40; Eph. 4:18).

7. The *thoughts* (Mt. 9:4; Heb. 4:12).

8. The *understanding* (Mt. 13:15; Rom. 1:21).

9. The *reasoning powers* (Mk. 2:6; Lk. 24:38).

10. The *imagination* (Lk. 1:51).

11. Conscience (Acts 2:37; 1 Jn. 3:20).

12. The *intentions* (Heb. 4:12; 1 Pet. 4:1).

13. *Purpose* (Acts 11:23; 2 Cor. 9:7).

14. The *will* (Rom. 6:17; Col. 3:15).

---

4. Excerpted from my book *Christian Meditation: Doorway to the Spirit,* chapter 22, "Faith—That Elusive Quality."

15. *Faith* (Mk. 11:23; Rom. 10:10; Heb. 3:12).[5]

Please take note that of the 15 attributes of heart mentioned above, 10 (a full two-thirds) have to do with *mental* activity! It is very clear in Scripture that heart=soul=mind. The eminent Greek scholar, Colin Brown, agrees with this conclusion:

> "A striking feature of the New Testament is the essential closeness of *cardia* to the concept of *nous*, **mind**.... Heart and mind (*noemata*, lit. thoughts) can be used in parallel (II Cor. 3:14) or *synonymously* (Phil. 4:7).[6]

Want to Change Your Ways? Change Your *Mind*!

I urge you therefore, brethren, by the mercies of God, to present your bodies a living sacrifice, acceptable to God, which is your spiritual service of worship. And do not be conformed to this world, but be transformed by the renewing of your mind... (Romans 12:1-2).

The solution that the apostle Paul offers for the sin problem is to be "transformed by the renewing of your mind." The mind of man is the great arena in which the furious battle between darkness and light is waged, and it is there that life in the Spirit begins—or ends.

Sometimes (as much as I hate to admit it) Satan is smarter than the children of God (see Lk. 16:8). He knows where the journey toward life in the Spirit originates, and what awesome power and authority awaits believers who arrive at its destination. Satan fears the extensive damage they will wreak upon his kingdom of darkness. Is it any wonder then that he exerts such great influence within the sphere of our minds? Why has Satan gone to such extremes to contaminate the minds of people, not just in the Church, but everywhere? Why has he confused the differences between soul (mind) and spirit in the minds of believers? Why has he lulled the clergy into refusing to preach about the mind, leaving that aspect of personality to worldly psychiatrists and psychologists? (It is a fact that psychiatrists have the highest suicide rate among all professionals. If they can't solve their own problems, how can they solve ours?) God said, "How

---

5. *Vine's*, 297.
6. Colin Brown, *The New International Dictionary of New Testament Theology*, Vol. 2, 182; emph. mine.

blessed is the man who does not walk in the counsel of the wicked" (Ps. 1:1a).

Can you see the big picture? Satan desires control of your mind and he is willing to pay any price necessary to gain it. The Church, on the other hand, is not willing to pay a commensurate price to retain spiritual control of the mind; thus we yield the whole man by default. Paul said: "But I am afraid, lest as the serpent deceived Eve by his *craftiness* [cunning use of his mind], your *minds* should be led astray from the simplicity and purity of devotion to Christ" (2 Cor. 11:3).

The mind is obviously the part of man that is led astray. Satan does the leading and the Church does the following. The Church is made up of good followers; we follow the world, the flesh, the devil, etc., yet *struggle* to follow the humble Nazarene. One reason for this is because the thoughts and attitudes of the world surround us daily and are automatically absorbed, while it takes a proactive effort on our part to fill our minds with godly thoughts and attitudes. That's *work*! Long before my mother became a believer or knew any (formal) theology, she would admonish me, "An idle mind is the devil's playground!" Truer words were never spoken. "For the weapons of our warfare are not of the flesh, but divinely powerful *for the destruction of fortresses*. We are destroying speculations and every lofty thing raised up against the knowledge of God, and we are taking *every thought captive* to the obedience of Christ" (2 Cor. 10:4-5).

One major purpose for which God gave us these divinely powerful weapons is to accomplish "the destruction of fortresses." From the context of these verses it is evident that the fortresses mentioned are located in the mind. These fortresses are strongholds from which the enemy relentlessly wages war against us. Every evil, unbridled thought affords the enemy a secure hiding place from which to attack. These fortresses *must* be leveled to the ground!

The above verses are filled with great violence—violence aimed directly at undermining and ultimately destroying the kingdom of darkness. They speak of warfare and weapons, the destruction of fortresses and speculations. In the midst of all that violence appears this statement: "we are taking *every thought captive*." Does it seem like a strange place for the Holy Spirit to insert that phrase? It isn't. By doing so, the Holy Spirit is shining a searchlight on the true battlefield:

the mind. *Every* thought must be brought into submission to the mind of Christ within us (see 1 Cor. 2:16).

Paul admonished the Ephesian believers: "And that you be renewed in the *spirit* of your *mind*" (Eph. 4:23). That's an interesting phrase, "spirit of your mind." I believe this is a direct reference to the subconscious mind. After all, that's where all the programming (good and bad) takes place. We have spent a lifetime being programmed by parents, teachers, TV, Hollywood, news media of all sorts, friends, religious teachings, and all too often, our own negative outlook on life (just to name a few). Because of this programming, we are left with all kinds of bad habits, not-so-nice personality traits, evil thoughts, lust, pride, poor self-image, etc. After we come to Christ, we struggle valiantly to overcome these longstanding mental habits and personality traits. Often, having failed in the attempt, we settle back into the habitual mire of defeat.

> "The computer (brain) was meant to serve us, but through a lack of information, and wrong programming, we have become enslaved by the servant, who is often a cruel taskmaster...By the proper use of Christian meditation, we are able to reprogram (renew) our thought lives by aligning our minds with what the Word of God says about us, and experience the joy of transformation as referred to by the Apostle Paul in Romans 12:2b!"[7]

Hurry Up and Wait!

That seems to be the perpetual theme of the military—hurry up and wait. In God's army you think things should be different. We refuse to be subject to boot camp preparation (babies don't go to boot camp). We expect to be the recipients of instantly conferred perfection. That's because man is basically an impatient being (myself excluded, of course). We want things *yesterday*! We live in an instant society where everything is geared toward simplification. Instant mashed potatoes, instant foods of all kinds, spray-on shoe polish—you name it and somewhere it can most likely be found in its instant form. We carry this baggage of "instant everything" into our Christian lives and can't endure the rigors of *waiting* on God, or worse yet, the

---

7. Seavey, *Christian Meditation*, 153.

prospect of having to do something for ourselves. "Renewing of the mind" and "bringing every thought captive" are clearly and scripturally *our* responsibility. While we wait patiently (or not so patiently) for God to do the work, He waits for *us* to do it; and it takes both time and patience to bring about the renewing of the mind.

There are two interesting words used in Romans 12:2, which we translate as "transformed" and "renewing." Properly understood in the Greek, these words will shed light on the process by which renewal becomes feasible. The word in the Greek for "transformed" is *metamorphoo*, from which we derive our English word, "metamorphosis":

> "To change into another form (*meta*, implying change, and *morphe*, form). *Morphe* lays stress on the *inward* change. The present continuous tenses indicate a *process*. Second Corinthians 3:18 describes believers as being 'transformed into the same image, *i.e.*, of Christ.' "[8]

Strong emphasis is laid upon the fact that the desired change is a transmutation, something that takes place over a period of time. So, please don't become disheartened when you don't see the desired results immediately. Remember, growth is a process.

The second word to consider is "renewing," which is even more interesting in the Greek. The word is *anakainosis*, which, according to *Vine's*, means "renovation."[9] ("To restore to good condition; make new or as if new again").[10] Renovation requires tearing out what is now in place in order to restore what was there before. God wants His people to have the mind of Christ (see 1 Cor. 2:16; Phil. 2:5), which is the same mind our forefather Adam had before he fell into sin. As long as our minds are held captive to our old ways of thinking, we can never approximate the image God has of the Church! We will always be either defeated by Satan or continue to exist on the edge of "what might have been." The word *renovation* implies work—*hard* work—on our part. We content ourselves with housecleaning, simply dusting the furniture, when God requires renovation—tearing out the walls! The Church has somehow been caught up in the fantasy that God

---

8.   *Vine's*, 639; emph. mine.
9.   *Vine's*; 524.
10.   *Webster's Encyclopedic Unabridged Dictionary*.

does everything for us. Then, when we don't exhibit the called-for change, we feel justified in blaming God. After all, we did ask Him to change us, and since nothing happened, it must be His fault. It just isn't so! God has given us the equipment we need to renew our own minds—and He expects us to do just that.

Paul stressed the responsibility of the individual when he wrote: "...work out your salvation with fear and trembling; for *it is God who is at work in you...*" (Phil. 2:12-13). Since there is absolutely nothing we can do to effect the salvation of the spirit (except to believe, repent, and confess with our mouths), the above Scripture *must* refer to the salvation of the soul (mind). James 1:21b (which was written to those who were already Christians) reaffirms this contention: "receive the word implanted, which is able to *save your souls.*"

We've preached *free* grace for so long now that we have developed an aversion to anything with a divine price tag affixed to it. Over the outside of the gates to the Kingdom of God we read, "FREE—WHOSOEVER WILL, MAY COME!" This is an unassailable truth with which I am in total agreement. However, once you step inside the Kingdom of God and look back, the inscription on the inside reads, "Do you not know...*you are not your own? For you have been bought with a price*" (1 Cor. 6:19-20). It may be free to come through the door, but it will cost you everything to remain inside. Everything we are or ever hope to be belongs absolutely and irrevocably to Jesus Christ. We are His purchased property, and He alone is our Sovereign Lord and Master. Since we don't preach that strong gospel message much anymore, most Christians run their own lives, do as they please, and have absolutely no concept of the Lordship of Jesus Christ or His claim on their lives. That's why so many Christians claim salvation, yet have no sense of responsibility to the Kingdom of God except to await death or the rapture, whichever takes place first.

Why Satan Plays Mind Games With Us—The Answer May Surprise You

Even a cursory examination of the foregoing Scriptures identifies the mind as the arena of conflict between the forces of Light and Darkness. But why choose *this* arena? The answer is found in Romans 8:6: "For the *mind* set on the flesh is death, but the *mind* set on the Spirit is life and peace." The verse can be more clearly understood when we consider an in-depth examination of Hebrews 9:8: "The Holy Spirit is signifying this, that the way into the holy place has not yet been disclosed, *while the outer tabernacle is still standing*."

That verse was always an enigma to me, until I researched its full meaning in the Greek text. (An enigma is a saying that contains a hidden meaning, like a riddle, according to Webster's dictionary.) Indeed, there was a hidden meaning in this verse that would shed new light on the process of renewing the mind. It's found in the statement that there was "no access to the holy place while the outer tabernacle was still standing" (see Heb. 9:8). Yet we know that the outer tabernacle provided the only access to the Holy of Holies.

Please understand that when the writer of Hebrews speaks of the holy place he is referring to what we commonly know as the Holy of Holies. This is borne out in Hebrews 10:19-20: "Since therefore, brethren, we have confidence to enter the holy place [holiest of all] by the blood of Jesus, by a new and living way which He inaugurated for us *through the veil* [the veil served as a barrier to the Holy of Holies], that is, His flesh." The blood was applied only in the Holy of Holies (see Heb. 9:1-3,7,24), and in no other place.

Chapter Sixteen

Meta"more"phosis (Metamorphosis Continued)

The Enigma Unveiled

There are three created heavens: the atmosphere, the ionosphere, and outer space. The first (atmospheric) heaven is where man has his existence. Thus, it corresponds to man's *flesh*. The second (ionospheric) heaven is situated above the earth's atmosphere (between it and the third heaven) and corresponds to man's *mind*. (It is not accidental nor coincidental that the evil hosts of Ephesians 6:11-12 reside in this stratum.[1] From this vantage point they relentlessly wage war against man's mind.) The third heaven (outer space) is where God dwells, the place Paul called Paradise: "I know a man in Christ...such a man was caught up to *the third heaven...was caught up into Paradise...*" (2 Cor. 12:2,4). The third heaven, the dwelling place of God (who is spirit according to John 4:24), corresponds to man's *spirit*.

God manifests Himself in three persons—Father, Son, and Holy Spirit—referred to by many as the Trinity. Man is a tripartite (consisting of three parts) being: spirit, soul, and body. There is a heavenly tabernacle,[2] composed of three parts, which was the pattern of the earthly tabernacle:

---

1. An in-depth explanation can be found in my 4-tape series on spiritual warfare: "Strong Man to Straw Man."
2. See Hebrews 8:1-2,5; 9:11-12,23-24; 10:19-20; Revelation 15:5.

*We have such a high priest, who has taken His seat at the right hand of the throne of the Majesty in the heavens, a minister in the sanctuary, and in **the true tabernacle**, which the Lord pitched, not man* (Hebrews 8:1b-2).

*Therefore it was necessary for the **copies** of the things in the heavens to be cleansed with these, but **the heavenly things** themselves with better sacrifices than these* (Hebrews 9:23).

The typology of the tabernacle is so rich that manifold volumes have been written about it; but we will concern ourselves only with its design (three divisions), and how that relates to the renewing of the mind. The tabernacle was a sacred tent wherein God manifested His Presence to Israel. It consisted of two rooms, the outer of which was referred to as the holy place (or the outer tabernacle) and the inner sanctum was known as the Holy of Holies. The entire tabernacle was holy but the Holy of Holies was especially so because that was where God chose to abide, and from there He manifested His Presence. Immediately outside the tabernacle proper, surrounded by a linen fence, there was a large open area referred to as the outer court, where animals were slain to atone for the sins committed by the people. The tabernacle was a portable structure used until King Solomon built a permanent temple to house the Presence of God. The temple, though far more elaborate, also followed the precise format of the tabernacle; it too had an outer court, the holy place (the outer tabernacle), and the Holy of Holies. Two other temples followed Solomon's, both of which also were constructed according to the precise pattern of the tabernacle.

The Holy of Holies (Presence of God) was restricted to all but one person, the high priest, and then only on one day a year: Yom Kippur, the Day of Atonement. Upon entering the Holy of Holies, the high priest would sprinkle the blood of atonement on the mercy seat, minister before Jehovah, and leave. In keeping with God's restrictiveness, only one path was provided into His Presence: through the outer court (where the sacrifices were offered), through the outer tabernacle, and through the veil, into the Holy of Holies. There was only *one* God and there was only *one* approach to Him!

Throughout the Old Testament era God hid Himself from the common people, revealing Himself only to those who were called to high offices of religious or civil authority (*i.e.*, prophets, priests, and kings). Then Jesus came, of whom John said, "And the Word became flesh, and dwelt among us…" (Jn. 1:14). The word "dwelt" literally translated from the Greek is tabernacled. Jesus became God's tabernacle (a sacred tent of God's Presence) among men. The Bible expands upon that revelation by explaining that, "…God was *in* Christ reconciling the world to Himself…" (2 Cor. 5:19); yet no one seemed to recognize the Father's Presence. Even Philip, who knew Jesus intimately, requested, "Lord, show us the Father, and it is enough for us" (Jn. 14:8b). Jesus' reply was in itself a question, "…Have I been so long with you, and yet you have not come to know Me, Philip?" (Jn. 14:9a). Jesus' answer to Philip was a revelation that would be fully understood only after His resurrection: "Then He opened their minds to understand the Scriptures" (Lk. 24:45). What prevented Philip, who had known Jesus personally for approximately three years, from being aware of the Father's Presence? Similar to the veil that precluded the people of Israel from entering the Holy of Holies (thus viewing the Presence of God), a veil also hindered Philip from recognizing the Father's Presence in Jesus. In the case of Israel a fabric veil was the barrier; with Jesus it was His flesh: "Since therefore, brethren, we have confidence to enter the holy place by the blood of Jesus, by a new and living way which He inaugurated for us through the veil, that is, His flesh" (Heb. 10:19-20).

Jesus' flesh has a twofold typological application. First, it was analogous to the outer court where lambs (and other animals) were offered for sin. John the Baptist recognized this when he spoke prophetically of Jesus, "Behold, *the Lamb of God* who takes away the sin of the world!" (Jn. 1:29b). Jesus' flesh also served as a veil that prevented anyone from seeing or entering into the Father's Presence. Thus, Jesus' Spirit was the inner sanctum, the Holy of Holies, the dwelling place of Almighty God.

This being understood, the sacrifice of Calvary takes on a whole new significance for us. Our understanding opens to the fuller meaning of Jesus' death on the cross. As stated earlier, the primary function of the cross was not to remove us from hell and take us to Heaven—those were its by-products. When His body was torn by the cruel nails and Roman spear, it was in reality the rending of the veil (His flesh), allowing all mankind free access to the Holy of Holies, into the very Presence of God. Jesus' body being torn on the cross is the *type*; the Father's simultaneous rending of the temple veil (see Lk. 23:45-46) is the *antitype*, or fulfillment. Jesus' cry, "It is *finished*," immediately coincided with the Fathers' rending of the temple veil because they are synonymous events. The very purpose for which Jesus had come was intricately and minutely fulfilled at that precise moment in time; the way into the Holy of Holies had now been opened to whosoever will! The Holy Presence is still accessible to all who will believe. The Father has made Himself accessible, and has invited us to boldly (in the Greek that means with confidence) enter the Holy of Holies and experience not only His Presence, but His *essence*.

The Tabernacle Called Man

Now we are confronted with the question, "Why did God create man as a tripartite being: spirit, soul, and body?" Even a cursory examination of Scripture would reveal that from the very beginning of time it was God's intention that redeemed men should be the dwelling place of the Holy Spirit: "Do you not know that *you are a temple of God*, and that the Spirit of God dwells in you? ...for the temple of God is holy, *and that is what you are*" (1 Cor. 3:16-17; see also 1 Cor. 6:19a; 2 Cor. 6:16). God had commanded Moses to construct the tabernacle precisely according to the blueprint He had given him while on the mountain (see Ex. 25:9,40; 26:30; 27:8), which was a duplicate of the pattern of the heavenly tabernacle. The three subsequent temples were all constructed in strict accordance with the same pattern revealed to Moses. Since God's ultimate plan was for man to be the temple of the Holy Spirit, it was imperative that he should also be created according to the pattern of the heavenly tabernacle. Thus, man was made a tripartite being—spirit, soul, and body.

Once we understand why man was created a tripartite being, God's analogy is easily understood. God is spirit (see Jn. 4:24) and His dwelling place was in the Holy of Holies (see Heb. 9:24). Thus, it remains that man's spirit (his innermost being) is analogous to (a type of) the Holy of Holies. The outer court was the outermost part of the tabernacle and was open to everyone, even Gentiles; all flesh was welcome there. It was the place of sacrifice and is analogous to (a type of) the flesh, man's body. The intermediate place between these two was the outer tabernacle (the holy place), which is analogous to (a type of) man's heart (which is the same as his soul and/or his mind). The correlation between man's tripartite being and the tabernacle can be clearly seen. Yet, part of the mystery remains: "...the way into the holy place has not yet been disclosed, *while the outer tabernacle is still standing*" (Heb. 9:8).

The phrase "while the outer tabernacle is still standing" presents a problem. Even though the first (Mosaic) tabernacle was replaced by three subsequent temples, there was never any change of design, let alone the removal of the outer tabernacle (the holy place). To resolve this confusion I read the verse in the Greek text and was quite surprised by the literal meaning of the word "standing." The Greek word is *stasis*, which W.E. Vine translates as "by implication a *popular uprising*" (emph. mine). Further search revealed a similar, even stronger, translation: "dissention, *insurrection*, riot, *sedition*, standing, uproar."[3] Let's read Hebrews 9:8 again, replacing the word "standing" with the words "in insurrection": "...the way into the holy place has not yet been disclosed, while the outer tabernacle is still *in insurrection.*"

We know that the outer tabernacle corresponds to man's heart (soul, mind), which is the repository of man's will, intellect, and emotions. It is also a fact that, since his fall in the Garden of Eden, man's mind has been in open rebellion against God. It is not coincidental then that Satan's fall from Heaven was characterized by five "I will's" (see Is. 14:13-14). The introduction of sin into the cosmos was initiated by an insurrection in the *mind* of Satan himself! It is no wonder then that when Satan initially enticed Eve to sin, it was on a mental level (see Gen. 3:4-6). Man followed Satan's example; his initial sin was in the realm of the mind (exercising his will) as he ate of the tree of the *knowledge* of good and evil. Since God does nothing by chance, notice that Jesus was crucified on Calvary,[4] which translated means, "place of a skull," the very receptacle of the brain (mind). "But I am afraid, lest as the serpent deceived Eve by his *craftiness*, [cunning use of his mind] *your minds should be led astray* from the simplicity and

---

3. Bauer, Arndt, and Gingrich, *A Greek-English Lexicon of the New Testament and Other Early Christian Literature*, Second Edition (1979), 764; emph. mine.
4. In Hebrew, *Golgotha*; in Latin, *Calvarius*, which is translated in English, "Calvary." See Luke 23:33.

purity of devotion to Christ" (2 Cor. 11:3; see also Gen. 3:1-7). Because thoughts always precede actions, as the mind goes, so goes the individual. Jesus Himself said that external things do not defile the man, but those things that proceed from within, from the heart (soul, mind). (See Matthew 15:15-20.)

Access to the Holy of Holies was always by the same route: one would enter the outer court, pass by the altar (a type of the cross) where sacrifice for sin was made, move forward into the holy place where prayer and praise were emphasized (in the types of the table of shewbread and altar of incense), and proceed past the veil into the Holy of Holies, into God's manifest Presence. There was no back door to the Holy of Holies. One either approached via God's prescribed path, or didn't come at all! As believers, our ultimate objective should be to enter the Holy of Holies and experience the effulgence of His Presence.

Unknowingly, we follow the divine pattern of the tabernacle in the format of our worship services, which often begin with lively singing, clapping, raising of hands, and verbal praise (and in some churches, dancing before the Lord). Thus, we begin praising God through the use of our flesh (our physical bodies—a type of the outer court). We may not even feel like entering into praise, but we direct our flesh and it obeys. Proceeding further into the service, we move into the area of our heart/soul/mind (a type of the holy place) as we become emotionally involved with what we are doing. Soon praise becomes spontaneous as, from deep within, it bubbles up like an artesian well. It's as though a fountain within the depths of our soul had been uncapped. Praise then yields to worship and we enter the dimension of our spirit (a type of the Holy of Holies), where the Presence of God pervades the consciousness. John 4:24 tells us that "God is *spirit,* and those who worship Him *must worship in spirit....*" Thus, whenever believers gather together in His name, our foremost desire must be to worship in spirit. Nothing short of this should satisfy us. Worship—making love to God—is preparation for us to receive the Word (seed) of God in our spirits.

Mind—A Bridge Over Troubled Waters

The mind of man is noncorporeal (not of flesh), yet it works with and through the brain, which *is* corporeal (fleshly). Possessing such unique facility, it functions equally well within the physical *and* spiritual dimensions. The mind (soul), though not spirit, is so closely linked to spirit that only God's Word can make the distinction as to their juncture. "For the word of God is living and active and sharper than any two-edged sword, *and piercing as far as the division of soul and spirit...*" (Heb. 4:12).

When God wishes to communicate with us He speaks directly to our spirit. But what my spirit knows will be of little consequence to me if my brain isn't made aware of it. Thus, it is vitally important that what is communicated to my spirit have some means by which it is ultimately imparted to my brain, so that my physical being (body) can act upon that knowledge. For simplification, follow this path: (1) the Holy Spirit speaks to your spirit (Holy of Holies); (2) that information is then passed along from your spirit (Holy of Holies) to your soul/mind (holy place); (3) which then communicates it to your flesh/brain (outer court) in order for your body to physically act upon it. So we see that all three parts of our being cooperate in the divine drama—or at least they are supposed to.

I *Am* a Spirit—I *Possess* a Soul—I *Live* in a Body!

This is God's divine order. Yet, many Christians are controlled by their flesh (body), which dictates habits, likes and dislikes, sleep patterns, occupations, desires (which are often lusts), eating patterns, physical laziness, and spiritual apathy, *ad infinitum*.

God created mankind with the ability to experience a threefold consciousness: (1) A physical body (a type of the outer court), which possesses five wonderful senses: sight, smell, taste, touch, and hearing. These physical senses enable us to experience the physical world—to have *world*-consciousness. (2) A heart/soul/mind (a type of the holy place). We have been given intellect so that we may experience the mental realm of reason and logic—to have *self*-consciousness. (3) A spirit (a type of the Holy of Holies), the only means by which man can have any comprehension of God is on the level of spirit (see Jn. 4:24). Mankind was created as a spirit so that, by perceiving God's Presence by the Holy Spirit, we can intercommunicate. Thus, the *created* could come to know his *Creator* intimately—to have *God*-consciousness!

We all know of some sorry Christians whose actions and decisions are controlled solely by the intellect. Yet Scripture is clear that no one has ever known God through the intellect. Intellect (in and of itself) is, in fact, a barrier to knowing God (see 1 Cor. 2:14; Rom. 8:8). Whenever we attempt to gain understanding of spiritual verities through purely physical or intellectual means, we are set on a self-defeating course. The Spirit illuminates our understanding, apart from which we can never comprehend spiritual things. Attempting to understand things of the Spirit simply by human reason (intellect) alone does not work.

> *For those who are according to the flesh set their **minds** on the things of the flesh, but those who are according to the Spirit, the things of the Spirit. For the mind set on the flesh is death, but the mind set on the Spirit is life and peace, because the mind set on the flesh is hostile **toward God**; for it does not subject itself to the law of God, for it is not even **able** to do so; and those who are in the flesh **cannot please God*** (Romans 8:5-8).

It is evident from these verses that the carnal (fleshly) man sees no further than carnal (earthly) things. That is why the apostle Paul wrote: "Set your *mind* on the things above, not on the things that are on earth" (Col. 3:2).

Back to Romans 8:6

"For *the mind* set on the flesh is death, but *the mind* set on the Spirit is life and peace" (Rom. 8:6). With our new understanding of the tripartite nature of man, we can appreciate why it is man's *mind* that is the central arena in which most of the battles between light and darkness are fought. In warfare, opposing forces fight the hardest to conquer the highest hill, because from that vantage point the entire countryside can be observed and controlled. To the forces opposed to the Kingdom of God, the mind of man is that highest hill!

The mind has the unique ability to function in either dimension: *inward* toward the spirit (in which case we become spiritual); or it can operate *outward* toward the flesh (in which case we become of the flesh, fleshly). In the King James translation, Romans 8:6 reads, "For to be carnally minded is death...." The word "carnally" comes from the Greek word *sarx*, meaning "flesh," or "meat." Since the mind is in man's head, one of today's more casual versions might translate "carnally minded" as "meathead." (I simply couldn't resist that pun! Although written in jest, it is painfully close to the truth.) "Meatheads" can never understand the things of the Spirit, yet many Christians foolishly expect to become spiritual without changing the carnal minds that have enslaved them to the lower level of their flesh.

The Holy Spirit is calling for believers everywhere to renew their minds by bringing them into conformity with the Word of God. Only as we do so can we possibly begin to live up to His expectations of us. God's desire is for us to think the way He thinks. Why should we consider that unattainable when Scripture tells us "we have the *mind* of Christ"? (See First Corinthians 2:16b.) The mind of Christ resides in our spirits, and our spirits have been kept in subjugation to our rebellious minds. The "outer tabernacle" has been allowed to "remain standing" in seditious uprising against the rightful rule of the spirit. It is time for the people of God to halt the insurrection of the ages by exercising their God-given control over their minds, demanding that the reins be surrendered to the spirit within. The Holy Spirit will then joyfully accept full responsibility for the total control of our minds, and our bodies (flesh) will dutifully follow.

Chapter Seventeen

Thy Kingdom Come

The very first petition in the Lord's Prayer[1] is "Thy kingdom come." The thought of a coming kingdom wasn't new to Jewish thinking, since this theme formed the central core of Judaic teaching. Many seers had peered down the corridors of time not yet born, and prophesied of a Messianic kingdom that would encompass the world "as the waters cover the sea" (see Is. 11:1-9). Then, in the fullness of time Jesus came, and the Kingdom of God burst upon the world scene!

When you understand the importance that New Testament theology places on the concept of the Kingdom of God, much of its teaching becomes eminently clear. Every truth contained in its pages hinges upon one salient fact: the Kingdom of God has arrived. I understand that there are three tenses to God's Kingdom: past, present, and future; and I will leave the exegesis of the past and future time frames to greater scholars than I.[2] Within this chapter my main concern will be to deal with the Kingdom of God as it pertains to the present.

Occasionally people try to pigeonhole me by asking, "Do you believe what is referred to as 'Kingdom Now' doctrine?"[3] (Let me go on

---

1. Actually, what we call the "Lord's Prayer" is the *disciple's* prayer. The *Lord's* prayer is the entire seventeenth chapter of John's Gospel.
2. Here are two books on this topic I recommend: *Kingdom Now, But Not Yet*, by Reverend Tommy Reid; and *The Gospel of the Kingdom*, by George Eldon Ladd.
3. While evangelicals generally hold to a belief that Jesus' Kingdom is relegated *only* to the future, there are many who view His Kingdom as being also in the *now*. *Extremists* teach a militaristic approach to the establishment of Jesus' Kingdom. I do not! See the books in the previous footnote for extended teaching on this topic.

record here that I definitely do not believe in the militaristic stance taken by some who call themselves proponents of Kingdom Now theology.) To those who ask, my reply is simply a scriptural quotation: "Thy kingdom is an *everlasting* kingdom, and Thy *dominion* [kingdom; reign] *endures throughout all generations*" (Ps. 145:13). Since the Psalmist said God's Kingdom is everlasting (*i.e.*, eternal), that time frame would obviously include *now*!

John the Baptist was the forerunner who prepared the way for the advent of the Messiah, the Lord Jesus Christ. His message was basic and to the point: "Repent, for the kingdom of heaven is at hand" (Mt. 3:2). Jesus' message repeated John's central theme: "Repent, for the kingdom of heaven is at hand" (Mt. 4:17b). The major emphasis of Jesus' gospel also stressed the advent of the Kingdom: "And Jesus was going about all the cities...proclaiming the gospel of the kingdom..." (Mt. 9:35). Jesus' accentuation of the Kingdom never abated, as His post-resurrection message reiterates: "appearing to them over a period of forty days, and speaking of the things concerning the kingdom of God" (Acts 1:3). His followers also continued to proclaim the centrality and importance of the Kingdom message. The apostle Paul "went about preaching the kingdom" (Acts 20:25; see also 14:22; 19:8; 28:23,31); and the Book of Acts records Philip's message: "...they believed Philip preaching the good news [the gospel] about the kingdom of God..." (Acts 8:12).

In 1977, I prophesied that the next great theme of the Church would be that of the Kingdom of God. The passage of time has validated my prediction as a true word from God. To deny that God's Kingdom is presently here is to argue against one of the most documented facts of the scriptural record.

Sometimes the Word of God uses the phrase "kingdom of heaven," and at other times the phrase, "kingdom of God." These are not contradictory terms, as can be proven by our Lord's usage of both phrases interchangeably (see Mt. 19:23-24) in the story of the rich young ruler.

"The difference between the two phrases is to be explained on linguistic grounds. The kingdom of heaven is the *Semitic* form and the kingdom of God is the *Greek* form of the same phrase.... The terminology in Matthew 19:23,24 makes it quite clear that the two phrases are interchangeable and that no difference of meaning is to be sought between them."[4]

Are We at the End, or the Beginning, or the Beginning of the End?

"And this *gospel of the kingdom* shall be preached in the whole world for a witness to all the nations, and *then* the end shall come" (Mt. 24:14). I claim no particular expertise in the area of eschatology (study of end-time prophecies), but I do have some insights into the above verse. Jesus said that the end *cannot* come until the gospel of the Kingdom has been preached for a witness in the whole world. That statement contains far greater truth than that the Church should simply preach the message of salvation. Yet, for the most part, that has been the sole extent of the gospel as preached by many. Granted, the world desperately needs to hear that Jesus saves. But the method by which God ordained for us to minister His Word is that it be accompanied by signs and wonders, thus demonstrating the power of the Holy Spirit! Without supernatural credentials, why should unbelievers accept the Christ of our Bible? Every religion has its own leader (be it The Buddha, Mohammed, Confucius, or Charlie Brown) and its own bible (sacred writings); so what makes our Christ and our Bible the *only* Christ and the *only* Bible? (Unbelievers want answers to these questions, and we must provide them by way of proof.)

We Christians have faith in Jesus and His Word, but that's our personal decision. We've lived our lives in a culture where (at least with lip service) the Bible is respected as the Word of God and Jesus is regarded as Lord. Why should the heathen (whether here or abroad) toss out their gods and their sacred writings (in which they've believed for centuries) in favor of ours? What will convince them that our God is bigger, stronger, and better than theirs? Our preaching must be accompanied by a demonstration of Kingdom power sufficient to convince the heathen beyond any shadow of a doubt that what we have is superior in *every* respect. Then they will not only

---

4. George Eldon Ladd, *The Gospel of the Kingdom* (Grand Rapids, MI: Wm. B. Eerdmans Pub. Co., 1959), 32.

want what we have, but will yearn to embrace it. John G. Lake said, "A God without power to heal a sick heathen's body is a poor recommendation of His ability to save his soul." (See Mark 2:10-11.)

During my many ministries overseas, the Holy Spirit has always performed outstanding miracles in the presence of the multitudes (even raising a dead boy in India), presenting incontrovertible evidence that our God is indeed alive and able to deliver. The supremacy of God's Kingdom was exerted over the kingdom of darkness in a manner no one could deny. The gods of the heathen are dead, lifeless images, powerless to deliver those who worship them. After witnessing these displays of divine power, multiplied thousands responded by accepting Christ in a single service.

The Church must learn that the gospel is not in preaching, presentation, production, and performance alone, but in *power* (see 1 Thess. 1:5), which persuades the heathen to forsake their gods and sacred writings for the *only* true and living God and His Word! (See First Corinthians 2:1-5). It isn't enough simply to *preach* to the world. We have a responsibility to *convince* the world by signs, wonders, and miracles.

Miracles—The Way to a Sinner's Heart!

Some years ago I was privileged to minister in Lagos, then the capital city of Nigeria, West Africa. A few months before that time, an evangelist from one of the world's leading Full Gospel denominations had conducted a revival crusade there. His denomination had advertised heavily with great fanfare and had managed to attract several hundred people. He faithfully preached salvation and at the end of the week his denomination was pleased to have counted approximately 50 or 60 converts to Christ. (I, too, thank God for every precious one who came to Jesus Christ; they represent that many less in the kingdom of darkness.)

Our crusade was also advertised heavily, but in addition we promised that God would perform miracles and heal the sick. Upon my arrival I was told that there was a national gasoline shortage and travel had been greatly restricted within the city. Buses were not only filled to capacity, but people clung to the outside and bus stops always had 30-40 people waiting for seats that weren't available. Yet, in spite of the fuel shortage, on opening night we arrived at the soccer field and found 20,000 people waiting to hear the good news.

The people were not disappointed as the Holy Spirit visited us, performing signs, wonders, and miracles. Each night we witnessed approximately 500 outstanding miracles, in addition to many more less notable ones. Shock wave after shock wave of the Holy Spirit swept over the waiting masses. As each one receded, reports poured forward that the blind had received sight; some who had never walked, walked for the first time; and the deaf could now hear the name of Jesus. Witch doctors ran to the front of the crowd, throwing their *juju* bags full of charms and amulets on the ground, crying out to be saved (see Acts 8:9-13). There was great rejoicing when I poured oil on the *juju* bags and burned them before the people (see Acts 19:17-20). What a testimony it was when the witch doctors confessed publicly that all their gods *combined* were not as powerful as the Lord Jesus Christ! Hallelujah!

The second night, the crowd swelled to 30,000 and the field was not large enough to accommodate any more people. Total conversions for the week exceeded 15,000; while the revival meeting that preceded ours had won only 50 or 60 converts. What made the difference? Could it be that the working of miracles provided the credentials for proclaiming the validity of the salvation message? (I'll let *you* decide.)

I've witnessed identical results, not just overseas, but here in the United States and Canada as well. This method (communicating the Word of God accompanied by signs and wonders) worked in the early Church (see Acts 8:4-13). Since it obviously still works today, why, in these times of ever-increasing evil, should we trade it for an alternative methodology? If it ain't broke, don't fix it!

Will the *Real* Church Please Take the Witness Stand!

The Greek word used for "witness" in Matthew 24:14 is a legal term, *marturion*. *Strong's* defines it as: "Something evidential, *i.e.*, (generally) *evidence* given, or (specifically) the Decalogue [Ten Commandments] in the sacred Tabernacle."[5]

> "It may refer to the two tablets with the Sinaitic commandments (Ex. 31:18; 32:15). It is also frequently used of the tent

---

5. *Strong's* #3142.

of the testimony (AV, 'the tabernacle of the congregation' Exod. 29:4). Its meaning almost inevitably had to shift from the act of encounter to the place of evidence, and from thence to the observance of the Law (the tablets standing as *pars pro toto* for the totality of the covenant ordering)."[6]

The word *witness* has at least a twofold implication: (1) It speaks of a *judicial*, therefore *legal* testimony. Those who spoke for Christ possessed firsthand knowledge whereof they spoke. They knew His power to deliver from sin and sickness. They had seen Him open prison doors and set captives free from demonic bondage. In their presence He had even raised the dead. Theirs was a witness that would stand up in any court. The Full Gospel church of today is faced with a major dilemma. Legal testimony cannot be given about an event that has not been personally witnessed firsthand. No court in the land will allow secondhand testimony to be entered into the record. The problem is that we now have a new generation in the Church who has never had a power encounter with the Holy Spirit. This new generation of Christians has never witnessed or experienced the power of the Holy Spirit working signs, wonders, and miracles. The clergy of today are, for the most part, members of that supernaturally barren generation; thus, they don't teach about, or even expect to witness, supernatural happenings. This represents the establishment of a dangerous, self-perpetuating cycle that will continue until it is deliberately broken. And break it we must!

(2) Surprisingly, the word *witness* has its roots in the tabernacle, the Holy of Holies, and the Ark of the Covenant (which contained the Ten Commandments). We Christians have become the tabernacle (temple) of the Holy Spirit (see 2 Cor. 6:16); therefore, the Holy of Holies now resides within us! It follows, then, that the commandments of God also abide in us. We have become His voice in this world, speaking forth the words of God: "…God is now declaring [commanding] to men that all everywhere should repent" (Acts 17:30). When we speak the Word of God to a lost world and declare the necessity for their repentance, we are under judicial constraint to the laws of Heaven to present them with evidence—irrefutable evidence. In

---

6. Brown, *New International Dictionary*, Vol. 3, 1040.

the Greek, the word translated as "signs" means: attesting miracles; the presentation of evidence, authenticating the veracity of that which was spoken; "...miraculous acts as tokens of divine authority and power (Jn. 2:11; 4:54)."[7] Webster defines the word *attest* thus: "to *bear witness* to, certify; declare to be correct, true or genuine; declare the truth of, in words or writing, esp. affirm in an official capacity."

Now let's consider the definition that Webster gives for the word *kingdom*: "The rank, quality, state, or attributes of a king; *royal authority*; *dominion*; monarchy; kingship."

> "The primary meaning of both the Hebrew word '*malkuth*' in the Old Testament and the Greek word, '*basileia*' in the New Testament is the rank, authority and sovereignty exercised by a king."[8]

Take note of the synonyms used to denote the word *kingdom* as Daniel spoke to King Nebuchadnezzar in the following passage; every one is an expression of authority: "You, O king, are the king of kings, to whom the God of heaven has given the kingdom [sovereignty], the *power*, the *strength*, and the *glory*" (Dan. 2:37). At the very heart of the meaning for the word *kingdom* is the authority to rule and it carries with it the assumption of sovereignty on the part of the one who rules. Psalm 115:3 helps us to further understand the word *sovereignty* as it applies to God: "But our God is in the heavens; *He does whatever He pleases*." The Bible is clear that Jesus came to assert His right to rule (kingdom) over all mankind, and that certainly includes His manifest right to rule the Church.

Many of the Old Testament prophets foretold a day when a Messianic kingdom would encompass the whole earth (see Is. 11:6; Hab. 2:14). Therefore the Jews held a firm, but misguided belief that when the Messiah came He would establish His kingdom on earth, with an earthly rule and a physical capital. They also believed that when the Messiah arrived He would remove all tyrannical dominance over the nation of Israel, thus the power (right to rule) of their oppressors (such as Rome) would be forever destroyed. Jesus' teachings upset the Jews' doctrinal apple cart. On one hand, He declared that the Kingdom of God had arrived within His own Person; yet at the same time,

---

7.   *Vine's*, 575.
8.   Ladd, *The Gospel of the Kingdom*, 19.

He refused to allow men to crown Him king and establish Him upon the throne of Israel (see Jn. 6:15). His actions contradicted every misconception they held concerning the Messiah. The Jews couldn't comprehend and wouldn't accept a Messiah who could declare, as Jesus did, "My kingdom *is not of this world*" (Jn. 18:36 KJV).

The Greek word used here for "world" is *kosmos*, which refers to the physical world. From Jesus' usage of that word, we understand that His Kingdom was not a physical one, but was instead spiritual in nature. Jesus was also explicit as to the Kingdom's location: "Nor will they say, 'Look, here it is!' or, 'There it is!' For behold, the kingdom of God is in your midst [within you]" (Lk. 17:21). The Greek phrase translated as "in your midst" may also be translated "within you." Both are equally correct usages, because if the Kingdom of God was to be within believers, it would most certainly be "in their midst." Jehovah had always reigned sovereignly over His Kingdom from within the Holy of Holies, first in the tabernacle, and later in the temple. In keeping with this firmly established tradition, He now exercises His kingship from the Holy of Holies (or spirit) within believers: "For *we are the temple of the living God*; just as God said, '*I will dwell in them and walk among them; and I will be their God, and they shall be My people*' " (2 Cor. 6:16b).

Chapter Eighteen

Power of the Kingdom

One noted author (whose person and works I otherwise deeply respect) has written a treatise on the Kingdom of God in which he states that when the Bible speaks about the Kingdom of God, it refers only to His *right* to rule. I must disagree with my esteemed colleague because that premise cannot be substantiated by Scripture and because logical analysis would lead to another conclusion altogether. Granted, implicit in the term "Kingdom of God" *is* the revelation of God's right to rule, but also implicit are the questions: when? over whom? through whom? and with what power? After all, what good is being a king if you don't have the power to back up your claim to kingship? And what sort of king would you be without subjects?

Every once in a while someone is honored by being appointed Mayor for the Day over a city. That's nice, and probably fun, but no one takes it seriously. In your wildest imagination can you ever envision that "mayor" presiding over a city council meeting, attempting to pass new legislation, or trying to radically change the structure of local government? Of course not! Why not? Because he or she (and everyone else) knows that Mayor for the Day is nothing more than an empty title of respect. Anyone who presumed to take it seriously would become the laughingstock of the local and perhaps even national news (film at eleven).

It takes awesome power to control a kingdom, and wielding that power is part of being king. Jesus cast out a dumb (not stupid, just dumb) demon, which had caused a man to be rendered speechless.

The Pharisees said that He was able to cast it out only because He did so by the power of Beelzebul, the ruler of the demons (see Lk. 11:14-22). In essence, even though they meant their remark to be an insult, it became a backhanded compliment. The Jews held to a tradition (not founded upon Scripture) that claimed that only a more powerful demon than the one inhabiting the person had the authority to cast it out. Thus, since Jesus was able to cast out any and *all* demons with no more than the spoken words "come out," they recognized He had more power than the ruler of all demons. And so He has!

In the same narrative Jesus declared: "But if I cast out demons by the finger of God, *then the kingdom of God has come upon you*" (Lk. 11:20). He affirmed that it was not Beelzebul, who had set the man free from the tormenting spirit—it was God. And the fact that demons were subject to His authority (right to rule) was proof positive that the Kingdom of God had arrived. Thus, when *we* exercise power over demonic forces, it is a sign (attesting miracle) that the Kingdom of God (His right to rule) is still present in the world and is being administrated by His emissary, the Church!

"By the finger of God" reveals the ease and simplicity with which demons should be cast out. Jesus expended no more effort than if one were to curl up a forefinger and simply flick an ant off the picnic table. (You don't need a sledgehammer to kill an ant!) There is no reason why believers should struggle for long periods of time to cast a demon out. It was only when I came to a scriptural understanding of my authority in Christ, and realized how truly easy it is to cast demons out (see Acts 16:18), that I joyfully accepted that aspect of the biblical commission: "And as you go, preach, saying *'The kingdom of heaven is at hand.'* Heal the sick, raise the dead, cleanse the lepers, *cast out demons*; freely you received, freely give" (Mt. 10:7-8).

My God Is Alive—I'm Sorry About *Yours*!

A well-known radio station in our area often broadcasts programming that attempts to prove that God no longer works miracles today. I stopped listening to that station because I was tired of hearing what God is *not* doing today! Just one unbiased reading of the Word of God (with an *open* mind) would reveal that the God of miracles is still alive and well and has great plans for His Church and for planet earth!

Our God is a God of power—awesome power—power beyond our limited human ability to comprehend. His power is so far above our capacity (or lack of it) to grasp, that an ant stands a far better chance of understanding quantum physics than we have of fathoming God's power. He is still the God who spoke and a universe poured forth; He parted the Red Sea, provided manna from heaven, healed the sick, cast out demons, and raised the dead—and that's just a fragment of His power. If your god does any less than that, you have my profound sympathy.

Many years ago, I heard a missionary relate an intriguing story. An evangelical, he didn't believe that miracles occur today. During his tenure in Africa, he had partially translated the Gospel of John into the local dialect. Because he was so busy preaching salvation, he had failed to tell his innocent native converts that God doesn't currently perform the miracles recorded by John. When Communist insurgents took over that area, he was forced to flee for his life, leaving behind that small segment of God's Word. Years later, when the area was liberated, the missionary returned and was shocked to discover that mighty miracles had become the norm. The sick were being healed, and there were even a few cases where the dead had been raised. Several large congregations had also been established—all because people believed that when God said it, He meant it—for all ages of time. This missionary's story proves what God will do when people take the Scriptures at face value, without having their faith in the Word of God watered down by those who proclaim that God doesn't work miracles anymore.

Satan Doesn't Want You to Read This

Luke 9:1 says "And He called the twelve together, and gave them power and authority over *all* the demons...." Contained in that single verse is the Church's "Magna Charta" in her ongoing struggle with Satan. Many argue that the power mentioned in that verse was delegated only to the 12 apostles, and ceased altogether with the death of the last apostle. *Au contraire!* Perhaps they've missed Luke 10:17-19: "And the *seventy* returned with joy, saying, 'Lord, *even the demons are subject to us in Your name.*' And He said to them, '...Behold, I have given you authority to tread upon serpents and scorpions [symbolic language for demons], and over *all* the power of the enemy....' " If

Jesus delegated His authority only to the apostles, then these 70 must have been apostles, which we know was not the case. The 70 were just believers (like you and me) who shared a common anointing and authority with Jesus. Thus, their results were identical to His. Every demon in the kingdom of darkness was subject to them. The Greek word for "authority" is *exousia*, which *Strong's* defines as "force, mastery, jurisdiction."[1] Also:

> "From the impersonal verb, *exesti*, "it is lawful." The power of rule or government; the power of one whose will and commands must be obeyed by others. *Judicial decisions* (John 19:10).[2]

In these two definitions alone, notice the frequent references to law: *jurisdiction*, (from the word, *juris*, from which we derive our word, "law"); *judicial*; *power of rule or government*; *lawful*.

In the last chapter we discovered that the word *witness* was a legal term, "evidence given, or (specifically) the Decalogue [Ten Commandments] in the sacred Tabernacle."[3] Our witness is to be delivered with power—*exousia*. At this juncture in our discovery process we can see the *judicial* aspect of the Church as she exercises her Holy Spirit-delegated authority over all the power of the enemy. The decrees of God issue forth from the Holy of Holies within us, as He serves His indictments against the powers of hell. The Bible says that "The Son of God appeared for this purpose, *that He might destroy the works of the devil*" (1 Jn. 3:8b). When believers exercise their judicial rights over demonic powers (binding or casting them out), they enter into the divine purpose that also motivated Jesus. But first must come a divine revelation of our rightful place of authority over all of the enemy's power.

On numerous occasions I've cast out demonic forces in the name of Jesus. Often they've come out screaming (see Acts 8:7). The Greek word for "scream" is *krazo*: "...cries, from fear, pain, etc."[4] Sometimes they've whimpered like a little child, *"Please don't make me go. Please*

---

1.   *Strong's.*
2.   *Vine's* #1849, 45; emph. mine.
3.   Strong's #3142.
4.   *Vine's.*

don't cast me out." Recently, one whined in a childlike voice, "It's checkout time! It's checkout time!" (All too often today it's Christians, instead of demons, who are whimpering and whining in defeat.) It's time for the Church to awaken to the fact that the powers of hell were forever shattered on Calvary (see Col. 2:15), and that we (the Church) have been given absolute mastery over every evil creature of darkness! Referring to the 1989 Commonwealth Conference, former British Conservative Prime Minister Margaret Thatcher was quoted as saying, "If it is once again one against forty-eight, then I am very sorry for the forty-eight."[5] She displayed fearlessness in the face of seemingly overwhelming odds. This is the same position of unbridled confidence to which God has called His Church when they face the archenemy.

"Go Ye Into All the World"—With All the Power

What Christian hasn't heard of the Great Commission?[6] How can anyone refer only to Mark 16:15-16 as the Great Commission when verses 17 and 18 list the necessary equipment to carry it out. Then, verses 19 and 20 describe the Commission in action—*with signs following.* Have you ever seriously contemplated what an overwhelming task God has entrusted to us? The enormity of the numbers of people who must be reached is matched only by the vast hordes of darkness who have marshaled themselves against the encroachment of the Church into (what they consider to be) their territory. Satan, as "god of this world" (2 Cor. 4:4), and his cohorts have controlled this planet for millennia, and they will not relinquish it without a great struggle!

Jesus came to earth to "destroy the works of the devil" (1 Jn. 3:8). Our Lord's objective was not fully achieved during His brief, three-year period of personal ministry. It is scripturally correct to conclude that His mission was planned to continue and ultimately be accomplished through His Church.

During the course of their three-year sojourn with Him, Jesus' disciples were eyewitnesses to incredible miracles: The blind received sight; the deaf heard; the crippled walked; the dead were raised; demons were cast out; water was turned into wine; the fury of storms

---

5.   *Daily Telegraph* (London: Oct. 25, 1989), Microsoft Bookshelf Quotations.
6.   See Mark 16:15-20.

abated; and multitudes were fed from a mere handful of food. All of the aforementioned miracles were performed by Jesus for the distinct purpose of destroying the works of the devil and/or building the faith of the disciples so that they also could destroy the works of the devil. When Jesus returned to the Father He did not abandon His mission of destroying the works of the devil; rather, He left His unfinished business to be accomplished by the Church. Jesus would not have committed the remainder of His mission (to "destroy the works of the devil") to the Church, and then have left them without the power necessary to accomplish it. John 14:12 explains what Jesus expected of His followers: "Truly, truly, I say to you, he who believes in Me, the works that *I* do shall *he* do also; and greater works than these shall he do..." (Jn. 14:12).

When we refer to the Church ultimately doing greater works than Jesus, there are always those who indignantly rise up and, in their most ecclesiastical tones, cry out, "Blasphemy!" Is it blasphemy to believe that Jesus said what He meant and *meant* what He said? Why should that be so difficult for Christians to comprehend? And why should it be labeled blasphemy? Some opponents argue that the Greek word for "greater" (*meizon*) only means "more" not greater in the sense of magnitude. It does mean "more," but it also means "larger," or in the classical sense, *greater.* In First John 4:4, John used the identical word when referring to God Himself: "...*greater* [*meizon*] is He [God] who is in you than he [the devil] who is in the world." Even if the word were to be translated "more," that would not diminish the meaning of Christ's statement that we would perform greater works. The Greek word for "works" (*ergon*):

> "Is related to the work of Christ (Matt. 11:2 and Luke 24:19),
> where it embraces His effective working in deed and word....
> *Jesus understands His working as the fulfillment of His divinely-
> appointed mission* (cf. Jn. 5:36; 9:4; 10:25), which aims to
> awake faith in the One who has been sent as the Revealer of
> God. *Jesus' miracles also serve to this end* (Jn. 14:11). The be-
> liever, on the other hand, is given the promise that he will do
> *even greater works than Jesus* (Jn. 14:12). Works done 'in
> God' *en theo.*"[7]

---

7.   Brown, *New International Dictionary*, Vol. 3, 1150; emph. mine.

Since the works of Christ attested to His being the Messiah, we know that they were works of power (miracles), especially since the Greek word for "signs" means "attesting miracles." With that in mind, we might translate John 14:12 thus: "Truly, truly, I say to you, he who believes in Me, the works [miracles] that I do shall he do also; and greater [more; bigger] works [miracles] than these shall He do...."

Jesus Entrusted Us With the Same Task—And the Same Anointing

Looking forward to the day when He would return to the Father, Jesus began to prepare and equip believers to carry on His unfinished task. In His physical absence, His followers would be left neither comfortless (see Jn. 14:18) nor powerless. "Jesus therefore said to them again, 'Peace be with you; as the Father has sent Me, *I also send you.*' And when He had said this, He breathed on them, and said to them, 'Receive the Holy Spirit' " (Jn. 20:21-22). The essence of what Jesus said to His followers was, "In the same manner, in the same power and anointing as the Father has sent *Me,* I am now sending *you.*" Following that statement, He breathed on them. Just as God breathed His Spirit into Adam and he received life, Jesus breathed on His disciples and said, "Receive the Holy Spirit." (The Greek aorist tense means "receive *now!*") In that moment He imparted the indwelling Holy Spirit to them—*and the Church was born.* But on the day of Pentecost they would have yet *another* encounter with the Holy Spirit. In Acts 1:8, Jesus said to His disciples, "But you shall receive *power* when the Holy Spirit has come upon you; and you shall be My *witnesses....*" Here is that word *witnesses* again, incorporated in the same sentence with the word *power.* Is that a coincidence, or does God intend for us to see a connection between our witness and our power? What it's saying is that God requires us to be *power witnesses* (before the world and the forces of darkness), and thus serve as a testimony that the kingdom of God has arrived.

Who Has the Kingdom, the Power, and the Glory?

The Book of Daniel contains profound revelation concerning events that will transpire in the end times, prior to the return of the Lord. Some of that revelation has to do with the highly exalted position and rank that God has bestowed upon the Church. If anyone doubts the awesome standing of the Church in the eyes of her Creator, let them consider the following:

> *But the saints of the Highest One will **receive** the kingdom and **possess the kingdom forever, for all ages to come.** ...until the Ancient of Days came, and judgment was passed in favor of the saints of the Highest One, **and the time arrived when the saints took possession of the kingdom.** ... Then the **sovereignty** [kingdom], **the dominion, and the greatness** of all the kingdoms under the whole heaven **will be given to the people** of the saints of the Highest One; His kingdom will be an everlasting kingdom, and all the dominions will serve and obey Him (Daniel 7:18,22,27).*

Verse 22 tells us that a day would come when the saints would take possession of the kingdom—no small promise in itself. Verse 18 sets the time frame for this accomplishment: "the saints of the Highest One...will possess the kingdom *forever*." Please take particular note of verse 27 where three interesting words—sovereignty, dominion, and greatness—are used when referring to the rule of God's saints. Daniel boldly wrote that "the sovereignty, the dominion, and the greatness...will be given to...the saints of the Highest One." Let's take a look at the meaning of those three words in the Hebrew:

1. **Sovereignty**: "Royalty, reign, *kingdom*."[8]

2. **Dominion**: "Have the mastery, have *power*, bear rule, be ruler."[9]

3. **Greatness**: "Increase of *dignity*, greatness, **majesty** (*glory*)."[10] (The Greek word for "glory" is *doxa*, one meaning of which is "dignity.")

Many centuries before the advent of Jesus, Daniel declared that the day would come when God would cause His Kingdom, His power, and His glory to be received by His saints. Without question then, the beginning of the kingdom era arrived in the Person of the Lord Jesus Christ!

---

8. *Strong's* #4437; emph. mine.
9. *Strong's* #7985; emph. mine.
10. *Strong's* #7238; emph. mine.

In Matthew 6:13b, at the conclusion of what has come to be called the Lord's Prayer, we read: "For Thine is the *kingdom*, and the *power*, and the *glory*, forever...." I am aware of the fact that it is accepted among most scholars that the above clause is omitted in the earliest manuscripts. Yet the truth remains firmly established in Scripture that the kingdom, the power, and the glory all belong unequivocally to God and His Christ! (See First Chronicles 29:11). That being established, let's go on to discover some pertinent, though often overlooked, facts concerning these three royal possessions. For these I quote Jesus as the absolute authority.

When instructing His disciples one day, Jesus said, "For your Father has chosen *gladly* to give *you* the *kingdom*" (Lk. 12:32b). Not only did the kingdom belong to Jesus, but the Father rejoiced to share it also with believers. We discovered earlier that *kingdom* means "right to rule," and that right to rule belonged exclusively to Jesus as King of kings and Lord of lords. He proved that the Kingdom had arrived in His Person, by exercising His right to rule with indisputable power over the realm of darkness. He held absolute power and authority over every filthy, slimy, harmful, hateful, detestable, ugly, evil thing that ever oozed its way out of the kingdom of darkness and into the lives of humanity. They were *all* subject to Jesus because the Kingdom of God had arrived! Hallelujah! All the forces of hell combined (Satan included) could not withstand the power of Jesus' awesomely simple command: "Come out!" Demons met more than their match when they met Jesus. Toward the end of His earthly ministry, He began the process of turning over the Kingdom to His followers in order that they might complete His mission of destroying the works of the devil. He entrusted His power and authority to ordinary people just like you and me, because God delights in taking *ordinary people*, and doing *extraordinary* things through them (see 1 Cor. 1:26-31).

Some argue that the word for "kingdom" isn't the same as the word used in the phrase "kingdom of God." Not so! The Greek word in both references is *basileia*, implying that the kingdom Jesus possessed was the very same kingdom He transferred to His followers. Now we know *where* the kingdom (the right to rule) is resident—*in the Church*!

Where's the Power?

(After all I've written thus far, I really shouldn't have to ask that question.) Jesus received a fantastically enthusiastic progress report from His 70 disciples upon their return from their seek-and-destroy-the-works-of-the-devil mission. They reported excitedly that demons had been subject to (forced to obey) them and had come out whimpering and whining. "And He said to them, 'I was watching Satan fall from heaven like lightning. Behold, I have given you authority to tread upon serpents and scorpions, and over all the power of the enemy, and nothing shall injure you' " (Lk. 10:18-19).

Anyone who reads the New Testament with a totally honest and open mind can arrive at *no* other conclusion: that Jesus conveyed His own power to believers and that this same power should be resident in the Church of this century. Our evangelical friends would have us believe that the power ended with the death of the last apostle, John. (That contention is about as difficult to prove as it would be for a blind man in a dark room to find a black cat that isn't there!) The writings of the early Church fathers record that the power and Presence of the Holy Spirit were still present and performing miracles well into the third and even fourth centuries—until the Church began to backslide! It remains a historical fact that every great outpouring of the Holy Spirit since the day of Pentecost has been accompanied by supernatural signs and wonders.

Don't Touch the GLORY!

No one can dispute the fact that the glory of the Father rested upon Jesus. One would have to ignore far too many verses in the Bible in order to deny Jesus His rightful glory. Yet, the average church member and many clergymen haven't the foggiest notion *what* the glory is. Thus, they build theological walls around the word *glory* in order to confer upon it some mystical quality that God never intended.

> " 'Glory' comes from the Greek *doxa*, from which we derive our English word, 'doxology.' It is used of the nature and acts of God in *self-manifestation*, *i.e.*, what He essentially is and does, as exhibited in whatever way He reveals Himself in these respects, and particularly in the person of Christ in whom essentially His 'glory' has ever shone forth and ever

will do, John 17:5,24. It [the glory] was exhibited in the character and acts of Christ in the days of His flesh (John 1:14; 2:11).[11]

The glory, then, is the *manifested Presence of God!* Jesus, as the manifest Presence of God, was the *glory* of God. He now lives in us, His temple.

When John recorded Jesus' extraordinary miracle of turning water into wine, he added the following reflection: "This beginning of His *signs* [attesting miracles] Jesus did in Cana of Galilee, *and manifested His glory*" (Jn. 2:11a). Glory and supernatural happenings always go hand-in-hand. You cannot have one without the other. If God manifests Himself, that is unquestionably a miracle. And when a miracle occurs, it is always a manifestation of God's Presence, which *is* His glory. I've said all that to dispel the commonly held notion that glory has *only* to do with praise. It does have to do with ascribing worth to Him, but it has much greater implications than that narrow band of interpretation and far more often falls under the definition explained in the preceding paragraphs.

The seventeenth chapter of John's Gospel is the actual Lord's Prayer. This prayer reveals His heart of compassion for his believers, not only those present with Him then, but for us who were yet unborn (see Jn. 17:20). The chapter is a delight to read and is filled with references to the glory of God. In His prayer, Jesus explained to the Father what He had done with the glory that the Father had bestowed upon Him: "And the glory which Thou hast given *Me* I have given to *them* [believers]" (Jn. 17:22a). Thus the mystery as to the current location of the glory is now solved. Jesus transferred the glory to the Church at large. He had previously transferred the kingdom and the power to the Church, and He now did likewise with His glory. So, there we have it; the kingdom, the power, and the glory all currently resident in the Church, the Body of Christ. Since the Church is *truly* the Body of Christ (see Eph. 1:22-23), why would anyone argue that His glory should not be upon Himself?

Do I smell heretic fires burning? If you are preparing to burn me at the stake, please be patient for a little while longer. First of all, *I* didn't say it—*Jesus* did! Secondly, these statements will all fall beautifully

---

11.   *Vine's*, 267; emph. mine.

into place like an intricate mosaic in chapters yet to come. This is not an attempt to take anything away from our Lord Jesus Christ; quite the opposite is true. I'm endeavoring to bring glory to God by exhorting believers to believe *everything* Jesus said—even if their denominations have never taught them those truths. I want to see the day when believers will dare to take the Word of God at face value, then live it out before the world. India's former Prime Minister Mohandas (Mahatma) Gandhi is quoted as having said, "I would have no trouble believing in your Bible—it's those *Christians* who get in the way."

The Church must awaken to the fact that more is at stake than lost souls waiting to hear the gospel of salvation. Bringing souls to Christ is our most important task, but it is only a fragment of our commission. There are multitudes who are also in need of deliverance: blind eyes longing to see; deaf ears yearning to hear; wasted, crippled limbs crying out to feel and function; and those in intense pain waiting for someone to bring them their only hope of relief. The list of desperate needs goes on and on. Have the Church's ears become so deaf that we can no longer hear the cries of the hurting; or have we backslidden so far that we no longer possess the power and anointing necessary to set the captives free? Peter said to the lame man in Acts 3:6, "I do not possess silver and gold, *but what I do have I give to you*: In the name of Jesus Christ the Nazarene—*walk!*" Peter was short on finances, but long on the anointing. The wealthy Laodicean-like Church of this century can no longer echo Peter's statement. It is a Church of wealth and prestige, but for the most part the anointing has long ago vanished. *Ichabod* ("The glory has departed," First Samuel 4:21) is written over many Full Gospel churches of our time. The glory of the supernatural, which once was our hallmark, can seldom be found. They might as well say to the sick, hurting, wounded multitudes, "*We no longer possess the power of God; but here's a ticket to the musical our church is presenting this Sunday.*" Yes, the world is sick and hurting, but the Church is even *more* so. If the Church of this generation is all that God intended for it to be, then He owes the world an apology—but, the Church *is* not, and He *does* not! Actually, God has great aspirations for His people. Thankfully, the negative description I've given above is soon to change, for the Holy Spirit *shock wave* is poised to sweep through His Church!

Chapter Nineteen

Weapons of the Kingdom

"Like *a mighty army*, moves the Church of God," wrote Martin Luther centuries ago. Having looked beyond the limitations of frail humanity, he recognized our position and victory in Christ and described the Church as a mighty army—an army at war. Perhaps he was equally inspired by the following New Testament words pertaining to war, and by the frequency of their use: war (13), warfare (3), fight (8), wrestle (1), destruction of fortresses (1), destroying speculations (1), taking every thought captive (1), resist (2), sword (11), armor (4). Forty-five references to warfare, its weapons and methods, are strong indicators that God intends for the Church to be a vital, aggressive force in the Spirit world. Certainly, in our relationships with each other we should exhibit the kind and gentle spirit of Christ; but in our dealings with the devil we should be as mean as a junkyard dog! When entering into conflict with the enemy we must sound the bugle command, "no quarter" (which means give no mercy, take no hostages).

Identifying the Enemy

During the Vietnam War, one of the greatest frustrations experienced by our armed forces was the inability to clearly define the enemy. In most of America's previous conflicts there had been visible opponents and evident battlefronts—not so in Nam. More often than not the enemy remained unseen. Subterranean tunnels were everywhere, providing the enemy with concealment and ease of escape. A veteran related the following story to me:

155

"There was heavy machine-gun fire coming from a small clump of trees in the middle of a large field. We responded with intense fire; leveling everything in sight so that not even a tree was left standing. We were certain that every living thing in that area was now dead. We proceeded forward to make a body count. But, as had been our experience countless times before, there was not a single body to be found. It was as though we were fighting with ghosts. Morale was low and continued that way. The feeling was, if only we had been able to see and identify the enemy, the war and its outcome might have been different."

This is the general lament of all Vietnam veterans. The result of this frustrating situation was that people on the same side began to fight with each other as tempers flared and resentments grew. The desire to strike out became increasingly difficult to control and eventually was misdirected toward comrades in arms—all because the *real* enemy was so elusive.

Brawl in the Family

That canny general, Satan, sees to it that the same scenario is repeated often on the battle lines of the local Church. Because we have failed to identify the real enemy, inner aggressions become misdirected toward the brethren, and we end up fighting among ourselves. Countless churches have closed their doors because of unresolved church conflicts *caused* by an unseen enemy (Satan), but *fought* face-to-face by brethren in Christ. Such scenarios have left a trail of spiritual carnage throughout Church history, while the enemy laughs behind the scenes as he surveys the devastating results. The apostle Paul wrote: "For our struggle *is not against flesh and blood,* but against the rulers, against the powers, against the world forces of this darkness, against the spiritual forces of wickedness in the heavenly places [literally, *in the heavenlies*]" (Eph. 6:12).

Satan strives to keep us blinded to the fact that our struggle is not against flesh and blood (people). He manipulates our thinking and causes us to focus our attacks on one another. Actually, he's delighted when we attack anyone or anything as long as our warfare isn't directed against *him*. The Church's ignorance of his devices (see 2 Cor. 2:10-11) has allowed the devil to stir up massive strife within the Body of Christ without encountering much resistance himself. When trouble starts in the Church, we are quick to point the accusing finger at the offending individual and fail to recognize that the true source of the conflict is Satan. From that moment of deception the battle lines begin to form where they ought not to be. When brethren fight each other, they ignore the evil forces that initiated the strife, leaving them (the evil forces) free to further attack the weakened Body.

The apostle Paul continues this thought in Second Corinthians 10:3-4: "For though we walk in the flesh, we do not war according to the flesh, *for the weapons of our warfare are not of the flesh,* but divinely powerful for the destruction of fortresses." It would make sense then, since our struggle is not against flesh and blood (people), that our weapons also should not be of the flesh (carnal). *Spiritual* battles cannot be fought with *fleshly* weapons. Tanks, artillery, rifles, arguments, lawsuits, and various other carnal implements will never succeed in our battle against "the world forces of this darkness" (Eph. 6:12). Knowing this, when some disturbance erupts within the local Church, we still resort to the arm of flesh to provide a solution. Yet, even when it appears that matters are resolved by carnal means, they often are not. Feelings usually lie buried beneath the surface, seething, waiting to burst forth at some later date, and the whole vicious cycle begins all over again. A battle fought with improper weapons against the wrong enemy is doomed to failure even before it begins.

Power and Authority

"And He called the twelve together, and gave them *power and authority* over *all* the demons, and to heal diseases" (Lk. 9:1). Jesus delegated both power *and* authority to His disciples. Power is the ability to accomplish a task—which in our case is the establishment of the Kingdom of God. It was no ordinary power that Jesus entrusted to His followers; it was the supreme power of the Holy Spirit. This is borne out by the use of the Greek word for "power,"—*dunamis*—which *Strong's* defines as: "specifically, miraculous power; ability."[1] (Unfortunately, the Full Gospel denominations, which once experienced the anointing of the Holy Spirit in signs, wonders, and miracles, have

---

1. *Strong's* #1411; emph. mine.

gradually traded the power of the supernatural for the machinery of the flesh.)

But what good is power without the authority to use it? Such a situation could only lead to frustration. The Greek word for "authority" is *exousia*, which according to *Vine's*: "denotes 'authority' (from the impersonal verb *exesti*, 'it is lawful'). The power, or rule of government. The power of judicial decision. *The right to exercise power.*"[2] (Note that there are various legal terms incorporated in the definition of the word *authority*: "It is *lawful*"; "power or *rule of government*"; and "power of *judicial decision*." All of the foregoing emphasize the kingdom (rule) of God on earth as expressed first in Jesus and now exercised, by His delegation, through His Church. Basically, authority means "the right to do something." So, Jesus not only endowed His followers with the power of the Holy Spirit, He also entrusted to them the authority, the right to use that power over *all* the power of the enemy.

Power of Prayer

In ancient times, a king's subjects were permitted to come into his presence only when he extended his scepter toward them. To walk into the king's presence on one's own initiative was to invite certain death. One of our greatest privileges in Christ is that we have been given the right to immediate access into God's Presence, without fear or intimidation. The King of kings has extended His royal scepter to all believers, and not only are we granted access to His Presence, we are encouraged to come into the throne room of Heaven with boldness! "Let us therefore draw near *with confidence* [boldness] to the throne of grace, that we may receive mercy and may find grace to help in time of need" (Heb. 4:16).

In chapters 14-16 of his Gospel, John made recurrent references to the believer's use of prayer. One cannot help but be impressed with the frequency with which John used the words "whatever" and "anything." For example: "And *whatever* you ask in My name, that will I do, that the Father may be glorified in the Son. If you ask Me *anything* in My name, I will do it" (Jn. 14:13-14; see also John 15:7,16; 16:23-24).

---

2. *Vine's*, 45; emph. mine.

The "whatevers" and "anythings" in the above Scriptures have often been misunderstood by some overly zealous individuals, much to their own detriment. It isn't my purpose here to expound on prayer, since far more able men than myself have done so;[3] but I have learned that praying effectually is far more than a compilation of politically correct words recited in highly religious tones. In Scripture, God has revealed at least six prerequisites that must be met before He will answer prayer. First, you must pray; "You do not have because you *do not ask*" (Jas. 4:2). Pray according to the will of God (1 Jn. 5:14-15). Pray in faith (Jas. 1:5-6). Ask largely (Jn. 14–15). Ask persistently (1 Thess. 5:17; Lk. 16:1-8). Ask in Jesus' name (Jn. 14:13-14).

Unfortunately, we have reduced praying "in Jesus' name" to a mere formula or ritual, using that phrase as a magic incantation. According to tradition, every prayer must end with that phrase. In truth, asking "in Jesus' name" has absolutely nothing to do with closing our prayers with those words. "Name" signifies authority—that is, all of the authority invested in that person's name. (For instance, "Stop *in the name of the law!*" really means, "Stop *in the full authority invested in me* as an officer of the law!") Thus, praying in Jesus' name denotes that whatever we petition for, we do so in Jesus' authority! Please note that four of the five Scriptures quoted from John's Gospel have "in My name" as the operative phrase. The equation is simple: if your request is not in accord with His will, He doesn't authorize it; and if Jesus doesn't authorize it, you don't receive it! The hard fact is that unless you pray according to the will of God, *He doesn't even hear you* (see 1 Jn. 5:14). All other aspects of prayer are subordinate to these two simple yet profound rules.

It never ceases to amaze me that *every* (even the weakest) believer has immediate access to the ear of God! Herein lies the only power of the Church, because prayer (mixed with faith) alone moves the hand of God. Someone has well said, "All the hosts of hell tremble when the least of God's children bends the knee to pray." All the forces of the universe, including the total power contained in every hydrogen bomb, are as *nothing* compared to the awesome power unleashed when we pray. Prayer, as outlined above, enables us to tap into the unlimited resources of the Holy Spirit, and through His power we are

---

3.   I heartily recommend *Destined for the Throne*, by Paul F. Billheimer, as the finest treatise on prayer that I have ever read.

enabled to enforce the will of God on earth. The hosts of hell tremble when we pray because they recognize that the Church is the arm and the rod of God on earth, armed with His authority to execute His judgments against them. Everyone who has made an impact upon his or her generation has understood the vital link between prayer and the Christian's victory over all the power of the enemy. Prayer is the key to the throne room of Heaven. The Father invites you into His Presence; the Bible declares your right to enter there; and Jesus Himself has prepared the way. The Holy Spirit awaits to usher you in and introduce you to the Father personally. *Will you come?*

Chapter Twenty

People of the Kingdom

"These *that have turned the world upside down* are come [here] also!" (Acts 17:6 KJV). What a marvelous testimony to the power of the Holy Spirit working through believers! Many cities had already felt the awesome shock wave of the Holy Spirit's visitation, and Paul and Silas' reputation had preceded them to Thessalonica. The powers of hell quaked as these men of God approached, because whenever Paul and Silas exited a city, they left behind massive destruction to the kingdom of darkness. In their wake, the fortresses of darkness lay in ruins, and bastions of the Kingdom of God now stood where once the powers of evil had been firmly entrenched. Wherever Christians went, hell was forced to relinquish its death grip over mankind: masses of people were redeemed; the sick were healed; demonized ones were delivered; and the dead were raised. It's no wonder then that Satan and all his evil hordes so greatly feared the invasions of Holy Spirit-anointed believers. When they were finished, no city was ever the same again!

The only major difference between the first-century Church and today's Church is an unwavering faith in the Word of God and an intimate relationship with the Author! The first-century Church believed that everything Jesus said was true. They possessed the confidence of a people of destiny, and this released God's supernatural power to work through them. Those early believers were armed with far more than religious rites and rituals. They enjoyed a living, vital relationship with the resurrected Christ. He was real. His Word was real. The

161

Great Commission was real, and His promise of "power and authority over all the demons" (Lk. 9:1) was equally real. Believers *knew* who they were in Christ, and they performed supernatural exploits to prove it. The Church of today has an identity crisis; they do not understand or believe the astonishing things God's Word has to say about them. When they are informed of the untapped potential, unrealized power, and unused resources that are promised in the Word of God, they cry, "heretic!" This response by believers is all the more frightening when we consider that the *only* meaningful resistance Satan will ever encounter—the only *enforceable* challenge to his absolute rule in this world—can come *only* from the Church! And, for the most part, the Church that has been charged with this task has a veil of ignorance over its face. It suffers from terminal closed-mindedness.

The devil delights in lying to God's people, deceiving them into settling for second best and playing second fiddle. Sadly, he has often used ministers of the gospel to spread his words of defeat and demoralization throughout the Church. Far too many ministers have unwittingly sat down at the peace table and negotiated a truce with the enemy. They have urged the Church to lay down her arms and trade relationship for *religion*. Multitudes have obediently followed their religious advisors in the same way teeming numbers of lemmings mindlessly and unquestioningly accompany their leaders into the sea—to certain destruction. Thankfully, God still has His prophets— anointed men and women who are possessed with the courage to stand up and declare the truth exactly as God said it.

Viewing Demonic Forces Through God's Eyes

Almost everyone has seen at least portions of *The Wizard of Oz*. In the movie the wizard awesomely presented himself as a disembodied, bald head that floated in midair and was surrounded by huge puffs of orange smoke. His voice thundered, echoing frighteningly throughout his throne room. He used all of these mysterious trappings in order to convince people that he was indeed the wonderful Wizard of Oz. His ruse worked and everyone feared him, until Dorothy finally looked behind the curtain. For the first time, she saw the real wizard—who wasn't at all the awesomely powerful personage portrayed by his projected image. Instead, behind the curtain sat a short, fat, bald-headed man who manipulated all the mechanical gizmos that made everything run and animated the fearsome, awe-inspiring, wonderful Wizard of Oz. Once Dorothy saw the Wizard for what he really was, all her fears melted away and she was filled with new boldness.

Like Dorothy, believers must dare to tear aside Satan's curtain and penetrate his smoke screen. In order to do this we must understand what God has to say about the enemy and realize our position of power over him. Satan is a defeated foe; he was totally disarmed by Christ at Calvary. "When He had disarmed the rulers and authorities, He made a public display of them, having triumphed over them through Him" (Col. 2:15). Compared to the surpassing greatness of the power resident in believers, Satan's power is as nothing! The fact is, the only power he now has is the power surrendered to him by believers who allow him to walk roughshod over their lives. "Your tormentors, who have said to you, 'Lie down that we may walk over you.' You have even made your back like the ground, and like the street for those who walk over it" (Is. 51:23b). Most believers (like those to whom Isaiah referred) who suffer defeat at the hands of the enemy, do so simply because they don't understand their identity and position in Christ.

Understanding Our Position in Christ

From the beginning of time, God's intention was to raise up a nation of worshipers, to establish His people as regents[1] reigning under Him: "And God blessed them; and God said to them, 'Be fruitful and multiply, and fill the earth, and *subdue* it; and *rule* over the fish of the sea and over the birds of the sky, *and over every living thing* that moves on the earth'" (Gen. 1:28). "The heavens are the heavens of the Lord; *but the earth He has given to the sons of men*" (Ps. 115:16).

Had the pair in the Garden not fallen from grace, their offspring would have multiplied into a righteous nation. That failed to happen. Later, God raised up Israel as a nation of people through whom He could accomplish His will in the earth. His initial design for Israel

---

1. (When referring to the reign of Adam's race as God's kingdom people, I use the term *regent* rather than *vice regent* which is a misnomer. Webster defines *regent* as "one who exercises the ruling power in a kingdom during the...absence of the sovereign." Thus, the usage of the term *regent* throughout this book.)

was quite different than the altered plan for which they eventually settled. God's *primary* plan, His perfect will for Israel as a nation, can be easily missed when reading the Bible because it is briefly (but clearly) stated in only one verse: "And you shall be to Me *a kingdom of priests and a holy nation*" (Ex. 19:6a). God's design was for the entire nation of Israel to enjoy the twofold ministry described in the phrase "kingdom of priests"; they were to minister *to* Him and *for* Him.

A look at the design of the headgear worn by the Levitical priests makes the dual nature of a priestly ministry even clearer. "And you shall set the turban on his head, and put the holy crown on the turban. *Then* you shall take the anointing oil, and pour it on his head and anoint him" (Ex. 29:6-7). The turban speaks of priesthood—ministering *to* the Lord—while the crown speaks of ruling—the authority to minister *for* the Lord. Lastly, the anointing speaks of spiritual equipping for service. The order in which each piece of the headgear was donned should be particularly noted: the turban went on first and the crown last. The Holy Spirit reveals to us, through this beautiful typology, that worship must always precede any attempt to reign in Christ. Many Christians today would like to wear the crown without the turban, but God will not permit that. He is searching for true worshipers, those who will worship Him in Spirit and in truth! Only those who follow this scriptural pattern can be trusted to reign. God decreed that both the turban and the crown must first be in place—then (v. 7) and *only* then was the priest anointed with the holy oil.

Having a Form of Godliness

Many of our Full Gospel churches have maintained a form of worship, but that's often all it is—a form. No more than 20-25 minutes are usually allotted to the worship part of the service, which in reality has become no more than a sing-along. (The announcements are often given more time than the worship of Jehovah!) How many times have you attended a service where the Holy Spirit had complete control and spontaneous worship filled the service? Alas, many preachers limit praise to a set time slot because they are afraid the Holy Spirit might gain control, and they wouldn't have time to preach their carefully prepared sermons. (Perish the thought that the service might go beyond noontime and the saints be inconvenienced!) I have heard countless pastors apologize because the service continued a few minutes past noon. Yet, they still call it a *worship* service. *I don't think so!*

How can any activity that limits the freedom of the Spirit be truthfully referred to as worship? (I have many fond recollections of services where we worshiped the King for hours, and no one cared about the time, or about meals, or appointments. Having been ushered into the very Presence of the Almighty God, worship became our only appropriate response.)

Worshipers, and worshipers alone, will reign under Christ! Therefore, this generation of believers must receive a revelation of their position as worshipers and begin to freely ascribe the praise and worship due to the Lord Jesus Christ. Let us prostrate ourselves before Him crying, "Holy, Holy, Holy, is the Lord of hosts, the whole earth is full of His glory" (Is. 6:3b).

Turning Point

In Exodus 19:17, Moses brought the people (the future priests and kings) to Mount Sinai in order to meet their God. Exodus 20:18 relates how the people were overcome with fear and verse 19 records their response to Moses: "...Speak to us yourself and we will listen; *but let not God speak to us*, lest we die." How foolish! Priests must be able to hear the voice of God! Since the entire nation refused their right to individual priesthood, God established the Levitical priesthood. Out of the 12 tribes, only one specific tribe would minister to Him and for Him. Nevertheless, in a limited manner He still used the nation of Israel to display His kingdom (right to rule) on earth. One reason for which Jesus came was to once again offer the nation of Israel the opportunity to accept their rightful position as a nation of individual worshipers and priests. Again, they rejected Him. "He came to His own, and those who were His own did not receive Him" (Jn. 1:11). When the chief priest and the elders of Israel challenged His authority (see Mt. 21:23), Jesus answered them with a lengthy, scathing indictment that concluded with, "Therefore I say to you, the kingdom of God will be taken away from you, and be given to a nation producing the fruit of it" (Mt. 21:43). Notice once again that Scripture refers to the kingdom of God as a nation. Jesus said explicitly that the kingdom of God would be removed from Israel and transferred to a *nation* that would "produce the fruit of it." If *kingdom* means "the right to rule," then one of the signs (fruits) of the nation to whom it is given will be that they are a people who *rule*. To which nation then did Jesus transfer the right to rule? There is no present nation on earth that lives righteously or exhibits His power. One of the reasons a search for the nation of God comes up blank is because our natural definition of *nation* is a political entity with geographical boundaries—borders that delineate it from all other nations of the world. God is not so constrained by semantics. He called Israel a nation even while they wandered in the wilderness for 40 years with absolutely no homeland and no geographical boundaries to separate them from all the other nations. It was not where they lived, but their worship of the one true God that set them apart from the rest of the world!

Search as you will, you can't find a geographical nation of people who are ruling under God. So, who are these mysteriously elusive people to whom God relegated His Kingdom rule? The answer to that question will not be found in the physical world, but in the Word of God.

"Do not be afraid, little flock, for your Father has chosen gladly to give *you* the kingdom" (Lk. 12:32). Jesus' handful of believers, which He endearingly called His little flock, were those upon whom the Father had conferred the kingdom (right to rule). He transferred the kingdom into the hands of a few fishermen, a tax collector, two zealots, a doubter, and a soon-to-be traitor. What a strange lot to lead this new nation. When screening applicants for His kingdom (fortunately for most of us), God doesn't make His selections according to outward appearances or educational backgrounds (see 1 Sam. 16:1-13; 1 Cor. 1:26-31). In James 2:5, we are told that even the poor have a part in God's kingdom; and that God's kingdom (right to rule) was not limited to the first-century Church, but was for "those who love Him" throughout all generations: "...did not God choose the poor of this world to be rich in faith and heirs of the kingdom which He promised to those who love Him?" (Jas. 2:5; see also Dan. 7:22,27)

First Peter 2:9-10 reveals even more of God's great plan for believers: "But you are a chosen race, *a royal priesthood, a holy nation,* a people for God's own possession, that you may proclaim the excellencies of Him who has called you out of darkness into His marvelous light; for you once were not a people, *but now you are the people of God....*" Please note again that God refers to the Church as a "royal *priesthood,* a holy *nation.*" Peter's revelation is similar to that of the apostle John as recorded in Revelation 1:6a: "And He has made *us* to be *a kingdom, priests* to His God and Father." The literal translation is: "And He has made *us* to be *a kingdom of priests* to His God and Father." Let the record show that the Holy Spirit described the Church with the identical terms used to distinguish Israel's calling in Exodus 19:6—a *nation*, a *kingdom of priests*! From henceforth God would deal with the Church as a nation, *a nation of priests*!

> *For you have not come to a mountain that may* [not] *be touched and to a blazing fire, and to darkness and gloom and whirlwind, and to the blast of a trumpet and the sound of words which sound was such that those who heard begged that no further word should be spoken to them* [see Ex. 20:19]. *For they could not bear the command, "If even a beast touches the mountain, it will be stoned." And so terrible was the sight, that Moses said, "I am full of fear and trembling." But you* **have** *come to* **Mount Zion** *and to the city of the living God, the heavenly Jerusalem, and to myriads of angels, to the general assembly and church of the firstborn who are enrolled in heaven, and to God, the Judge of all, and to the spirits of righteous men made perfect, and to Jesus, the mediator of a new covenant, and to the sprinkled blood, which speaks better than the blood of Abel.* **See to it that you do not refuse Him who is speaking. For if those did not escape when they refused him who warned them on earth, much less shall we escape who turn away from Him who warns from heaven** (Hebrews 12:18-25).

In the above verses the contrasts between Israel (the Church in the wilderness) and the New Testament Church are obvious: Moses (a type of Christ) led Israel (the Church in the wilderness) to Mount Sinai which could *not* be touched; while Jesus has led us (the Church) to stand before Mount Zion, which *may* be touched. Our God is approachable! As Moses presented the people before God so that they might receive their commission as a "nation of priests," so Jesus leads the Church before Mount Zion that we might receive our commission as a "kingdom of priests" (Rev. 1:6). The Israelites adamantly refused to hear God for themselves, and elected instead to have Moses and Levites (priests) hear God's voice for them, and then relate it to them secondhand. Most Christians have blindly chosen the same path. Let us heed the warning of Hebrews 12:25a: "See to it that you do not refuse Him who is speaking."

It was never God's original plan that Israel have an *elite* group (the Levites), which would perform all ministries. Rather, it was His desire that the entire nation would minister to Him and for Him as priests. The Church of today finds itself in a similar situation to that of ancient Israel: Having refused to minister, they relinquished that right to an elite group of clergy (Levites) who minister in their place. This arrangement should not exist. Once we understand our position in Christ (that we are a kingdom of priests), it becomes the duty of every believer in Christ to stand as a priest before God and the world. The fivefold ministries (apostle, prophet, evangelist, pastor, or teacher) then function as leadership offices within the nation of priests.

This holy nation (the Church) was ordained to move in irresistible power against the citadels of hell as one person, with one mind, sharing one purpose: the passion of Jesus to "destroy the works of the devil" (1 Jn. 3:8). The Church has now inherited the divine commission that Israel rejected: "Go in and possess the land" (Deut. 1:8). We have not yet taken up the challenge; in fact, quite the opposite is true.

Satan knows God's plan for the Church and has diligently worked to thwart God's master program. (There are those who argue that Satan doesn't know the future, let alone the future of the Church. Not so. God's design for the Church is clearly delineated in the Bible and, since Satan knows the Bible better than most Christians, he is well aware of it.) Old slewfoot has managed to fragment the Church into numerous entities (denominations), each with manifold doctrinal differences, thus creating apparently irreconcilable schisms in the Body of Christ (see 1 Cor. 1:10-13).

Hear Martin Luther's description of the ideal Church in "Onward Christian Soldiers": "We are not divided, all one body we; *one in hope and doctrine,* one in charity." As the Church stands today, few statements could be further from the truth. When he penned those words, there was only one Protestant denomination (Lutheran) with only one doctrinal statement. Throughout the centuries since Luther's day, countless denominations have arisen. Each of them has brought new revelation and unique insight into some (old) new truth.[2] But each

---

2.   For an in-depth insight into this topic, see my book, *Christian Meditation: Doorway to the Spirit,* chapter 2, "An Eye for an Eye, and a Truth for a Truth."

revelation spawned yet another denomination, which in turn added to the already existing confusion. (That is not to say that any of these new revelations from God's Word were wrong, simply that they were not accepted by the establishment.)

Beginning with Luther, it was generally not the intention of those who received new insights into the Word of God to secede from their denominations. On October 31, 1517, Luther nailed his 95 theses to the door of the Cathedral at Wittenberg hoping to reform the Catholic church. In 1521, the Catholic church convened the Diet (council) of (the city of) Worms, where they condemned Luther as a heretic. The Catholic church, having refused to accept that "The just shall live by faith" (Rom. 1:17b KJV), left Luther no alternative but to withdraw and minister to those who believed the new revelation. Thus, it has continued down through the ages. Fragmentation occurs when the Old Guard locks horns with those who receive new light from the Word of God. The new kids on the block are not usually the ones who foment these factions, but division becomes inevitable when denominations adamantly refuse to budge from their doctrinal trenches and *open-mindedly* examine new revelation.

Living Stones, I Presume

Visualize this tragic scene: the Master Architect, with blueprints in hand, stands back and observes the building site which is the world. Scattered everywhere are building blocks of every description, shape, size, and color imaginable. They aren't ordinary building blocks—these are *alive*. "And coming to Him as to *a living stone*, rejected by men, but choice and precious in the sight of God, *you also, as living stones, are being built up as a spiritual house for a holy priesthood,* to offer up spiritual sacrifices acceptable to God through Jesus Christ" (1 Pet. 2:4-5). Each living stone has been assigned to a unique position, but many are not in place. Most of them are busy fuming, fussing, and fighting over how to preserve doctrinal purity, debating whether or not certain stones even have a right to *be* in the building. Meanwhile, demonic forces run among the building blocks stirring up strife and discord; reinforcing each building block's right to be right; urging them onward toward further divisiveness and isolationism. (You can almost hear one church singing, "Will There Be Any Stars in My Crown?"; while the church across the street sings their reply, "No,

Not One, No, Not One." (Most Christians enjoy fellowship, just as long as it's in *their* ship.) The powers of darkness thus manage to keep Christians so busy fighting each other that they have little time (and even less energy or desire) to fight the real enemy. The vicious cycle becomes self-perpetuating. The Architect compares His magnificent design for His Church with its present stage of construction, and sees mostly barren land choked with Satan's weeds. He views His expensive (blood-bought) building blocks haphazardly scattered—*and, with a broken heart, He weeps.*

It angers me that Satan is apparently smarter than most Christians (see Lk. 16:8). Satan recognizes the absolute authority Jesus has invested in His Church and fears the invincible army that we have the potential to become (if we ever get our act and ourselves together). In Mark 3:24 Jesus said, "...If a kingdom is divided against itself, that kingdom *cannot* stand." Although the immediate reference concerns Satan's kingdom, Jesus therein established a principle. He said, "That kingdom [*any* kingdom divided against itself] *cannot stand!*" That statement is an absolute and applies even to the kingdom of God within His Church. Because Satan is a master military tactician who understands the power of the "divide and conquer" maneuver, he has used it to great advantage in his relentless assaults on the Church. And divide and conquer he has. After centuries of his persistent attacks, all that remain are scattered pieces of the whole.

One thing that Satan understands (and greatly fears) is how Scripture describes the synergistic effect[3] of unity. "Five of you will chase a hundred, and a hundred of you will chase ten thousand, and your enemies will fall before you by the sword" (Lev. 26:8). Knowing the strength and the anointing for service that unity brings, he will do his utmost to sow disharmony among brethren in the Church.

Genesis 11:1-9 records man's effort to build a tower to Heaven, and God's angry response. He could have sent fire from Heaven or a whirlwind or an earthquake to halt construction. In actuality, the solution was far less drastic than any of the aforementioned. Up until that moment everyone spoke the same language—but not *after* that moment. God simply divided them into many different language groups and the grand project came to a dead stop. From that time onward

---

3. Where the sum total of two forces is greater than their combined numbers.

they were scattered over the face of the whole earth. Using the same technique, Satan causes believers to speak different "languages" (doctrine), thus scattering us into our various exclusive camps (denominations). Scripture refers to our faith as a "confession" (see Heb. 4:14; 10:23). *Confession* means, "agreement, to speak the same thing as another," also, "acknowledgment of the truth."[4] More than frustrating, it would be impossible to convince every individual in each denomination to begin saying (confessing) the same things, wouldn't it? *Or would it?* Perhaps it could be easily accomplished if instead of attempting to convince groups to convert doctrinally (that is, to join *our* camp), we determined to maintain an open mind, listened for what the Spirit of God is saying to His Church, and then agreed with (confessed) what *He* says. Then, and only then, we would all speak *the same language*! My prayer echoes the chorus, "Make us one, Lord, make us one!"

Since Scripture refers to Israel in the wilderness as a type of the Church, and Israel consisted of 12 tribes, some argue that this endorses a multiplicity of denominations. I disagree. True, there were 12 tribes, but they all maintained one doctrine: the Law of Moses. The cry of the Holy Spirit is for the present-day denominations to lay down their differences and *unite*. If they will not, then God will raise up a new company of believers who *will* accomplish His plans and purposes in the world by living out the scriptural description of the New Testament Church. They will be God's judicial representation in the world. "In God's eternal purpose the Church, as Christ's Eternal Companion, is to occupy the highest position in the universe short of the Godhead itself. As the Bride of the Eternal Son she is to share with Him universal sovereignty."[5] "Or do you not know that *the saints will judge the world?* ...Do you not know that *we shall judge angels?*" (1 Cor. 6:2a-3a) "And he who overcomes, and he who keeps My deeds until the end, *to him will I give authority over the nations*" (Rev. 3:26).

Judging the world and angels and having authority over the nations is reserved for later, but what is the Church's current mission? She is intended to be the reflection of God and His eternal purposes in

---

4.   *Vine's*, 120.
5.   Paul E. Billheimer, *Destined for the Throne* (Ft. Washington, PA: Christian Literature Crusade, 1975), 48.

and to the world. Just as a mirror gives a true representation of the one reflected, the Church should clearly reflect the nature and attributes of Jehovah. God's plan (that the Church represents Him in this world) is clearly delineated in Ephesians 3:10: "In order that *the manifold wisdom of God* might now be made known *through the church* to the rulers and the authorities in the heavenly places." Jesus Christ has commissioned the Church to declare His unbounded wisdom to the rulers and authorities in the heavenlies. "Rulers and authorities" are the identical words used elsewhere to describe the evil forces of the enemy that reign in the heavenlies (see Rom. 8:38; Eph. 6:11-12; Col. 2:15). The word *known* in the Greek means "declare." Webster defines *declare* thus: "To make known clearly, especially in explicit or formal terms—to announce officially."

The same word is also translated "declare war." When Jesus began His ministry, He openly declared war on Satan's kingdom. The people of God have likewise been ordered to stand strong in the face of the enemy, reaffirm Jesus' declaration of war on all the forces of hell, and reflect the manifold wisdom of God. One way the manifold wisdom of God is revealed in us is that He uses people (not angels—but redeemed, Spirit-filled, yielded *people*) to carry out His plan to tear down Satan's strongholds on this earth. He doesn't use denominations or institutions; He uses *people* to set the captives free, to heal the sick, and to raise the dead. These are the people of the kingdom. This is the Church!

All too many believers lament their lack of ability as a lame-duck excuse for nonparticipation in God's program. The fact is that God cares little about your ability or inability. His major concern is your *availability*. He can impart what you lack; but He will not force your participation!

Chapter Twenty-one

(A Brief Parenthesis)

Over the centuries, many great revivals have taken place. These shock waves of the Holy Spirit have impacted the Church, and in some instances, the world. Joel spoke prophetically concerning three powerful future waves of the Holy Spirit that would leave indelible impressions on planet earth. These are of present concern to us. In Joel 2:28-32, God said that one day He would send a supernatural outpouring of His Spirit on all flesh. On the day of Pentecost, when believers were baptized in the Holy Spirit, Peter referred the people to Joel's prophecy: "But this is what was spoken of through the prophet Joel" (Acts 2:16). That Holy Spirit visitation is commonly referred to as the "former rain."

The analogy of rain was readily understood in Israel. After seed planting, heavy rains fell to prepare the soil; this was referred to as the "former rain." Moderate rains came occasionally during the growing season, and shortly before harvest there were heavy rains that brought about rapid growth. This was referred to as the "latter rain." Both rains were absolutely essential to the completion of a fruitful harvest. At the birth of the Church, the Holy Spirit began planting the supernatural seed of the Word of God; so God poured out the supernatural former rain of His Spirit on the day of Pentecost to nourish the new seed.

When He Reigns—It Pours

In his New Testament epistle, James also introduced the subject of the latter rain: "Be patient, therefore, brethren, until the coming of the Lord. Behold, the farmer waits for the precious produce of the soil, being patient about it, *until it gets the early* [former] *and late* [latter] *rains.* You too be patient; strengthen your hearts, *for the coming of the Lord is at hand"* (Jas. 5:7-8). James identified the former and latter rains with the return of the Lord and the spiritual harvest that would precede that event. At the turn of the twentieth century, the world witnessed a great shock wave of the Holy Spirit that continued until it reached its zenith in the great healing/miracle revivals of the 1940's through the 1960's. The attention of the world focused on the supernatural events that accompanied that move of the Holy Spirit, and many believed the Lord would appear at any moment. If the day of Pentecost was the former rain, then this move was clearly the latter rain.

The belief that the Lord could return at any moment was more a product of fervent desire than it was scriptural. Acts 3:20-21 is most clear concerning the subject of Christ's return: "And that He may send Jesus, the Christ appointed for you, *whom heaven must receive* until the period of restoration [*apokatastasis*] of all things about which God spoke by the mouth of His holy prophets from ancient time." Heaven *must* receive Jesus *until* the period of *restoration of all things*! In the Greek, "restoration" is *apokatastasis*:

> "The verb '*apokathistemi*' meant originally 'to restore to a previous state.' A derivative of the verb is the later noun '*apokatastasis*.' Only the verb is used in the LXX...meaning 'to turn back...restore.' In the New Testament the verb is found eight times (mostly in the Synoptic Gospels[1]), and the noun only once (Acts 3:21)."[2]

In almost every instance the Greek usage refers to restoration to a former condition—the healing of the sick for example (see Mt. 12:13; Mk. 3:5; 8:25; Lk. 6:10). Many hold the belief that the restoration spoken of has to do with returning the earth to its original condition, and in a limited sense this is true. The earth will be restored to its *Edenic* condition; and so also believers will be restored to the Adamic position of authority over all creation. Toward that purpose

---

1. Matthew, Mark, and Luke.
2. Brown, *New International Dictionary*, Vol. 3, 146-147.

the next great outpouring of the Holy Spirit will be directed. And *then* He will come!

Much of the Church has recognized the former and/or latter rains, but has somehow overlooked a *third* future outpouring: "...for He hath given you the former rain moderately, and He will cause to come down for you the rain, *the former rain, and the latter rain in the first month*" (Joel 2:23 KJV).

According to Joel's prophecy, God has plans for planet earth to experience one last great shock wave of the Holy Spirit. The scope and intensity of this outpouring will be a combination of both the former and the latter rains, which will be poured out *together* within a brief framework of time (figuratively speaking, "in the first month").

It is evident that this final shock wave will be totally unprecedented in the annals of history! Mankind will witness supernatural power greater than any prior visitation of the Holy Spirit ever experienced by mortal man. We've considered the synergistic effect produced when the total impact of two forces is greater than their combined numbers. Try to envision what this final, greatest visitation of the Holy Spirit will be like, when both the former and latter rains are combined in a synergistic effect—and then *multiplied*. That is what God has planned for the final earthly days of His Church! For a prophetic look into this next shock wave of the Holy Spirit, carefully examine (throughout the Book of Acts) the results of the former rain that began at Pentecost Sunday. Then examine the results of the latter rain visitation that began at the turn of the twentieth century.[3] As He did at the wedding at Cana of Galilee, Jesus has once again saved the *best* wine for last!

---

3.   To learn more about this topic, read *With Signs Following*, by Stanley H. Frodsham—available from the Gospel Publishing House, Springfield, Missouri.

Chapter Twenty-two

Sons of the Kingdom

The next shock wave of the Holy Spirit will produce a unique brand of people, the like of which the world has never seen, except in the person of our Lord Jesus Christ! I approach this concept with a certain amount of trepidation because in the past, lesser revelations than this have elicited vitriolic responses from both denominational and Full Gospel leaders. But I am also aware of a keen sense of reverential awe, knowing that I will be handling manna from Heaven in much the same way the disciples handled the broken loaves and fishes when feeding the multitudes. I have been assured by the Holy Spirit that though some will decry me as a heretic, He has already prepared many who are presently hungering for "the bread that came down out of heaven" (Jn. 6:41). I am aware of the heavy responsibility that is mine, for Scripture says: "...And from everyone who has been given much shall much be required; and to whom they entrusted much, of him they will ask all the more" (Lk. 12:48). I have been likewise commissioned to deliver what the Holy Spirit has revealed from His Word.

The Aliens Return

The human race started out in perfection, but soon degenerated into the depths of depravity and moved far away from God. Refusing to abandon His creation, the Father immediately initiated a program of redemption (see Gen. 3:21) whereby mankind would someday be brought back into the heavenly family: "And although you were formerly *alienated* and hostile in mind, engaged in evil deeds, yet He has now reconciled you in His fleshly body through death, in order to present you before Him holy and blameless and beyond reproach" (Col. 1:21-22).

Under inspiration, John Newton penned the classic song of redemption and expressed it as *"Amazing* Grace." God's grace is truly amazing, because He has taken those of us who were alienated from Him—who were actually His enemies—and not only redeemed us (bought us back) from lives of sin and degradation, but made us His *friends.*

In order to understand the substantial significance God places upon friendship, we should examine His relationship with Abraham: "And Abraham...was called *the friend of God"* (Jas. 2:23b). The cup of God's wrath was about to overflow and destroy five great cities of the Plain, including Sodom and Gomorrah (see Gen. 18). In the impending judgment, multiplied tens of thousands would die. Yet God hesitated, momentarily delaying His wrath, before He reduced those cities to ashes. The reason for God's hesitancy? "And the Lord said, 'Shall I hide from Abraham what I am about to do?'" (Gen. 18:17). Herein lies a principle of friendship as timeless as God Himself: *Friends share their deepest and innermost secrets with friends.* It was unthinkable to God that He would destroy those two great (though wicked) cities, without first revealing His plans to His friend Abraham. I believe it is God's desire to have at least *one* trusted friend in each major city of the world—someone in whom He can confide before earthquakes, floods, or other (super)natural disasters take place. This forces me to wonder: If God was about to destroy the city in which I reside, before releasing His judgment, would He first reveal His plan to *me*? To you? I wonder...

This theme of friendship is expanded upon in Amos 3:7, where God reveals that prophets are considered among His special friends: "Surely the Lord God does *nothing* unless He reveals His secret counsel to His servants the prophets." The enormity of what we have just read overwhelms the imagination. By His own choice, the infinite God who formed the universe, does nothing unless He first reveals it to His friends!

Jesus reflected on divine friendship: "You are My *friends*, if you do what I command you. No longer do I call you slaves, for the slave does not know what his master is doing; *but I have called you friends, for all things that I have heard from My Father I have made known to you*" (Jn. 15:14). Jesus reaffirmed the depth of intimacy present in the believer's friendship with God by explaining to His disciples that absolutely everything the Father had revealed to Him, He had in turn made known to them. Because of their friendship with Jesus, the disciples were privileged to live every day in the light of revelation knowledge. This same privilege is available to us also.

The key to this relationship can be found in the first two phrases, "You are My friends, *if you do what I command you.*" Conversely, the opposite is also true; if you refuse to do what He commands, then you are not considered a friend. God doesn't stop *loving* you because you fail to do what He tells you, *but He does stop being your friend.* He ceases to confide in you His innermost secrets and desires. Those are reserved for His intimate friends—those whom He can *trust.* If you desire to be on the inside track of what God is doing in the world, *be His friend.* The path that leads to His friendship is clear enough; simply do whatever He tells you to do. Is it your longing to be a part of today's supernatural visitation? The requirements are the same as they have always been: "*Whatever* He says to you, *do it*" (Jn. 2:5b)!

More Than Friends—SONS

Through the new birth, by the blood of the Lamb, God has brought us into His family and made us sons, children of God. Although most evangelicals and fundamentalists agree on the new birth, their understanding of all that it entails is rudimentary in nature. They accept the fact that God has, in some *generic* sense, made us His sons, and that this relationship entitles us to marvelous spiritual benefits, powers, and glory. But their understanding is that most of these wonderful things can be ours only in Heaven, after death or the rapture. Meanwhile, God's children have apparently been left to muddle through this earthly life in a vacuous limbo of human frailty, devoid of spiritual power and authority. Although many churches may not always practice the power of the Holy Spirit, they at least offer lip service to the existence of the supernatural in this present life.

In our quest for a broader understanding of true scriptural sonship, our investigation must commence with God's Word. Scripture is replete with references concerning our standing as sons before God and all the privileges and responsibilities that encompasses. Yet a major barrier standing between us and our becoming all that God says we are, is our inability to simply *believe* what God has said about us. Whenever we begin to consider our awesome standing in Christ, Satan immediately sends a spirit of incredulity to steal the seed of God's Word before it can take root in our hearts (see Mt. 13:19). Understanding this, please resist him and attempt to keep an open mind while we review what God Himself has to say about our sonship: "See how great a love the Father has bestowed upon us, that we should be called children of God; *and such we are.* ...Beloved, *now* we are children of God..." (1 Jn. 3:1-2; see also John 1:12). These verses clearly establish our *present* standing as sons before God, not that we will *become* sons after death.

Many struggle with the doctrine of true sonship because of their misunderstanding that God had (has) only *one* Son. Scripture is abundantly clear that *it was never God's intention to have only one Son.* He would, however, have only one Messiah! There can never be another Redeemer. Jesus is the *only* Lamb of God. But God's desire to father a multiplicity of sons is expressed clearly and repeatedly in His Word: "For it was fitting for Him, for whom are all things, and through whom are all things, in bringing *many sons* to glory..." (Heb. 2:10; see also Rom. 8:29).

Long before an assembly line turns out duplicate products, a prototype must be designed. Once this design has been tested and proven, the prototype becomes the first of many subsequent items of the same kind. The purpose of all assembly lines is to generate many replicas of the original—perfect copies of the prototype.

In the field of genetics the human equivalent of a prototype is a *genotype.* According to the Word of God, Jesus was the genotype from whom God intended to generate an entirely new breed of people, each of whom would be an exact replica of His Son. We earnestly sing, "O, to be like Thee. O, to be like Thee, blessed Redeemer, pure as Thou art." Yet how many of us really believe for a moment that it is possible. The implied content of much of today's preaching is "even though God has instructed us to become like Jesus, it really isn't possible; so continue on in defeat, and at the last trump we will all be miraculously changed into His image." That's not God's plan for the Church! Wimpy, watered-down preaching of that caliber spawns lukewarmness and loose living because "after all, *no one* can be like

Jesus." If we can't totally reflect the life and ministry of Jesus, then at what point should we stop growing into His image and settle for second, third, or perhaps one hundredth best for our lives? What then *is* the standard to which Christ purposes to bring us?

"For both He who sanctifies [Jesus] and those who are sanctified [believers] *are all from one Father*; for which reason He is not ashamed to call them *brethren*" (Heb. 2:11). The preceding Scripture clearly declares that Jesus and we are *all* from one Father (God, Elohim). First Peter 1:3 and First John 5:1,18 continue this truth by declaring that all believers have been born (*begotten*) of God. The very word used in Scripture to denote *our* being "begotten" is identical to the word used to refer to Jesus' having been "begotten" (Acts 13:33; Heb. 1:5; 5:5). The Pharisees (the don't-want-to-sees) of our day, who contend that we can never be like Jesus, defend their position by quoting Scriptures that refer to Jesus as "the *only* begotten" (Jn. 1:14,18; 3:16,18; 1 Jn. 4:9). The words "only begotten" come from the Greek word *monogenes*, which is used only five times in the New Testament, and that only by John. In an attempt to portray Jesus as a *singular* child, translators have rendered it "only *begotten*." This is biblical exposition at its worst. There is no way, in all good conscience, that anyone could translate *monogenes* as "only begotten."[1] In reality, what the Greek word *monogenes* is trying to establish is that Jesus is unique! "*Monogenes*: 'of a single (*monos*) kind (*genos*).' " The virgin birth established Jesus' uniqueness forever. Even if *billions* of sons are subsequently born into the Kingdom of God, there will *never* be another virgin-born, *incarnated* Son of God. There will *never* be another Messiah. Jesus is unique!

Satan will see to it that we struggle with this concept in the Word of God. Whenever someone preaches that we can totally reflect the

---

1. "There is little linguistic justification for translating *monogenes* as 'only begotten.' The latter practice originated with Jerome who translated it by the Latin *ugenitus* to emphasize Jesus' divine origin in answer to Arianism. The word '*monogenes*' reflects the Hebrew *yahid*, only 'precious' (Gen. 22:2,12,16, of Isaac), and is used in Heb. 11:17 of Isaac who was *unique* in the sense of *being the sole son of promise*, but who was *not the only son* whom Abraham begot. Perhaps the word may best be translated as '*unique*.' John clearly intends to distinguish Jesus' unique relationship with the Father from that of others who become children of God through Him; (cf. Jn. 1:14 with vs. 13 [emph. mine]."— Brown, *New International Dictionary*, Vol. 2, 75-76.

life and ministry of Jesus, the heresy flags go up amidst cries of "Blasphemy! Blasphemy!" It is neither heresy *nor* blasphemy. Rather, it's a simple childlike faith that takes God's Word at face value, believing that He said what He *meant,* and that He meant what He *said.* Arguing with Scripture will only wear out *many* hammers on the anvil of God's Word.

"For you are not just mortals now, but sons of God; the live, permanent word of the living *God has given you His own indestructible heredity"* (1 Pet. 1:23; Phillips translation). That verse being true, then through the new birth we have been granted God's own *heredity.* (Webster defines *heredity* as: "the transmission of genetic characters from parents to offspring.")

The following verses further establish that the very *nature* of God has been transmitted to us through His Word:

> *Seeing that His divine power has granted to us **everything pertaining to life and godliness,** through the true knowledge of Him who called us by His own glory and excellence. For by these He has granted to us His precious and magnificent promises, in order that by them **you might become partakers of the divine nature...*** (2 Peter 1:3-4).

> > "This union goes beyond a mere formal, functional, or idealistic harmony or rapport. It is an 'organic relationship of personalities' (Sauer). Through the new birth we become bona fide members of the original cosmic family (Eph. 3:15); actual generated sons of God (I John 3:2); 'partakers of the divine nature' (II Peter 1:4); begotten by Him, impregnated with His 'genes'; called the seed or *sperma* of God (I John 5:1,18; I Peter 1:3,23); and bearing His heredity. Thus, through the new birth—and I speak reverently—we become the *next of kin* to the trinity, a kind of *extension* of the Godhead.[2]

At the new birth, our backslidden spirits were reunited with the Holy Spirit and became *one* with Him: "But the one who joins himself to the Lord *is one spirit...*" (1 Cor. 6:17). The ideal scriptural scenario is that from the moment of the new birth the Holy Spirit begins to live out the life of Christ from within each believer, and the nature, character, and attributes of Jesus become apparent in their everyday

---

2. Billheimer, *Destined for the Throne,* 35.

lives and ministries. When we were born again from above, God implanted His very nature (Himself, the Holy Spirit) within us. He could impart no more of Himself to us than what we received at the new birth. (I will establish this scripturally in the following chapter.)

The Church has lived in timidity and fear for so long that we have paralyzed the working of the Word of God in our lives, rendering it powerless to transform us. Although the Bible is replete with them, the truths presented here are foreign to most Christians because they stagger our finite mortal minds. Because of this, some will strain to assign them to rhetoric or place them in the catchall of the symbolic. But we must not ignore the cardinal rule of scriptural interpretation (which any first-year Bible college student could explain): It is imperative that the Bible is accepted as completely literal, unless it is *clearly evident* that what is written is a *parable or is poetical, symbolical, or figurative.* Thus, when God's Word says that we are sons of God, it *means* that we are sons of God. When it says, He who "joins himself to the Lord is *one spirit"* (1 Cor. 6:17b), it *means* that God's Spirit and ours are now *one* spirit. There can be no closer union than this—two spirits merging into one, each sensing and experiencing the heartbeat, desires, and emotions of the other.

> *The God of our Lord Jesus Christ, the Father of glory, may give you **a spirit of wisdom and of revelation** in the knowledge of Him. I pray that the eyes of your heart may be enlightened, so that you may know what is the hope of His calling, what are the riches of the glory of His inheritance in the saints, **and what is the surpassing greatness of His power toward us who believe** (Ephesians 1:17-19a).*

Chapter Twenty-three

In His Image

"Then God said, 'Let Us make man in Our image, according to Our likeness....' And God created man in His own image, in the image of God He created him; male and female He created them" (Gen. 1:26-27).

At the dawn of creation God took a handful of earth and formed man in His own image. This was not a physical likeness, because "God is spirit" (Jn. 4:24a) and does not have a *physical* form. He fills the entire universe: "Being then *the offspring of God*, we ought not to think that the Divine Nature is like gold or silver or stone, an image formed by the art and thought of man" (Acts 17:29). Paul's emphasis is that man's physical likeness cannot portray God. God took a part of Himself and created man as a *spirit*. Even though a physical flesh-and-bones body was also created, the *real* Adam (who was *spirit*) came into being only when God breathed His Spirit into him (see Gen. 2:7). Adam (spirit) *possessed* a soul (mind) and *lived* in a body. The first man was, in every sense of the word, led by the Spirit, because he *was* spirit.

Adam was created to serve (in God's stead) as regent, with delegated authority to rule over all the inhabited earth (see Gen. 1:27-28). Ultimately, sin severed man's intimate relationship with the Father, and Adam's kingdom and authority were forfeited (see Gen. 3:22-24). God planned man's redemption from before the foundations of the world—long before His creation ever sinned (see Eph. 1:4; 1 Pet. 1:18-21). Redemption included reparation for mankind's fallen condition, the renewal of the image of God within, and his reinstatement to his God-given place of rulership.

Christ, the Perfect Image

Paul wrote: "...Christ, who is the *image of God*" (2 Cor. 4:4); also, "...*He is the image of the invisible God, the first-born of all creation*" (Col. 1:15). These verses show that Jesus was the visible manifestation of the invisible Father-God. All our knowledge concerning the Father's nature and attributes should come through observation of Jesus' words, life, and ministry. The author of Hebrews wrote of Him: "...He is...*the exact representation* of His [the Father's] nature" (Heb. 1:3). In the Greek, the term "exact representation" means "exact copy"; therefore, seeing Jesus was the same as seeing the Father! Second Corinthians 5:19 continues this theme by saying: "...*God was in Christ* reconciling the world to Himself." When Philip asked Jesus to "show us the Father" (Jn. 14:8), Jesus replied, "...Have I been so long with you, and yet you have not come to know Me, Philip? He who has seen Me *has seen the Father*" (Jn. 14:9). "Look at Me, Philip," Jesus said, "and see the Father." If you desire to understand God's nature then diligently study the life and ministry of our Lord.

The Church has no problem believing that Jesus was the exact reflection (archetype) of God's nature, being, and attributes, but it has great difficulty accepting what the Bible clearly reveals about *us*: "And have put on the new self...*according to the image of the One who created him*" (Col. 3:10). "For whom He foreknew, *He also predestined to become conformed to the image of His Son*, that He might be the first-born among *many* brethren" (Rom. 8:29). "And just as we have borne the image of the earthy [Adam], *we shall also bear the image of the heavenly?* [Jesus]" (1 Cor. 15:49). (See also Romans 13:14; 2 Corinthians 3:18; and Ephesians 4:23-24.)

How could any honest, *open-minded* person miss (or refuse to acknowledge) the fact that God's ultimate plan for believers is to usher them to the place where they reflect perfectly the image (nature, being, and attributes) of Jesus Christ in the same manner that He reflected the nature, being, and attributes of the Father?

Perhaps the answer to this question may be found in one of my mother's favorite proverbs: "There is no man so blind as he who does not *want* to see!" Unfortunately, this aptly describes the majority of the people in the Church regarding this truth. For centuries Satan blinded the eyes of the Church and buried this important revelation in the archives of darkness and obscurity—along with the doctrines of justification by faith, sanctification, water baptism by immersion, the baptism in the Holy Spirit, and the gifts of the Holy Spirit. The bottom line then is that he has hidden every major truth. The healing of the Church's eyesight has not been accomplished by means of an instantaneous miracle, but through gradual restoration. We have received new light one doctrine at a time—a little here and a little there. At times the Church could be likened to the blind man who said to Christ, "I see men, for I am seeing them like trees, walking about" (Mk. 8:24b). He began to see, but not distinctly. So Jesus ministered to him again, and then his vision was perfect. I pray that we will submit (and, if necessary, resubmit) our blindness to the Lord and allow Him to minister sight to us. Divine revelation is rejected by a closed mind even as sight is rejected by closed eyes. If, at first, you can't see these truths clearly, ask Him to touch you again. He will—*and you will see!* "I pray that the eyes of your heart [mind; understanding] may be enlightened, so that you may know what...are the riches of the glory of His inheritance in the saints, *and what is the surpassing greatness of His power toward us who believe*" (Eph. 1:18-19a).

Restricted by the limitations of language to convey—and understanding the inability of finite carnal minds to fathom divine truths— Paul realized that only a divine revelation would enable us to comprehend God's magnificent plans for us, His Church. I'm likewise restricted in my attempt (through finite language) to convey what the infinite mind of God has conceived for His Church (see 1 Cor. 2:9-12; 2 Cor. 12:1-4). Yet, as difficult as it may be for you to accept, God's primary purpose for our lives is that we become an exact image of Jesus Christ, accurately reflecting His kingdom, His power, and His glory to the world. It is His ultimate objective that everyone who is touched by our lives will sense that they have had a personal and intimate encounter with Jesus Christ (see Acts 4:13). Jesus declared to Philip, "He who has seen Me has seen the Father" (Jn. 14:9). He could say that because the Father was unobstructedly living out His life through Him (see Jn. 14:10). Insofar as we also yield ourselves to Christ and allow Him to freely live out His life through us, to that extent people with whom we come in contact should recognize having seen Him.

God's New Breed of People

As Adam, who was created in God's image, reigned as regent under God, even so the Church is destined to exercise its dominion and authority with the same fullness of power and glory that Jesus (second/last Adam) manifested. Remember, we are Adam's redeemed descendants, and we have been returned to the original state that his children would have occupied had the fall not occurred. And, like Adam, we were recreated to reign (as the Bride of Christ) as regents (co-sovereigns) of the universe.

Perfect Union

When God created man and woman, He named them *both* Adam: "He created them male and female...and named *them man...*" (Gen. 5:2). "And named them man" is not the literal translation. "Man" should be translated "Adam"; thus the passage should read, "And God named *them Adam.*" Likewise, also, Genesis 1:27 should read: "And God created *Adam* in His own image, in the image of God He created him; *male and female He created them.*"

Putting Adam in a deep sleep, God took the woman from his side. In the same manner, the Church (Jesus' Bride) was taken from His wounded side as He slept the sleep of death, out of which came resurrection life. Acts 2:24 says of Jesus: "And God raised Him up again, putting an end to *the agony* of death...." The Greek word for "agony" is *odin*, which *Strong's* defines as "a pang, or throe, *especially of childbirth.*"[1] Thus we understand that the pains endured on the cross were more than death pains; they were also birth pangs, because through His death He birthed many sons into glory.

That God viewed the first couple as *one* is established by the fact that He gave them only one name, Adam. Had mankind not sinned, every descendant of Adam would have been called by the same appellation, Adam. As direct descendants of the second Adam (Jesus), we are so united with Him that we share his name, Christian (which means Christlike). "For this reason, I bow my knees before the Father, from whom every family [*spiritual* family] in heaven and on

---

1. *Strong's* #5604.

earth derives its name" (Eph. 3:14-15). Further proof that God viewed them as one flesh is reflected in Jesus' comments concerning the intimate union of marriage (see Mt. 19:3-6).

Before the fall, Eve had no separate identity (or identity crisis), nor did Adam. The fact is, she didn't even have her own name. She was simply referred to as "woman," finding her fulfillment, identity, and equality in a totally perfect union with her husband. Whatever he was, she was—not *because* of him, but *with* him. And by no means was hers a demeaning position. On the contrary, she was—in every sense of the word—equal to him. If he was regent of the world, she was also. Scripture says nothing to indicate any lesser status on her part before God. (In the Garden of Eden, the only reference to her individuality was a sexual one.) After the fall, the extremely intimate union of oneness with God was severed, as was the woman's oneness with Adam. Along with her new identity she received a new name, Eve (see Gen. 3:20). The new name identified her individuality (her separateness) in her relationship with both God and Adam.

Everything Begins in Jesus

Many heatedly dispute the fact that Christians constitute a new breed of people ordained of God to represent Him as regents on earth, even as their forefather Adam did. They contend that since Scripture declares Jesus to be the *"last* Adam," it is impossible for us to consider ourselves little Adams. That could easily be debated simply on the merits of our identification with Christ (last Adam) and our absolute union with Him (see 1 Cor. 6:17). But there is other, equally compelling evidence in Scripture that supports this belief.

To have seen Jesus was to have seen what the first Adam was like before he fell into sin. In Scripture, God refers to Jesus as "second man" (or second Adam) (1 Cor. 15:47). Whatever the first Adam failed to become because of sin, Jesus was by virtue of His inherent righteousness. The first Adam failed the test of temptation (see Gen. 3); the second Adam was victorious (see Lk. 4:1-14). The first Adam relinquished to Satan his right to reign on earth (see Lk. 4:5-6) and surrendered his scepter. In so doing, the first Adam handed over the keys to the city—every city—to Satan! The second Adam took back the throne, disarmed Satan's spiritual rulers and authorities, made a public spectacle of them, and triumphed over them (see Col. 2:15). Whatever the first Adam surrendered in the Garden of Eden, the second Adam, Jesus Christ, reclaimed on Calvary!

In order to fully grasp this truth, consider what the Bible says in reference to Jesus' relationship to Adam, and our relationship with Jesus. "The *first* man [Adam] is from the earth, earthy; the second man [Jesus] is from heaven" (1 Cor. 15:47). Also, "...'The *first* man, Adam, became a living soul.' The *last Adam* became a life-giving spirit" (1 Cor. 15:45). It is important to note that Jesus is referred to jointly as "*second* man" (literally, second Adam) and "*last* Adam." He is second by lineage; that is, He follows immediately after the first, thus establishing that there are no pretenders to the throne between the first Adam and Jesus—He is second. He is also referred to as the "last Adam." Here is where so many have difficulty seeing the forest for the trees. They maintain that if Jesus is the last Adam, then there will never be another Adam to follow Him. Thus, the Church can never become the exact image of Jesus Christ.

I agree at least on the point that there can never be another "last Adam." Doubtless, Jesus *is* the last Adam. But in order to comprehend what that involves, we must first understand Adam's unique position. Adam was *the first being* of the new creation. His name, Adam (mankind), attests to this. Jesus shares that uniqueness as the last Adam. He is *the first being* of the new creation, God's new order of people. "And He is *the image of the invisible God* [the first Adam also was "in the image of God"]; *the first-born* of all creation" (Col. 1:15). The reference to Jesus as the "first-born of all creation" has absolutely nothing to do with the original creation because His birth occurred several thousands of years later. So, the "all creation" mentioned here must refer to something else entirely. The Bible defines believers as the "new creation" of God: "Therefore if any man is in Christ, he is a new creature [literally, new creation]" (2 Cor. 5:17a).

The Greek word *ktisis,* translated "new creature," should have been rendered "original formation...creation."[2] This ties in with Jesus (the second Adam) being "the first-born among many brethren" (Rom. 8:29b). When we are born from above, we are restored to the original formation/original creation. I believe Paul had this in mind in Ephesians 2:15 when he referred to the "new man." All of the pieces fit together to form a beautiful mosaic of God's magnificent plan for the Church.

---

2. *Strong's* #2937.

All the Way Back to Adam

Everything Adam forfeited because of transgression, the last Adam (Jesus) retrieved by righteousness and made it ours. As the last Adam and the first-born among many brethren, Jesus commands a mighty army—the Church. Their mission: *to destroy the works of the devil and possess the land for God*! Adam was commissioned by God to subdue the earth. (The Hebrew word translated as "subdue" in Genesis 1:28 means to "bring under submission by force.") The Church has been commissioned to do likewise in the spirit realm.

In earlier chapters we learned that the Church has been ordered to possess the land, even as Israel was. Israel failed to accomplish that under Moses. It was not by chance that Moses was not the man to lead Israel, a type of the Church (see Acts 7:38), into the Promised Land. It was God's plan to use Joshua (the Hebrew name for *Jesus*) to lead them in the conquest of the land. (Please read the third chapter of Joshua.)

After 40 years of wandering in the wilderness the long-awaited day arrived when Israel would enter and begin their conquest of the Promised Land. The people of God sanctified themselves in preparation for what lay ahead, for God had promised to work wonders in their midst. Many obstacles stood between the people and their fulfillment of God's commission, not the least of which was the River Jordan. There were no ferry boats or bridges to facilitate the crossing of two to three million people. To make matters worse, the river was at flood stage. The people watched in awe as God miraculously parted the waters. Scripture records: "The waters which were flowing down from above stood and rose up in one heap, a great distance away *at Adam*" (Josh. 3:16a). Nothing was ever recorded in Scripture by accident. The Bible says the last barrier (Jordan) that stood between the people of God and their possession of the land was rolled all the way back to Adam! Granted, in this instance *Adam* was a city, not a person. But God could have rolled the river back to *any* geographical area or city He desired. Yet He specifically selected the city whose name was *Adam*, and made particular reference to it. Coincidental? I don't think so. This is the only scriptural reference to a city called Adam. It's noteworthy that this singular reference is within the context of Joshua (Jesus) leading God's people (the Church) into the

Promised Land—where they were subsequently to claim their God-given possessions.

Throughout the ages a barrier has prevented God's people from entering into the fullness of their inheritance in Christ—a barrier that obstructed access to their Promised Land. Since it has its roots in the original sin, that barrier extends all the way back to our forefather, Adam. If the land is still to be taken for God (and it *is*), then our Jordan must be crossed. Our Joshua (Jesus), the Captain of our salvation, has prepared the way. Will we dare to become the Joshua Generation that crosses over Jordan into the place of victory, possession, and fulfillment?

Remember, in typology the Jordan River speaks of the baptism in the Holy Spirit. It might be argued that people have been receiving the baptism in the Holy Spirit since the day of Pentecost; so what's new? Although the baptism in the Holy Spirit has commonly been considered an end in itself, the fact is that it is but the first step in the conquest of our Promised Land. It is one thing to enter the land, but quite another to take *possession* of it. Many believers receive the baptism in the Holy Spirit (crossing Jordan), then promptly become contented and satisfied with having arrived. Then they sit down on the other side of the river—*powerless to advance further*. Their attitude seems to be, "After all, we now speak in tongues; what more could there possibly be?" The fullness of the Holy Spirit's power and anointing awaits them, yet they sit idly by, contented with their meager portion.

Jesus never intended for the baptism in the Holy Spirit to be an end in itself, but He intended it to serve as the portal through which we enter into the vastness of God. Think of it as a gate that opens into lush pastures of the Holy Spirit: "and [they] shall go in and out, and find pasture" (Jn. 10:9b). Some interpret that to mean, "they shall go in—and then come out again." Never! Just as there was no back door to the Holy of Holies, there is likewise no *revolving* door to the Kingdom of God. What Jesus implied here was, "They shall go in (enter), and then go farther out out into the abundant pastures of the Spirit." "The Lord is my shepherd.... He makes me lie down in green pastures" (Ps. 23:1-2a). Have you ever noticed what the pasture is like in the immediate vicinity of the gate? It's an area where heavy traffic has created a rut. (Believers who linger around the gate of the kingdom of God always end up in a rut, which is nothing more than a grave with both ends kicked out.) What little grass there may be around the gate is always stunted, dusty, and scarcely fit to eat. Cattle don't congregate around the gate; they always advance into greener pastures. Yet many of the Lord's sheep park themselves by the gate, where they barely exist on the dusty, stale trappings of form and tradition. Could it be that cows are more intelligent than most Christians? Look around (and within) and judge for yourself.

Chapter Twenty-four

Mystery of the Kingdom—Revealed

Everyone loves a mystery—as long as it's eventually solved. Among many other things, the Bible is a book of mysteries, parables, and hidden sayings.[1] The words *mystery, mysteries, hid,* and *hidden* occur repeatedly throughout the New Testament. Although mysteries do exist in Scripture, and certain knowledge is hidden from casual view, it is not God's intention that it remain that way. Jesus said: "For nothing is hidden, except to be revealed; nor has anything been secret, but that it should come to light. If any man has ears to hear, let him hear" (Mk. 4:22-23).

Even though God desires that His children see clearly into the hidden things, these mysteries will not be understood by everyone in the Church. They can be, but they won't be because "The secret of the Lord *is for those who fear Him,* and He will make *them* know His covenant" (Ps. 25:14). God reveals His innermost heart to "those who fear Him." *Fear,* in this context, doesn't mean "to be afraid of" in the classical sense, but rather "to have reverential awe of." Today's Church does not stand in absolute wonder before Almighty God; instead, He is commonly perceived as a casual friend or buddy. Some songwriters have even displayed a heedless disrespect by referring to

---

1. For a fuller understanding of scriptural mysteries, see my book, *Christian Meditation: Doorway to the Spirit,* chapter 6, "Looking Into the Mysteries."

Jehovah God as "the Man upstairs" and other terms of inappropriate familiarity.

Mark 4:22-23 explains to whom the hidden secrets of the Word may be revealed: to those who have "ears to hear." The Greek word for "hear" is *akouo* and may also be rendered "understand," which sheds a slightly different light on Jesus' statement: "He that has ears to understand, let him understand." Jesus repeated the same command a total of seven times to the churches of the Book of Revelation. They were also the last words He spoke to the Church at large: "He who has an ear, *let him hear what the Spirit says* to the churches" (Rev. 2:7a; see also 2:11,17,29; 3:6,13,22). The Holy Spirit searches intently for those Christians who have understanding hearts, and whose minds are not closed to His ever-unfolding truth. If Satan's greatest tool is a *closed mind*, perhaps God's greatest tool is an *open mind*. The following paragraphs may stagger the imagination, but you will see that God has laid an extremely strong Scriptural foundation upon which these concepts are built.

The Mystery Demystified

In Second Corinthians 3:18, the apostle Paul wrote: "But we all, with unveiled face beholding as in a mirror *the glory of the Lord*, are *being transformed into the same image from glory to glory*, just as from the Lord, the Spirit." An honest reflection on the above Scripture raises the question: Does that describe the Church of today? Are we "being transformed into the same image [of Christ] from glory to glory" on a consistent basis? I think not. Yet, God has set in motion the transformation of this defeated ragtag group of military misfits into the glorious image of their Warrior-King, Jesus, the Captain of their salvation.

The devil will always do his utmost to keep the revelation of this intended transformation a mystery. One of the most successful methods he uses is to keep the Church blinded to *all* new revelation. Satan knows far better than we what awesome spiritual potential lies buried within each believer. He fears the vast devastation that will be unleashed upon his kingdom when the saints finally awaken from their Rip Van Winkle-like slumber, lay aside their ignorance and apathy, and clothe themselves with the whole armor of God.

In Ephesians 3:3-6, the apostle Paul revealed that the Gentiles would become fellow heirs of the grace of God. The Jewish Christians had missed this truth altogether until the time of Paul's revelation. Paul elaborated on this theme in Colossians 1:26-27:

> *...the mystery which has been hidden from the past ages and generations; but has now been manifested to His saints*, *to whom God willed to make known what is the riches of the glory of this mystery among the Gentiles*, **which is Christ in you**, *the hope of glory* (Colossians 1:26-27).

The mystery was not only that Christ would be in the Gentiles (that was only *half* the mystery), but that Christ Himself was dwelling in *all* believers! "Do you not know that *you are a temple of God*, and that the Spirit of God dwells in you?" (1 Cor. 3:16). Although God chose to reveal this truth among the Gentiles, it applied to the entire Church. We clearly see two distinct mysteries unfolded here: (1) that Gentiles were also heirs of the grace of God; and (2) that Christ was resident within every individual member of His Church.

We understand what "Christ in you" means, so let's examine the last part of the sentence in the light of the Greek text. "Hope" can also be translated "expectation." "Glory" comes from a very simple Greek word, *doxa*, yet close examination reveals a more complex meaning than expected. In its simplest form, *doxa* means "praise." Since there is an abundance of Scriptures in which the word *glory* clearly denotes praise, I will not elaborate on them. Yet, there are other Scriptures where the current rendering of *doxa* cannot mean praise.[2] In every one of the footnoted Scriptures, *glory* indicates something seen, heard, or experienced—*the manifest Presence of God!* From this, then, we understand that "glory" often indicates the manifest Presence of God. With that in mind, "Christ in you, *the hope of glory*" might well read, "Christ in you, *the expectation* of the *manifest Presence of God!*" Since *expectation* means eager anticipation, we should actually spend each day in eager anticipation of personally manifesting His Presence before the world.

There are three distinct aspects to this expectation: (1) *God* expects us to manifest His Presence, both in the Church and before the world. (2) *We* should expect to manifest His Presence at every opportunity. (3) The *world* has a right to expect that we will manifest His Presence in signs, wonders, and miracles.

---

2. Please read these Scriptures before proceeding: Lk. 9:31-32; Jn. 1:14; 2:11; Rom. 3:23; 6:4; 8:18,21; 1 Cor. 2:7; 2 Cor. 3:7-11,18; Eph. 5:7; Col. 1:27.

Let's return to Ephesians 3:9-10, which will shed additional light on verses 3-6:

> *And **to bring to light** what is the administration of **the mystery** which for ages has been **hidden in God**, who created all things; in order that the manifold wisdom of God might now be made known **through the Church** to the rulers and the authorities in the heavenly places.* (Ephesians 3:9-10).

The Greek word for our English word "administration" is *koinonia,* which means "communion, fellowship, *sharing in common.* From the Greek word, *'koinos,'* common."[3] As used above, the thought of sharing in common has nothing to do with Gentiles and Jews sharing a common Lord. It has to do with a mutual sharing of power and authority between the risen Christ and His Church. This is further borne out in the phrase, "in order that *the manifold wisdom of God might now be made known through the Church* to the rulers and the authorities in the heavenly places." The rulers and authorities referred to here are the same ones mentioned in Ephesians 6:10-18, where the Church is admonished to militantly resist the evil powers who dominate the heavenlies.

Another great mystery that Paul revealed here is that God, though He could have dispatched angels, chose to use born-again, Spirit-filled *people,* to carry out His magnificent plan of the ages. Since God appointed us believers to mount a relentless attack against the citadels of evil, we should ask ourselves: Are we faithfully attending to our appointed task?

One comedian recently commented about Christians: "I find it hard to believe that God, the greatest power in the universe, *would choose these Bozos* [clowns] to do His PR [public relations] work!" The audience displayed their approval of his mockery by laughing and applauding loudly. God has chosen the Church to reveal His manifold wisdom—and the world *dares* to call us *clowns!* Perhaps the Church's present anemic condition has given them just cause for mockery, but they won't have a legitimate reason to laugh at us much longer!

Though we have been called by God to execute His judgments against the superpowers of darkness, it seems we have somehow

---

3.   *Vine's,* 233; *Strong's* #2842.

experienced a reversal of roles—the Church grovels while Satanic powers gain the upper hand and remain largely unchallenged. The Church stands without excuse in allowing this, for Scripture plainly declares, "Christ...who is not weak toward you, *but mighty in you*" (2 Cor. 13:3b). One translator renders the above verse, "The Christ you have to deal with is not a weak person outside you, but *a tremendous power inside you*" (Phillips).

This is the revelation of the mystery—*Christ in you*! You may ask, "What's so special about that? Ever since I became a Christian, I've known that Christ came into my heart." When many Christians speak of the "Christ in you" concept, they imply that His *influence* is there because something good, moral, and righteous has entered into them. On the contrary, not some*thing*, but *Someone*, has entered them and that Someone is Christ! God was not speaking rhetorically when He declared that Christ is resident in us. He meant precisely what He said: At the moment of salvation, the Lord Jesus Christ, King of kings and Lord of lords, He who sits at the right hand of the Father, *literally* came to reside within us—not some representative, not some impersonal force, but Christ Himself! He who spoke and the universe came into being; He who healed the sick, raised the dead, walked on water, and stilled the storm with a word—He personally lives inside you! In Galatians 2:20, Paul defined it this way: "I have been crucified with Christ; *and it is no longer I who live, but Christ lives in me*; and the life which I now live in the flesh I live by faith in the Son of God, who loved me, and delivered Himself up for me."

The Real Mystery Is: Why Are Christians So Blind?

If Jesus Christ is truly resident within every believer, then why are there so many defeated Christians? Why is Satan allowed to run roughshod over the saints and advance the kingdom of darkness here on earth? And why does it appear that God's plan for His Church has failed and will never come to fruition? Why? Because "Christ in you, the hope of glory" is still a total mystery to most Christians. Through their ignorance, they have allowed Satan to keep them blinded to all that "Christ in you" really means. Paul attempted to communicate this revelation to the Church, but his words must be studied with an *open mind* and a sincere desire to allow the Holy Spirit to awaken your understanding (see Eph. 1:17-23). Then the full revelation of "Christ in you" can bear fruit.

Instead of Being Full, the Church Is Running Close to Empty

Having read the New Testament, how could any believer fail to recognize the awesome position, power, anointing, and authority that Christ has provided for His Church? Yet by failing to see it they live out their lives as perennial beggar-princes—possessing *all*, yet claiming *nothing*. Christians often listen to Satan's lies instead of God's revealed truth concerning them. When Satan tells them they are nothing, they readily believe him. Yet, when God's Word tells them of their exalted position in Christ, they seem unable to grasp it. Nevertheless, the Bible declares the undeniable fact that we are sons of the living God, and as such have been endowed with His resident nature, power, and anointing! With that in mind, let us resume our search of Scripture and discover more about our place, power, and position as believers in Christ.

In order to understand our position in Christ, we must first understand *Christ's* position before the Father. Colossians 1:19 and 2:9 say of Jesus, "…it was the Father's good pleasure for *all the fulness* to dwell in Him" and, "…in Him *all the fulness of Deity* dwells in bodily form." Antagonists of the believers' identification with Christ often quote the above Scriptures as proof texts to bolster their position. They contend that the gap between Jesus and believers is established in their concept that He possessed *all* the fullness of the Holy Spirit, *and we do not.* They also argue that we have only been given a portion of the Holy Spirit. Their doctrinal position is in direct contradiction to revelation in John 3:34: "For He whom God has sent [Jesus] speaks the words of God; for *He gives the Spirit without measure.*" Their groundless arguments also fall far short of explaining John 1:16a: "For of His *fulness* we have all received."

The Holy Spirit is a Person, not a thing or a substance. He can't be divided into pieces, so that one person can be given a large portion while another receives only a small helping. Every person receives the same amount (all) because Jesus "gives the Spirit without measure," which literally translated is: "for He does not give the Spirit by measure."[4]

---

4.   NASB marginal note.

When we observe that only a small percentage of Christians actually accomplish spiritual exploits, while the vast majority of the Church sits idly by, it is easy to understand why there are those who maintain that varying portions of the Holy Spirit have been given to different people. (This is often used as an excuse for lack of service: "I can't do that because I don't have as much anointing as so-and-so," etc.) This disparity of service does not reveal differing *portions*, but differing degrees of *yieldedness* and *commitment* to the Holy Spirit who dwells in all of us! The question isn't, "How much of the Holy Spirit do *you* have?" The question should be, "How much of *you* does the Holy Spirit have?" What would appear to be how much *we* have of God, is in reality determined by how much *God* has of *us*. (Currently, He has been given precious little by most Christians!) Since we have all received the Holy Spirit "without measure," being filled with the Spirit has nothing to do with quantity, but has everything to do with the degree (and quality) of our yieldedness—that is, how much of ourselves we have been willing to surrender to the control of the Holy Spirit.

Many Christians live in spiritual squalor far beneath their God-given privileges, while the Master continually calls to them, "Come and dine." Heaven's table is spread with every good thing—nothing is lacking. But, like those in the Bible who were invited to a feast, they offer lame excuses (see Lk. 14:16-24) and continue to exist on starvation fare. Sadly, like the Laodicean church of Revelation, they believe they are doing very well. (There's that lying mirror again!) They reinforce this position by comparing themselves with other churches or denominations (some of which are spiritually bankrupt), and grow increasingly more contented with the status quo. Thus, the downward spiral is perpetuated.

Does the Church Know What Time It Is?

With the advent of radio, various on-air services were introduced, such as weather forecasts, current time, etc. Each morning on his way to work, the keeper of Big Ben (the world's most famous clock) became accustomed to setting his watch by the time announced over the radio. When he arrived at work, he would then set Big Ben by the time on his watch. Gradually, but consistently, Big Ben's time became increasingly errant and corrections were often necessary. The mystery was solved when it was learned that the radio announcer set *his* watch by Big Ben every morning on his way to the station.

This true illustration hadn't happened when the apostle Paul wrote Second Corinthians 10:12b, but the concept of fruitless comparisons was certainly valid: "But when they measure themselves by themselves, and compare themselves with themselves, they are without understanding" (2 Cor. 10:12b). Paul enjoined us not to use others as a basis of comparison, but to use Jesus as the only yardstick by which to measure ourselves.

New Testament doctrine leaves no room for speculation; God commands His children to grow up and begin to act like Jesus. Nothing less is satisfactory. In Ephesians 3:19b, Paul prayed: "that *you* may be filled up *to all the fulness of God.*" It is inconceivable that Paul would pray for something (see verses 14-21) that was not the will of God, or enjoin believers to strive for that which was impossible to attain. Yet Paul prayed for believers to come under the absolute control of the Holy Spirit. And this *is* attainable because "...the one who joins himself to the Lord is *one* spirit with Him" (1 Cor. 6:17).

One Spirit

Christians do not have two spirits, but *one* Spirit. God's Word declares it to be so. God said it—that settles it! I may not understand it, but I must believe it. The Word of God is emphatic: *one* Spirit. The Greek word for "one" is *heis*: "*heis*, is used to signify 1) 'one' in contrast to many; 2) emphatically, *a single ('one'), to the exclusion of others.*"[5] At the new birth, what takes place is not a *bonding* of two distinctly different spirits (the Holy Spirit and ours), but rather a homogenous *blending* of spirits. Our spirits, which were alienated from God, are regenerated when the Holy Spirit takes up residence, and a new man (see Eph. 2:15) comes into being. When we become a part of the family of God, His seed enters us;[6] our spirits are melded with the Holy Spirit, and thus become *one* spirit. By receiving the Holy Spirit, we actually become an extension of God. This is hard for most Christians

---

5. *Vine's*, 446; emph. mine. *Strong's* #1520.
6. "...because His seed [*sperma*] abides in him...because he is born of God" (1 Jn. 3:9).

to grasp because we have been taught for centuries that the Church will diminish and evil will grow worse, until the point is reached where the weakened, desperate Church must be rescued (raptured) from the overwhelming evil of the world. Such a scenario is not entirely scriptural. True, the presence of evil will increase in the world, but righteousness and power will also increase among true believers (see Rom. 5:20). There will indeed be a rapture of the saints; but they will not be some discouraged, browbeaten, scattered people—but rather, "a glorious Church, without spot or wrinkle" (see Eph. 5:27)!

We do not currently resemble that ideal. In its present state, the Church needs a trip to the cleaners—with a good pressing included! When I refer to the ideal Church of Scripture, I'm not talking about some disheveled old bag lady who hasn't seen a shower in more than a decade. I point instead to the glorious Bride of Christ who is seated in Him, at the right hand of the Father—she who serves as co-sovereign of the universe (2 Tim. 2:12; Rev. 5:10; 20:4-6; 22:5) and who will judge angels (see 1 Cor. 6:3).

Instead of being filled with the Holy Spirit, many Christians are filled with doubt, suspicion, and unbelief. God purposely created us in such a way that we can never understand infinite values with our finite, carnal, fleshly minds (see 1 Cor. 2:5-16; Rom. 8:5-8). Whether it is a local deacon board or a group of denominational leaders who vainly define boundary lines for Holy Spirit revelation, these attempts are exercises in futility. The depths of God's Word can be understood only when we open our minds to the revelation of the Holy Spirit and allow Him to impart truth to us. No matter how hard they try, fleshly, carnal minds *cannot* comprehend the things of the Spirit: "But a natural man does not accept the things of the Spirit of God; for they are foolishness to him, and *he cannot understand them, because they are spiritually appraised*" (1 Cor. 2:14; see also 2:11-12).

Chapter Twenty-five

God Said It—That Settles It!

We are about to consider truths that would challenge scriptural credibility, if we did not totally accept the accuracy and inerrancy of the Word of God. Everything we will explore is the Word of God; He spoke every word. (Be reminded that a closed mind is Satan's greatest tool.)

*What is man, that Thou dost take thought of him? And the son of man, that Thou dost care for him? Yet Thou hast made him **a little lower than God**, and dost crown him with glory and majesty! **Thou dost make him to rule over the works of Thy hands; Thou hast put all things under his feet** (Psalm 8:4-6).*

This passage is echoed by the author of Hebrews in chapter 2:6-8:

*... "What is man, that Thou rememberest him? Or **the son of man,** that Thou art concerned about him? Thou hast made him for a little while lower than the angels; Thou hast crowned him with glory and honor, **and hast appointed him over the works of Thy hands; Thou hast put all things in subjection under his feet." For in subjecting all** things to him, He left **nothing** that is not subject to him... (Hebrews 2:6-8).*

Although some translations of Psalm 8:5 read, "a little lower than the *angels,*" the above translation, "a little lower than *God,*" is actually and factually more correct. The word translated, "God" (and in some translations, "angels") is *Elohim*—the very first name attributed to deity in Scripture (see Gen. 1:1). It is interesting to note that there are occasions in Scripture where *Elohim* is also used to denote angels. Why would God employ the same word to identify both Himself and angels? Scripture teaches that "God is spirit" (Jn. 4:24); angels also are spirit (see Heb. 1:7,14); and man is likewise a spirit being (see Gen. 2:7). So we see that God made man and angels from His own substance—*spirit*. When Scripture says that man was created "a *little* lower than God," it means that God could not elevate His creation any higher, endue them with more power, bestow more glory upon them, or give them more authority without initiating them into the very centrality of the Godhead itself! Blasphemy? NO! Revelation? YES!

The revelation continues and expands with the words of the Psalmist: "I said, '*You are gods*, [Elohim] and all of you are sons of the Most High' " (Ps. 82:6). In John 10:34-36, Jesus reaffirmed what the Psalmist had written, thus placing His divine approval upon that revelation:

> *Jesus answered them, "Has it not been written in your Law, 'I said, **you are gods**'? If he called them gods, to whom the word of God came (**and the Scripture cannot be broken**), do you say of Him, whom the Father sanctified and sent into the world, 'You are blaspheming,' because I said, 'I am the Son of God'?"* (John 10:34b).

Jesus' argument to the Jewish leaders was, "God said to *men*, 'You are gods' [*Elohim*]; so why are you angry with Me for declaring that I'm the *Son* of God?" Jesus had no problem accepting the fact that His Father called redeemed people gods; after all, they had been born into the family of God.

It is important to note that the Psalms are poetical and not even remotely part of the Jewish Law. Jesus' words in Luke 24:44, "...all things which are written about Me in the Law of Moses and the Prophets and the Psalms must be fulfilled," prove that Jesus also made a clear distinction between the Law of Moses and the Psalms. Thus, Jesus' statement, "Has it not been written *in your Law*," clearly indicates the existence of an identical scriptural reference *prior* to that of Psalm 82:6. Obviously, then, the Psalmist's statement regarding men as gods was a quote from an earlier Scripture in the Law.

God endued Moses with impressive spiritual power and authority (see Ex. 4) and then commissioned him to represent Him before Pharaoh (who, remember, is a type of Satan). God spoke the following words to Moses: "Moreover, he [Aaron] shall speak for you to the people; and it shall come about that he shall be as a mouth for you, *and you shall be as God* [*Elohim*] *to him*" (Ex. 4:16). This theme is continued in Exodus 7:1: "Then the Lord said to Moses, 'See, *I make you as God* [*Elohim*] *to Pharaoh, and your brother Aaron shall be your prophet.'*" In both instances, when referring to Moses' role before Pharaoh, the Hebrew word used for "God" was *Elohim*. When referring to God Himself, the use of the name *Elohim* is overwhelmingly favored among writers of the Old Testament; it appears in their writings a total of 2,325 times. The truly amazing fact is that God shared not only His name (authority), but His nature and abilities with a mere mortal, and continues to do so today—not with just *any* mortals, but with those who are His offspring, those born from above who thus bear His image: "Beloved, now we are children of God" (1 Jn. 3:2a; see also John 1:12; Rom. 8:16). Being the "offspring of God" (Acts 17:28-29) why would we think it strange that our Father would speak of us in familial terms? To argue against this is to argue with God Himself because *He* said it.

Dethroning the God of This World

The Bible clearly refers to Satan is as "the god of this world" (2 Cor. 4:4), a title that God never authorized him to use. Therefore, the use of that title engenders serious questions. Since his title didn't originate with God, where did he get it, and what are the scope and duration of his reign? The answers begin to unfold in the narrative of Jesus' temptation as recorded in Luke 4:1-13. In verses 5-7 we read:

> *And he* [Satan] *led Him* [Jesus] *up and showed Him **all the kingdoms of the world** in a moment of time. And the devil said to Him, "I will give You all this domain and its glory; **for it has been handed over to me**, and I give it to whomever I wish. Therefore if You will worship before me, it shall all be Yours"* (Luke 4:5-7).

In this face-to-face encounter with Jesus, Satan boasted that *all* the kingdoms of the world and their glory were under his control. If his claim had any merit, it would undeniably establish his reign as god of this world. It is of serious note to us that Jesus did not dispute Satan's claim, which is tacit proof that he was indeed "the god of this world." To this, the apostle John adds his testimony: "The whole world lies in the power of the evil one" (1 Jn. 5:19b).

Let's address the first question: Where did he get this title? The answer has been in plain sight all along. Satan himself answers it for us in Luke 4:6: "For it has been handed over to me." The phrase, "handed over to me," ("delivered," in some translations) is from the Greek word, *paradidomi*: " 'To betray' (*para*, 'up,' *didomi*, 'to give'), lit. 'To give over,' is used in the sense of delivering a person or thing to be kept by another...to deliver over treacherously by way of 'betrayal.' (See Matt. 17:22; 26:16; Luke 9:44; 23:25; John 6:64.)"[1] "The basic meaning of the verb [*paredothe*] in the New Testament is to deliver up to judgment and death.... The devil also asserts that he can grant power to whomsoever he will, since it has been placed at his absolute disposal (Luke 4:6)."[2] Webster's Dictionary gives the following definition of *betray*: "To deliver or expose to an enemy by treachery or disloyalty."

There is nothing in the nature of God (or recorded in Scripture) to indicate that God gave, let alone delivered up, the kingdoms of this world to His archenemy. Yet *someone* obviously did. If not God, then *who*? Who possessed sovereignty over all the earth, and the authority to turn over that control? Since evil has reigned unbridled since the fall of man in the Garden of Eden, we are left with the only logical conclusion: *Adam betrayed the kingdom into the hands of Satan!*

"And God [Elohim] *created man in His own image*, in the image of God [Elohim] He created him...and God said to them, 'Be fruitful and multiply, and fill the earth, and subdue it; and *rule...over every living thing* that moves on the earth' " (Gen. 1:27-28). "The heavens are the heavens of the Lord; *but the earth He has given to the sons of men*" (Ps. 115:16). God established Adam as "god (Elohim; see Ps. 8:4-6; 82:6; Jn. 10:34-36) of this world" to reign under and be second only to Almighty God—even as the Church (redeemed mankind) will rule and reign on earth in Christ throughout eternity.

"And Thou hast made them [redeemed mankind; the Church] to be a kingdom and priests to our God; and *they* [redeemed mankind; the Church] *will reign upon the earth*" (Rev. 5:10). The Bible is quite clear that as Adam originally ruled (under God), redeemed (godly) men will once again rule (under God). Yet we are confronted with a huge gap of time when those (the Church; godly men) who ought to be

---

1. *Vine's*, 64; *Strong's* #3860.
2. Brown, *New International Dictionary*, Vol. 2, 368.

ruling, obviously are *not*. Perhaps we have missed something in the Word of God?

Our forefather Adam committed high treason against God when he handed over (delivered up) his kingdom to Satan. It is Adam's betrayal (handing over) to which Satan alluded (see Lk. 4:6) when he tempted Jesus in the wilderness. Everything that Adam forfeited in his act of high treason, Jesus Christ came to restore—including the kingdom. All-inclusive in Christ's victory was redeemed man's right to rule (under God) in that kingdom.

Matthew's Gospel placed Jesus' genealogy where one might expect to find it, before the birth of Jesus. Luke, on the other hand, inserted his genealogy in chapter three, sandwiched between Jesus' baptism by John and His temptation in the wilderness. Strange place for a genealogy? Perhaps not. The verse prior to Luke's genealogy of Jesus contains the Father's declaration, "Thou art My beloved *Son*, in Thee I am well-pleased" (Lk. 3:22b), and the genealogy itself ends with, "Adam, the *son* of God" (Lk. 3:38). It traces direct lineage backward from the second Adam (Son of God) to the first Adam (son of God). It is not coincidental that the mention of both the first and second Adams as sons of God should immediately precede Jesus' temptation in the wilderness (see Lk. 4:1-13). Luke's genealogy of Jesus is purposely parenthetical, and since there were no chapter breaks in the original manuscripts, we have a continuing narrative from the baptism of Jesus to the temptation in the wilderness. This is made clear in Mark's Gospel, "Thou art My beloved Son, in Thee I am well-pleased. And *immediately* the Spirit impelled Him to go out into the wilderness"(Mk. 1:11b-12).

When faced with temptation, the first Adam failed miserably. The consequences of his failure can be seen everywhere—the most notable of which are sin, sickness, and death. In order to secure His position as undisputed Sovereign over the kingdom, it was necessary that the second Adam not only be faced with temptations, but that He overcome them! Satan attempted to utilize the same hooks of temptation on the second Adam that he used, with great success, on the first Adam. And why not? They had worked so well in the Garden of Eden. As you will see in the following chart, the *modus operandi* he uses in his attempt to topple the Church (sons of Adam, to whom the retrieved kingdom has been entrusted) is identical to that used with the first and second Adams:

PROFILE OF TEMPTATION

FIRST ADAM	SECOND ADAM	SONS OF ADAM
"The woman saw the tree was:	"If You are the Son of God:	"For all that is in the world, the
1. Good for *food*	**1.** Tell this stone to become **bread**	**1.** Lust of the *flesh*
2. Delight *to the eyes*	**2.** *Showed Him* **all the**	**2.** Lust of the *eyes*
3. Desirable *to make one wise* she took...its fruit and ate...and her husband...and he ate" (see Gen. 3:6).	**kingdoms of the world** **3.** Cast Yourself down from here (temple pinnacle). (The implication in #3 is that multitudes would witness this event, thus it was an appeal to *pride*.)	**3.** Boastful *pride* of life is not from the Father, but is from the world" (see 1 Jn. 2:16).

The illustration above outlines Satan's stratagem which, apart from the second Adam, have served him well. Only the second Adam overcame by refusing to yield to Satan's enticements, and came through the crucible of temptation unscathed. Then, on Calvary He *sealed* His claim to the kingdom and redeemed everything the first Adam had handed over to the enemy.

When Adam relinquished the kingdom to Satan, in that moment all of mankind died (were separated from God—1 Cor. 15:22). For centuries Satan imposed his will upon the human race—*until the second Adam arrived on the scene*. For the first time the enemy's right to rule was contested—and he *lost!* The kingdom (reign, right to rule) was wrested from his control and restored to the redeemed sons of Adam's race (see Lk. 12:32).

In order to understand the scope of what believers have been given, one must first know precisely to what extent Adam reigned. (Since I covered that topic in great depth earlier, I'll not attempt a duplication here. But allow me to give a brief summation.) A careful examination of the scope of Satan's current influence will reveal the magnitude of Adam's dominion. Scripture refers to Satan as "the god of this world." He usurped that title, as well as the kingdom itself, from Adam, who was created in the image of Elohim—a son of God. As Adam was, so also are we. What was his is now ours, and we "will *reign in life* through the One, Jesus Christ" (Rom. 5:17b).

Every Christian is familiar with Revelation 11:15: "The kingdom of the world has become the kingdom of our Lord, and of His Christ; *and He will reign forever and ever.*" Yet, I wonder how many are equally familiar with Revelation 22:5b, "Because the Lord God shall illumine them; and *they* [believers] *shall reign forever and ever*"? God has ordained that the Bride of Christ should reign forever and ever, through Christ, as co-sovereign of the universe! As lost sinners it was "natural" to "reign in death," led about by every sinful whisper of the carnal mind. Now that we have been born from above, recreated in His image as sons of God, and have received His Spirit, His nature energizes our beings. Therefore, it should be totally "natural" to live as King's kids and reign "in life" and "forever"!

Will the Unimpeachable Witnesses Please Take the Stand

The following witnesses are all beyond reproach. The righteous Judge has added their testimonies into the record (the Bible) and they must stand unchallenged: **God** (Elohim) Himself had no difficulty declaring "You are gods [Elohim]." In the Law, **Moses** (under divine inspiration) likewise had no difficulty stating, "You are gods [Elohim]." (In John 10:34 Jesus quoted from the Law of Moses, although this quotation is not found in the manuscripts discovered to date.[3] Moses exhibited no difficulty in writing that God (Elohim) had instructed him (Moses) to become "as God [Elohim] to Aaron" (see Ex. 4:16) and "as God [Elohim] to Pharaoh" (Ex. 7:1). **David** also had no difficulty writing, "You are gods [Elohim]" (Ps. 82:6). **Jesus** Himself had no difficulty

---

3. Although I'm certain that Jesus spoke the words recorded of Him in Acts 20:35, no Gospel manuscript in our possession quotes them. Likewise, Matthew 2:23, Romans 9:17, Ephesians 5:14, James 4:5, and First Timothy 5:18b all record words from Old Testament manuscripts available to the first-century Church that we have not yet recovered. In John 10:34b Jesus said, "Has it not been written *in your Law,* 'I said, you are gods' "? Jesus could not have been alluding to Psalm 82:6, which was not included in the Law (Pentateuch, the first five books of the Bible). That Jesus distinguished between the Law and the Psalms is obvious in Luke 24:44b, "That all things...in the Law of Moses and the Prophets and the Psalms must be fulfilled." Psalm 82:6 opens with the words, "I *said,*" indicating that this is a *re*-quote of a prior statement of God. Jesus knew that some might argue that the Psalms were *poetical* books, but *no* one could (or *would*) argue against the Law of Moses. By quoting from the Law, Jesus was also offering "first reference."

stating, "You are gods [Elohim]" (Jn. 10:34) and by so doing He confirmed the prior testimonies.

It would seem that *we* are the only ones who find it difficult (if not impossible) to agree with God and His prophets. Could it be that we have *closed minds*? Or perhaps we don't understand the purpose for which mankind was originally created: to be sons of God, regents on earth. In past chapters we've discussed in depth that Jesus Christ Himself is literally living within all believers. Yet, He is more than living in us; His Spirit and ours have blended into one spirit (see 1 Cor. 6:17). Perhaps we would not struggle so with this scriptural concept if we had a better grasp of Paul's declaration in Galatians 2:20, which is far more than a mere rhetorical statement: "I have been crucified with Christ; and it is no longer *I* who live, *but Christ lives in me!*"

Spiritual Identification

The Church is as identified with Christ as *He* is with the Church. They are inseparable. The bond of Christ with His Church is absolute: We (the Church) were in Christ when He died on the cross, in Christ when He was buried, and in Christ when He was raised from the dead. Because we are in Christ now, we share in His life (see Gal. 2:20; Rom. 6:5; Phil. 3:10; Rom. 6:8-11) and even share in His throne: "And raised us up with Him, and *seated us with Him* in the heavenly places, in Christ Jesus" (Eph. 2:6).

Could our union be any more complete than for us to be in Christ, and Christ in us? Astonishingly, yes! In Jesus' High Priestly prayer the Lord extended our understanding of His union with redeemed people even further: "...even as Thou, Father, art in Me, and I in Thee, *that they also may be in Us.... I in them, and Thou in Me*" (Jn. 17:21,23a). The intent of Jesus' prayer was that we (the Church) would become *one* with the Father God and Jesus, as God the Father was one with Christ. What is implicit here is the circle of relationship: God the Father is in Jesus; Jesus is in His Church; the Church is in Jesus; and Jesus is in the Father! The new birth has brought us into a seamless union with both Jesus and the Father: "Christ in you, the hope of glory" (Col. 1:27). Because of our mystical union with both Jesus and His Father, we are *now* seated together with Christ on His throne. (Lest you are tempted to dismiss this out of hand, please be reminded again that Satan's greatest tool is a closed mind.)

Chapter Twenty-six

The Sons of God

"For I consider that the sufferings of this present time are not worthy to be compared with *the glory that is to be revealed to us*. For the anxious longing of the creation *waits eagerly for the revealing of the sons of God*" (Rom. 8:18-19). What is it about the above verses that makes Christians (especially preachers) cringe and break out in cold sweat? Those verses even send shivers up their spine. (Please allow me a little hyperbole here.) Most preachers take a detour around those verses and adopt the attitude, "If we ignore them long enough, they will go away."

Part of the revulsion to the concept of the "revelation of the sons of God" dates back to the mid-1940's and the birth of the Latter Rain Movement, which adopted those verses for its doctrinal core. To be sure, it was a movement fraught with excesses, and some of its extremists even believed that we (as little gods) would create galaxies, never taste death, etc. It became so easy to focus on the extremes, while overlooking the many good things that accompanied that great move of the Holy Spirit.

All of the major Full Gospel denominations repudiated the excesses of the Latter Rain Movement, and by association all but discarded Romans 8:18-19. Relegating these verses to scriptural limbo because there were serious flaws in the manner in which men applied them, is akin to throwing the baby out along with the bath water. Preachers are human—they fear what they don't understand—and in turn, they run from what they fear. If they would only take a closer look at the object of their terror, they might discover that it is not as terrifying as they had imagined.

"For we know that the whole creation groans and suffers the pains of childbirth together until now" (Rom. 8:22). All of creation, the entire universe, is groaning for a revelation of the sons of God (that's *us!*). The groans are caused by birth pains, an intense desire for the birthing of the sons of God—those who will "take the lid off" the Church and loose God's mighty army against the powers of darkness. Let's discover the true meaning behind, "...the anxious longing of the creation waits eagerly for the revealing of the sons of God" (Rom. 8:19).

The Greek word for "revealing," in Romans 8:19, is *apokalupsis,* which is defined as: "disclosure; appearing, manifestation, be revealed, revelation." It's derived from the word *apokalupto,* which means "to take off the cover, i.e.; disclosure: reveal."[1] Paul also used the word *apokalupto* in Second Corinthians 12:1,7 to describe the revelations the Holy Spirit had given him. There, and here, Paul clearly used the word to express that something previously hidden ("under a cover") had now been *uncovered,* and thus *revealed.* In the same manner, the Holy Spirit has now taken the cover off this mystery and is revealing new truth. This will be the next great mystery to be unveiled as God allows the world to witness His grand army, the Church, in all its power. The day is fast approaching when the Church will be all that God has planned for it to be.

Don't Let Appearances Fool You!

"Beloved, *now* we are *children of God,* and it has not yet appeared as yet what we shall be. We know that, *when He appears, we shall be like Him, because we shall see Him just as He is.* And everyone who has this hope fixed on Him purifies himself, just as He is pure" (1 Jn. 3:2-3). Verse two expresses the expectation that we shall be like Jesus: *homoioi auto esometha.* That has also been the major theme of this book: that we (the Church) shall someday, *in this world,* be like Jesus. Unfortunately, most Christians relegate the timing of these verses *only* to the second coming of the Lord, *after which* we will

---

1.   *Strong's* #602.

become like Him. While there may be a connection between these verses and the second coming, a serious look at the usage of certain Greek words in this passage indicates yet another interpretation. (Scriptural prophecies often have a duality of meaning, which may apply to these verses also.) I believe that my rendering of the meaning behind First John 3:2-3 is further strengthened by the same writer, in the same epistle: "Because as He *is* [present tense], so also are we in this world [now; present tense!]" (1 Jn. 4:17b). John made it abundantly clear that as Jesus is *now*, we are also—*now*!

The word translated "appear/appeared" is the Greek word, *phaneroo. Phaneroo* is a synonym for *apokalupsis.* "*Apokalupsis* has to do with *the revelation of mysteries,* as used by Paul in Rom. 8:18,19; I Cor. 14:6,26; II Cor. 12:1,7; Gal. 1:12; 2:2; Eph. 1:17; 3:3; and by John in Rev. 1:1."[2] It's not that *phaneroo* could not be used to describe the coming of the Lord. But there are other words that would far more aptly identify that event—words that were used several times in the Pauline epistles and once in the Book of James. Thus, if John's purpose had been to make it unmistakably clear that this reference pertained to Jesus' second coming, his first choice would undoubtedly have been the word *epiphaneia* ("appearing; brightness"), used by Paul in several places in his epistles to denote Christ's second coming (1 Tim. 6:14; 2 Tim. 1:10; 4:1,8; Titus 2:13). "*Epiphaneia*: A manifestation, ie; (specifically) the advent of Christ."[3] "Epiphaneia occurs with reference to the appearance of the Lord on earth at the end of history."[4] John's second choice would most likely have been the word, *parousia,* also used by Paul in reference to the coming of the Lord: "For this we say to you by the word of the Lord, that we who are alive, and remain until the coming of the Lord [*eis ten parousian tou kyriou*], shall not precede those who have fallen asleep" (1 Thess. 4:15). James also used *parousia* when reflecting on the coming of the Lord: "Be patient, therefore, brethren, until the coming of the Lord" [*heos tes parousias tou kyriou*] (Jas. 5:7).[5]

---

2. Brown, *New International Dictionary*, Vol. 3, 321.
3. *Strong's* #2015; emph. mine.
4. Brown, *New International Dictionary*, Vol. 3, 319.
5. Brown, *New International Dictionary*, Vol. 2, 901; emph. mine.

In the early Church, when either of the words *epiphaneia* or *parousia* was used, the hearers immediately understood that what was being conveyed pertained to the return of the Lord. The concept of *epiphaneia* or the *parousia* (the coming of the Lord) was at the heart of the Christian belief structure. Yet John (by the Holy Spirit) purposely chose to utilize neither of those two specific terms in describing the events of First John 3:2-3, using instead the nonspecific *phaneroo*. *Phaneroo* would hardly have been the word of choice had he wished to specifically refer to the coming of the Lord. (Yet, he was *quite* specific earlier in First John 2:28 where he used the word *parousia* to indeed describe the coming of the Lord.) By chapter three, however, he had changed his theme to emphasize the mechanics of living out the Christian life in the here-and-now. With that in mind, let's examine those verses in greater depth.

In First John 3:2, instead of the words *epiphaneia* or *parousia* (as one might expect, had his reference been to Jesus' second coming), John chose the word, *phaneroo*, which translated is, "appear/appeared."

> "*Phaneroo*: To be manifested in the scriptural sense of the word is *more than to appear*...To be manifested is *to be revealed in one's true character*; this is *especially* the meaning of *phaneroo*. The same word is used of believers, '...has not yet appeared....'

> "Paul used the same word, "*phaneroo*," no less than nine times in 2 Corinthians; especially in polemical[6] contexts. He used it of the *revelation* that comes about through his preaching (2 Cor. 2:14; 11:6)."[7]

*Now to Him who is able to establish you according to my gospel and the preaching of Jesus Christ, according to the **revelation** [phaneroo] of the **mystery** which has been kept secret for long ages past, but now is **manifested** [phaneroo], and by the Scriptures of the prophets, according to the commandment of the eternal God, **has been made known** to all the nations, leading to obedience of faith (Romans 16:25-26).*

6. *Polemic*, "a controversial argument, as one against some opinion, doctrine, etc." *Polemical*: "of or pertaining to disputation of controversy"—Webster.
7. Brown, *New International Dictionary*, Vol. 3, 322.

In every other reference in First John where the word *phaneroo* is used, it has the connotation of something not readily apparent (hidden) becoming obvious, or being *revealed* in its true nature and for its true purpose (see 1 Jn. 1:2; 2:19; 3:5,8; 4:9). Would John then make a 180-degree turn, and use it in an altogether different context in 3:2? Obviously, he did not.

As I mentioned above, John used the same word in reference to Christians as he did of Christ, thus further confirming that in this context *phaneroo* must mean more than "to return." In John's usage, it applies far more to the revelation of one's true character—who and what we (the Church) really are in Christ. Webster's Dictionary says that character, among other things, reveals the "status, and individuality which sets one person apart from all others." The true status of believers can be found in the phrase, "Beloved, now we are children of God..." (1 Jn. 3:2); *now*—not in some far-distant day of death or rapture.

John continued: "...it has not appeared as yet what we shall be" [as sons of God]" (1 Jn. 3:2a). This is because, at the time of his writing, the Church had not received the complete revelation (spiritual understanding) concerning "Christ in you, the hope of glory." Though the ultimate goal set forth in Scripture was for all believers to perfectly reflect the image of Christ as He lives His life through them, that had not yet become a reality in John's day.

Since the birth of the Church, Christ has always lived in believers, although for the most part He has been well concealed. That is, we have never allowed Him to manifest Himself through us in the fullness of His kingdom, power, and glory. (We talk about Him, but we don't fully reflect Him.) Hebrews 13:8 expresses the changelessness of Jesus: "Jesus Christ is the same yesterday and today, yes and forever." If He is truly the same, then He should still be doing everything He did when on earth—only now He should be doing it through His Body, the Church. To observe the anemic Church that bears His name, you would never know He is the same; but the time is rapidly approaching when Christ will fully reign in (and through) Christians, and the Church will truly reflect Christ in all His glory!

Notice Paul's usage of *phaneroo* in Colossians 3:3-4: "For you have died and your life is *hidden* with Christ in God. When *Christ*, who is our life, is *revealed*, then *you also will be revealed* with Him in glory." Once again, the theme is of something *hidden* that is about to be uncovered—in this case, both Christ and the Church—simultaneously. The word *hidden* (the Greek word *krupto*, "to conceal") cannot refer to our past life with all its sin because our sins are not *hidden*; they are *forgiven!* They have been removed from us as far as the east is from the west (see Ps. 103:12), buried forever in the sea of God's forgetfulness, never again to be remembered against us (see Mic. 7:19). There is no need to hide what no longer exists. In the context of what follows, the life spoken of here must be the dynamic, supernatural life of Jesus Christ, which has yet to be fully manifested (revealed) through the Church.

The next verse, Colossians 3:5, begins with the word *therefore*. (Remember, whenever you see the word *therefore*, ask, "What is it there for?") The theme of this chapter in Colossians deals with sanctification and putting on the new self. So, in verse 5 Paul wrote, "Therefore consider the members of your earthly body as dead to..."; then he lists several besetting sins. What Paul is saying is: "Therefore [because our desire is for Christ to be revealed in us in all His power and glory—and for us to be revealed in all His fullness], *put to death the sins of the flesh—sanctify yourselves.*" (See Joshua 3:5.) We are instructed to "kill" the flesh—that is, destroy its influence by bringing it under subjection to the spirit. However successful we are in accomplishing this, to the same degree Christ and His Church will be "revealed" (uncovered) for the world to see.

The time frame for the Church's transformation is clearly set forth in the words, "when He appears, we shall be like Him" (1 Jn. 3:2). We know that the word *appears* (*phaneroo*) has to do with the revelation of His character, ministry, and power, which are now resident (though *hidden*) in the Church.

The method by which it will come about is also clearly delineated: "because we shall see Him just as He is" (1 Jn. 3:2). There are two Greek words used for the word *see*. One is *horao*, "Figuratively, it comes to be used of intellectual or *spiritual perception*. 'Seeing' in the Greek and Hebrew Old Testaments can refer also to *perception by means of other senses....*"[8] We will see Christ *physically* at His return,

---

8.   Brown, *New International Dictionary*, Vol. 3, 513; emph. mine.

but we must first see Him *spiritually*—a clear-cut *perception* of His Lordship within the Church before that day arrives. While I agree that whatever our glory may ultimately be in this world, it will be far greater in the world to come; we dare not postpone the great transformation of the Church until the second coming of the Lord. What effect will our transformation at the coming of the Lord have on this sick and dying world, presently imprisoned under the control of the prince of darkness? Multitudes are in need of deliverance now and their cries for help fall on deaf ears. It is scripturally unreasonable to believe that God has deserted these people and left them in the hands of the enemy. God has a master plan that He will yet reveal through His Church (see Eph. 3:9-10).

Like Jesus

The goal of every believer should be to become exactly like Jesus. Watered-down preaching has prevented most Christians from having an awareness of their position and privileges in Christ. Thus they live out their lukewarm lives in ever-increasing defeat, and no wonder, "For as he thinks within himself, so he is" (Prov. 23:7a). We have been brainwashed into believing that we can never *really* become like Jesus. Yet Scripture says that the mind of Christ is resident in His Body, the Church (us), and all the knowledge of the universe is in that mind: "...the wealth that comes from the full assurance of understanding, resulting in a true knowledge of *God's mystery, that is, Christ Himself,* in whom are hidden **all** *the treasures of wisdom and knowledge*" (Col. 2:2-3). Paul unveiled the revelation that "*we* have the mind of Christ" (1 Cor. 2:16). John Wesley defined sanctification as, "Possessing the mind of Christ, and *all* the mind of Christ." And, because we do have the mind of Christ, the apostle John disclosed even further revelation: "...you have an anointing from the Holy One, *and you know all things*"[9] (1 Jn. 2:20).

Follow this simple train of logic: Christ is the head of the Church (see Col. 1:18; 2:19); the head is on the Body, and the Body is the Church. Therefore, all the knowledge contained in the head (Jesus) is accessible to His Body, the Church (us). We do not share God's omniscience

---

9. "So read some ancient manuscripts." NASB marginal note; emph. mine.

(having infinite knowledge; *ie.*, being aware of everything at all times), yet all of God's knowledge is available to us on a need-to-know basis (see 1 Cor. 12:8; Jn. 10:27; Rom. 8:14,26-27). The last words spoken to the Church imply that Jesus fully expects the Church not only to be *listening* for, but *hearing* (*ie.*, being *led by*) the voice of the Holy Spirit (see Rev. 3:22). Jesus promised His followers, "But the Helper, the Holy Spirit, whom the Father will send in My name, He will teach you *all* things, and bring to your remembrance *all* that I said to you" (Jn. 14:26). The following illustration may help you understand what having the mind of Christ is like.

This book is being written on my computer, which contains a hard drive (a series of disks that store information magnetically). Currently there are CD-ROM's (compact disks similar to those you play in your stereo system) capable of storing 300,000 pages of information. Developers are now experimenting with a shorter wave of red laser which, because of its narrower width, will allow the storage of ten times more information on one disk—3,000,000 pages. Within 20 years scientists are projecting that the use of even shorter wave blue lasers will allow them to store *one hundred times* more than today's capacity. If my math has served me well, that amounts to 30 million pages of information on one CD! That's an unbelievable amount of knowledge in an extremely small space. If you owned such a CD, would it mean you knew everything on it? Hardly. Yet, in one sense you would, because you'd have *access* to everything on that disk, whenever you had need of it.

This is similar to the way the brain operates. We have the information of a lifetime stored there; yet are not immediately aware of any of it until we have need for it. At that time the subconscious mind will project it to the surface (into the conscious mind) and cause it to become current (conscious) knowledge.

Even Jesus Himself (who certainly possessed the mind of Christ) wasn't immediately aware of everything at all times. He often expressed His total dependence upon the Father for leading and guidance. When speaking of His return, He said, "But of that day and hour no one knows, not even the angels of heaven, *nor the Son,* but the Father *alone*" (Mt. 24:36). Not even Jesus Himself knew when His return was scheduled. When praying in Gethsemane (see

Mt. 26:36-46), He asked the Father, *"If* it is possible, let this cup pass from Me" (Mt. 26:39). The word *if* implies imperfect immediate knowledge. Therefore, since He wasn't aware of God's will for the moment, He prayed *if.*

It's the Holy Spirit's job to function like the reading arm in my computer's hard drive, which scans over the disk (at incredible speed) in search of information. It doesn't bring up extraneous, useless data; it only produces relevant information for that precise moment. Yet, information that is irrelevant now, may be the exact information I need at some later date. In the same way, the Holy Spirit is able to dip into the great reservoir (the mind of Christ within us) and impart a "word of knowledge" (see 1 Cor. 12:8) when and where it is needed. Instead of accessing the mind of Christ, the Church too often settles for...

Stinkin' Thinkin'

"For as he thinks within himself, so he is" (Prov. 23:7a). The Lord Jesus Christ longs for every believer to be stamped with His nature and to exercise the mind of Christ. But for centuries the Church has been trained to live far beneath its privileges because our minds have been influenced by anemic, powerless preaching, which demeans and neutralizes Christ's power and demoralizes the Church. Those whose eyes are fixed on higher ground are often accused of being "proud elitists," "extremists," or "those Sons of God fanatics." We are tagged with those labels simply for believing what Jesus said about His Church. One day believers will truly become *believers* and permit the mind of Christ to think and reason through them. He will make His decisions and direct their lives by His Spirit. Then He will develop His nature within them, and they will be supernaturally empowered.

> *Seeing that **His divine power has granted to us everything pertaining to life and godliness,** through the true knowledge of Him who called us by His own glory and excellence. For by these He has granted to us His precious and magnificent promises, in order that by them **you** might become **partakers of the divine nature**... (2 Peter 1:3-4).*

Nature is the "particular combination of qualities belonging to a person...by birth..."—Webster. The Greek word for "nature" is *phusis* (from the word *phuo,* from which we derive the word *phule*), "natural production (lineal descent). An offshoot, *i.e.*, race or clan: kindred, tribe."[10] The implication is clear that we are God's offspring—of direct lineal descent through Jesus—and as such we share in His divine nature. We have inherited His mind, nature, kingdom, power, and His glory. What more could the Church desire? But there is more!

Let My People *Grow*

"My *children*, with whom I am again in labor *until Christ is formed in you*" (Gal. 4:19). Paul used the word *teknion*, which literally translated means "infants." The Church at Galatia was not at all a new (baby) church; they were old enough to have begun to backslide (see Gal. 1:6-7; 3:1). Their problem, a universal one, is also reflected in today's Church: They simply refused to grow up (become spiritual adults).

The Church has mastered the art of winning converts (birthing babies); at the same time she has miserably failed to produce grown, fully matured sons who perfectly reflect the image of their heavenly Father. Over the course of long years in ministry, I've attended many ministers' meetings. The subject would almost always arise as to how many souls were saved (birthed) in their church last week or month or year. Over all the years, and in all those meetings, I never heard even *one* minister say, "Last year we were pleased to help bring 'X' number of sons and daughters to spiritual maturity." So many are concerned about *birthing*; yet so few show genuine concern for *maturing*. Someday all who minister will stand before the Judgment Seat of Christ, where they will be called upon to answer the question, "How many sons did you help bring to *maturity*?" After all, we who minister are called upon to work in concert with the Holy Spirit to fulfill *His* vision of the Church—not our own. His vision of the Church is crystal clear:

> *Until we all attain to the unity of the faith, and of the knowledge of the Son of God,* **to a mature man,** *to the measure of the stature which belongs to the fulness of Christ. As a result,* **we are no longer to be children,** *tossed here and there by waves, and carried about by every wind of doctrine, by the trickery of men, by craftiness in deceitful scheming;*

10. *Strong's* #5449; #5453; #5443.

*but speaking the truth in love, **we are to grow up in all aspects into Him, who is the head, even Christ**, from whom the whole body, being fitted and held together by that which every joint supplies, according to the proper working of each individual part, **causes the growth of the body for the building up of itself in love*** (Ephesians 4:13-16).

Throughout Scripture the admonition to grow up is inescapable. In Ephesians 4:14 the word translated "children" is *nepios*: "infant—simple minded person—an immature Christian."[11] Paul didn't pull any punches; he called things the way he saw them. Paul reminds me of the baseball umpire who was being yelled at by a player (whom he'd just called out on strikes) and the team manager, both of whom were accusing him of being somewhat more than *slightly* blind. Without so much as batting an eyelid from intimidation, the seasoned umpire replied, "I just calls 'em da way I sees 'em!" Since the Church needs straightforward, truthful preaching that would point the way toward spiritual maturity, God give us more preachers who can likewise say, "I just calls 'em da way I sees 'em."

Paul was absolutely convinced that we, as sons of God, are commissioned to mature spiritually, and was equally clear as to the extent of this maturity: "the measure of the *stature* which belongs to the fulness of Christ" (Eph. 4:13). He further stressed that "we are to grow up in *all* aspects *into Him*, who is the head, *even Christ*" (Eph. 4:15). The word translated "stature" means, "*a comrade... i.e., as big as.*"[12] In every other New Testament reference where that word *stature* is used, it refers to physical size; but that can hardly apply in this context, so it must allude here to His *spiritual* stature. Into what fullness then does God expect His sons to mature? That can be found in the Greek word for "fullness," *pleroo*: "to make replete, ie (lit.) to cram..."[13] and *pleroma*: "(from *pleroo*) repletion or completion...what fills (as contents...copiousness...."[14] We are also instructed that our growth is to encompass "*all* aspects" (every facet of His being and nature) and that our growth is to be "*into him*, who is the head, even Christ" (Eph. 4:15). When we have been so filled with the nature of

---

11. *Strong's* #3516.
12. *Strong's* #2244; #2245; emph. mine.
13. *Strong's* #4137.
14. *Strong's* #4138.

Jesus, His power and anointing, that there is no more room for anything *but* Jesus, we will see the fulfillment of "Christ in you, the hope of glory!" This is what God recognizes as the "mature man" or the "fullness of Christ."

The following quotation is from Rev. Dr. John G. Lake (1870-1935), a man of God who demonstrated profound spiritual insights into the Word of God. I view him as a man who lived before his time.

> "I am glad that God has permitted man, even at intervals, to rise into that place of dominion in God, for it demonstrates the purposes of God. It demonstrates that He purposes that we should rise into the high place not only at intervals, but this should be the normal life of the Christian who is joined to God.

> "Christianity need not be apologized for. Christianity was the conscious life and power of the living God, transmitted into the nature of man until man's nature is transformed by the living touch. The very spirit, soul, and being are energized and filled by His life. Thus you become indeed as Christ intended, a veritable likeness of Him.

> "That startles some people. The ultimate goal of redemption is to save those enslaved by sin and the flesh, and recreate them in His own image, sons of God. Not sons of God on a lower order, but sons of God as Jesus was.

> "Paul declares, 'He gave some, apostles; and some prophets; and some, evangelists; and some pastors and teachers....' Why? 'Till we all come...unto a perfect man, unto the measure of the stature of the fulness of Christ' (Eph. 4:11-13). Not a limited life, but an unlimited life. The idea of God was that every man should be transformed into Christ's perfect image by his being joined to Him by the Holy Spirit. Christ within and Christ without. Christ in your spirit, Christ in your soul, and Christ in your body. Not only living His life, but performing His works by the grace of God. *That is the gospel of the Son of God.*"[15]

---

15. John G. Lake, *Spiritual Hunger and Other Sermons* (Dallas, TX: Christ for the Nations, 1987), 59; emph. mine.

Where Does This Path Lead?

In First Corinthians 13:8, Paul mentioned a time when the gifts of prophecy, tongues, and the word of knowledge would not be necessary. In verse nine, he defined the gifts of the Holy Spirit as fragments of the whole ("we know *in part,* and we prophesy *in part"*) and was explicit as to why and when they shall pass away: "For we know in part, and we prophesy in part; but *when the perfect comes,* the *partial* will be done away" (1 Cor. 13:9-10). Attempts have been made (in vain) to use these verses to bolster the argument that the gifts of the Holy Spirit are not for today. Proponents of this view claim that the phrase "that which is perfect" refers to the completed canon of Scripture, and since the Bible is now complete, we no longer have a need for the gifts. *Reductio absurdum!*[16] (Loosely translated, that means: "That dog won't hunt!")

Since the whole concept that the gifts are no longer necessary is linked to the phrase, "when the *perfect* comes," we must analyze the word *perfect* as it appears in the Greek. The Greek word for "perfect" is *teleios,* which means: "complete (in various applications of labor, *growth,* mental and moral character, etc.) completeness: *of full age,* [mature] man, perfect."[17] *Teleios* occurs five times meaning "mature, adult." In Ephesians 4:13 the Church is figuratively called a "grown man," and in Colossians 1:28, the *grown man* is the goal of the apostle's instructions.[18] The following Scripture illustrates how Paul used the term *teleios:* "Until we all attain to the unity of the faith, and of the knowledge of the Son of God, to a mature [*teleios*] man, to the measure of the stature which belongs to the fulness of Christ" (Eph. 4:13; see also Col. 1:28).

Teleios is used to mean "perfect" in some instances in the New Testament. The following will clearly establish why, in this instance (in 1 Cor. 13:10), it *cannot* mean "perfect." Verse 11 is a continuation of the thought established in the preceding verse (v. 10), and thus cannot (indeed *must* not) be separated from it. Notice that when these two verses are held together in context, verse 11 illustrates quite

---

16. Disproof of a proposition by showing the absurdity of its inevitable conclusion.
17. *Strong's* #5046; emph. mine.
18. Brown, *New International Dictionary,* Vol. 2, 62; emph. mine.

clearly what Paul meant in verse ten: "When I was a *child*, I used to speak as a *child*, think as a *child*, reason as a *child; when I became a man* [matured], I did away with *childish* things" (1 Cor. 13:11). Paul's meaning is eminently clear. The operative concept of these verses is established in the foundational thought of *spiritual maturity* (v. 10), as opposed to "something perfect," or "some perfect time." Notice that in verse eight he mentioned tongues (an oral gift) plus prophecy and knowledge (two mental gifts), while in verse 11 he also spoke of one oral ("speak") and two mental functions ("think, reason"). Coincidence? I think not. Referring to anything other than maturity would have been a radical departure from his prior metaphor. Paul's emphasis is not that the gifts are to be despised; on the contrary, He subsequently taught that they are to be coveted (see 1 Cor. 14:1). As Paul grew up physically, he certainly didn't cease to "speak, think, or reason." Actually, with maturity those faculties greatly improved. His accentuation is that maturity in Christ is to be our major goal; because at that point, something far greater than the gifts of the Holy Spirit awaits. The contrast in their ability to minister in the realm of the Holy Spirit will then be as marked as the baby's "ma-ma" and "da-da" are to the vocabulary of someone with a doctorate in languages.

I'm certainly not suggesting that we should now dispense with the gifts because the Church has already grown up—because it has not. What I *am* suggesting is that as individuals mature spiritually and the life of Jesus (instead of the self-life) becomes the motivating force in their lives, they will increasingly manifest the life and ministry of Jesus. They will find themselves functioning in the Spirit realm as Jesus did, in total yieldedness to the Father. Many Christians find it difficult to believe that mere flesh-and-blood people could function as Jesus did. In that context they are absolutely correct. Flesh-and-blood people *cannot* do these things. It is not they, but "Christ in you; the hope of glory," living out *His* life and working His wonders through them!

In order to understand these truths, we must grasp the revelation contained in Paul's declaration of faith: "I have been crucified with Christ; and *it is no longer I who live*, **but Christ lives in me**" (Gal. 2:20a). When believers finally yield all to the Lordship of Jesus

Christ, He will live His life through them—and He will do today the same things He did 2000 years ago (see Heb. 13:8).

Jesus explained His impending departure to his troubled disciples by saying: "It is to your advantage that I go away; for if I do not go away, the Helper [Holy Spirit] shall not come to you; but if I go, I will send Him to you"; also: "I go away, and I will come to you" (Jn. 16:7; 14:28). The Holy Spirit spoken of in John 16:7 and the "I" in John 14:28 are one and the same, because the Holy Spirit is the Spirit of Jesus (see 2 Cor. 3:17; Gal. 4:6; Phil. 1:19). Thus, with the advent of the Holy Spirit, Jesus did return (though not the second coming) and took up residence in believers, through whom He would continue to multiply Himself around the world for centuries to come. The literal translation of James 4:5 is, "Or do you think that the Scripture speaks to no purpose: 'The Spirit which He has made to dwell in us *jealously desires us.*' "[19] The Holy Spirit "jealously desires us," and we must not frustrate His efforts to hold the reins of our lives by insisting that we can do it better. The degree of our yieldedness to the Holy Spirit will determine the extent to which Christ lives His life through us.

---

19. NASB, side note; emph. mine.

Chapter Twenty-seven

Beyond the Gifts of the Holy Spirit

Have you ever wondered, "Did Jesus' ministry operate through the gifts of the Holy Spirit?" As a young minister, I used to think so, until a revelation from Scripture convinced me otherwise. Certainly, there are resemblances between His ministries and the common features of the individual gifts. On the surface, the following two instances would appear to be the gift of "the word of knowledge": Jesus spoke to the woman at the well and told her secrets from her past; and He told Philip that He had seen him (supernaturally) under the fig tree. When He healed people, it resembled the gifts of healings in operation.

Obviously, the results were the same, but were those really the gifts of the Holy Spirit in operation, or were they perhaps the result of some higher sensitivity to the realm of the Holy Spirit that Jesus possessed? It's critical that we gain insight here, because the Church will soon be moving in the same dynamics of that supernatural realm. Paul said that the gifts are fragmentary (see 1 Cor. 13:9), whereas Jesus' ministry was perfect. To understand Jesus' ministry (and someday soon, the Church's) we must rely on Scripture:

> *Jesus therefore answered... "Truly, truly, I say to you, **the Son can do nothing of Himself, unless it is something He sees the Father doing;** for whatever the Father does, these things the Son also does in like*

manner. For the Father loves the Son, and shows Him all things that He Himself is doing; and greater works than these will He show Him, that you may marvel" (John 5:19-20).

"*...I do nothing on My own initiative,* but I speak these things as the Father taught Me" (Jn. 8:28b; see also, Jn. 5:19,30; 14:10b,24b. Please read carefully and *prayerfully.*)

The Church's failure to identify fully with Jesus' life, ministry, power, and anointing is obvious. What may not be so obvious to the casual observer is the *why.* Perhaps we don't *do* what Jesus did, because we don't do *what* Jesus did! In our pursuit of understanding into *what* Jesus did, please notice certain distinct patterns that run consistently through the verses above:

1. Jesus was absolutely powerless without the Father's anointing; He refused to act on His own initiative: "The Son can do *nothing* of Himself" (Jn. 5:19b).

2. He spoke only the words that the Father inspired: "I do not speak on My own initiative" (Jn. 14:10b).

3. He did *only* what He saw the Father doing: "The Son can do nothing of Himself, *unless it is something* He sees the Father doing" (Jn. 5:19b).

4. Whatever Jesus saw or heard in the Spirit, He repeated exactly as seen or heard: "for whatever the Father does, these things the Son also does *in like manner*" (Jn. 5:19b).

Jesus was finely attuned to the voice of the Holy Spirit; He was a Man who lived and walked in two separate dimensions simultaneously— the physical, sense-dominated world, and the Spirit realm. He claimed to *see* and *hear* things that others standing nearby could not. Undoubtedly, Jesus was a visionary—a seer-prophet (see 2 Cor. 4:18). He spent every moment of every day aware of all that was transpiring in the world of the Spirit. Due to His spiritual sensitivity, He was able to respond instantly, consistently, and properly to every need. He constantly observed the Father at work, then physically *acted out* what He saw the Father doing. "For whatever the Father does, these things the Son also does in like manner [in the same way]" (Jn. 5:19b).

Led by the Spirit

I've often been asked why Jesus frequently healed everyone, yet at the Pool of Bethesda He healed only *one* person, and ignored a multitude of sufferers who were waiting for the moving of the healing waters (see Jn. 5:1-9,17). The answer is really quite simple: Jesus walked away because the Father walked away. In verse 17, Jesus said, "My Father is working until now, and I Myself am working." Having just worked one notable miracle, any one of us might have been tempted to continue the miracle service even after the Father was finished. But to have done so would have been to lay empty hands on empty heads, and achieve empty results. Contrary to many ministers today, Jesus cared absolutely nothing for crowds, fame, applause, or the accolades of men. His only desire was to please the Father who had commissioned Him. Just one chapter prior to the Bethesda incident, He said, "My food is to do the will of Him who sent Me, and to accomplish His work" (Jn. 4:34). Later, in John 8:29b, He said, "For I *always* do the things that are pleasing to Him." (Perhaps we don't *do* what Jesus did, because we don't do *what* Jesus did!)

For reasons known only to Him, the Father has chosen to work through the human instrumentality of believers (see Eph. 3:9-12). God has even refused to allow angels the privilege of preaching the gospel (see Acts 10:1-6, 21-22, 30-32). The Spirit of God desires to lead, guide, direct, and instruct us in what to do or say and when and where to do so, even as He did Jesus. "He jealously desires the Spirit which He has made to dwell in us" (Jas. 4:5b). But it remains our responsibility to become the instruments that carry out His will. First and foremost, we must *know* His will. This leads us back full cycle to, "He who has an ear, *let him hear* what the Spirit says to the churches" (Rev. 2:7a,11a,17a,29; 3:6,13,22) (Perhaps we don't *do* what Jesus did, because we don't do *what* Jesus did!)

The following is a frail (and very partial) attempt to explain how I believe the Holy Spirit worked in Jesus' ministry:

As the Father (who is Spirit) walked down a certain street, Jesus followed. (It was not mere rhetoric when Jesus said that He did *nothing* unless He saw the Father doing it.) When the Father stood before a sick person and laid His hands upon him for healing, Jesus then stood precisely where He had seen the Father stand, said the same words He had heard Him speak, and the person was healed.

This example is an intentional oversimplification, used to illustrate the spiritual dynamics at work in the ministry of Jesus—and the future ministry of the Church.

Where Is That Church *Now?*

Sinners love to taunt Christians with the question, "If God is such a loving God, how come there's so much sickness in this world?" The answer has nothing to do with an uncaring *God*, but has a great deal to do with an *unfeeling, uncaring, unhearing, and unseeing Church*. This is largely due to the Church's uncaring attitude, which in turn spawns apathy. To counter that spirit, it is imperative that we become sensitive to His voice and become able to hear and see into the dimension of Spirit. Only then will we be equipped with the same degree of spiritual sensitivity that Jesus possessed, and only then will healings and miracles of every description become the norm for the Church. Granted, there are many other scriptural reasons why some individuals don't receive healing. I wrote an entire book on this subject.[1] The following illustration will examine only one hypothesis. Consider this scenario:

> Christian, Johnny Doesn't-Care-to-See, is walking down the street. Coming his way is a paralyzed man in a wheelchair. The Father (who is Spirit and can't be seen by natural sight) stands beside the wheelchair with His hands laid upon the paralytic, prepared to heal him. It now becomes the responsibility of Johnny Doesn't-Care-to-See to be sensitive to the Holy Spirit. He must see (perceive) what the Father is doing and he must respond by walking over to the man and laying his own hands on him just as he had seen the Father do. As a result of his obedience, he would see the man healed (see Acts 3:1-9). Sadly, that *doesn't* happen. Instead of perceiving the intentions of the Holy Spirit, he yields to the flesh and is distracted by the bright red Corvette driving past. His attention thus diverted, the paralytic (and the opportunity to be used by God) passes him by. Probably no one will ever know of this invisible scenario. They will never know that a loving, caring God came by to heal. Because a non-sensitive believer missed his spiritual revelation, unbelievers will continue to blame the paralytic's plight on an unfeeling, uncaring *God*.

---

1. Burton Seavey, *Why Doesn't God Heal Me?* (Carol Stream, IL: Creation House Publishers, 1978).

Absurd? Absolutely not! God has chosen to involve His people in everything He has planned to do. Normal Christian living should include a keen awareness of the spiritual dimension. We should *expect* God to use us! *To whatever extent the Church fails to live in sensitivity to the Holy Spirit, to that degree a suffering world remains in pain.*

A friend of mine, who co-pastored a church with her husband, wept as she related the following story to me:

> While in prayer she had a vision of herself walking down a certain street in the town where she lived. As she stood on the sidewalk in front of a jewelry store, a paralytic on crutches approached her. She saw herself walk up to him, lay her hands on him, and in the name of Jesus, command him to be made whole. Immediately he dropped his crutches and was completely healed. Because of this miracle, a crowd rapidly gathered and she proclaimed Christ to them.

> A week later she found herself standing in front of the same jewelry store she had seen in the vision. The man on crutches approached. God was poised to visit that city with a spiritual shock wave of irrefutable power. Suddenly questions flooded her mind: "What if I've made a mistake? What if it's not God? What if the man doesn't get healed? I'll look so foolish! What if..." The "what ifs" prevailed and she disregarded the vision. As the crippled man continued on his way, he never knew how close he had come to receiving his miracle and an entire city never knew the blessings of its aborted divine visitation.

This was the means by which God had intended to bring a spiritual awakening to this local church and community. The church had grown prior to this time, but never grew again after the fruitless vision. (And who knows how many other churches would have been energized if a citywide revival had broken out?) These pastors continued on in an unfruitful ministry for several years. Disillusioned and broken in spirit, they eventually forsook their calling and returned to secular life. (Contrasted with "what might have been," note the fruits of obedience in Acts 9:10-19; 10:1-48.)

Friends of mine, Rick and Dottie Calhoon, while on their daily walk, happened to pass a Wesleyan church. They noticed a gentleman working on the church sign, and spoke briefly to him. They continued their walk, when all at once the Holy Spirit said, "Go back and pray for that man." In immediate response to the Holy Spirit's prompting, they returned and asked if they could pray with him. He warmly responded in the affirmative. In conversation he told them that he was the pastor of the church and his heart was desperately hungry for the things of the Holy Spirit. Rick (a layman) was asked to preach every Sunday morning for the next month, during which time he introduced the congregation to the Person of the Holy Spirit. I have since developed an ongoing relationship with that pastor, and have established a School of the Holy Spirit in his church. He recently testified that his church has more than doubled in size since the school came there. All this because believers were sensitive and obedient to the prompting of the Holy Spirit.

Because I have cultivated this sensitivity in my own life, the Holy Spirit often reveals to me the innermost secrets of strangers' hearts. He has often directed me to prophesy to people in restaurants, on airplanes, and even once at the scene of an automobile accident. In every instance, I've seen tears, as the Spirit of God (through the prophetic word) reached inside and touched areas of need, reminding them that He cared. (Perhaps we don't *do* what Jesus did, because we don't do *what* Jesus did!)

Visions

In a ministry that has spanned more than 38 years, I've experienced thousands of visions. Every single vision has come to pass precisely as the Spirit showed it to me. This is due, first of all, to the faithfulness of God. Secondly, it is due to the fact that I have always been careful to act out (by saying and doing) precisely what was shown to me in the visions—nothing more or less. An illustration here might be worth a thousand words:

It was a Saturday night, and I was ministering in Caribou, Maine. My head was bowed while the pastor led the congregation in prayer. Suddenly I was in a vision. I was in a dark valley, through which a river flowed. In front of me and to my left was a slightly built, balding man dressed in an olive green suit. He was kneeling over a tree stump (at a 45-degree angle to me), weeping heavily as he prayed. As I watched, an angel descended, caught him up in his arms, and flew down to the middle of the river, where he baptized him. As the angel brought him up out of the water, the man raised his hands in praise, and immediately the valley became as bright as noonday. Then the vision disappeared.

The Holy Spirit said, "The valley is a valley of sickness and despair, and the man is one of My little ones who is ill. The river is a healing stream, and the angel is My ministering messenger." I then asked, "When will this take place?" Immediately I felt a tap on my shoulder. A deacon stood before me and requested that I come downstairs to pray for a Brother Belanger who was extremely ill. The Holy Spirit spoke to me instantly saying, "This is it. Go, doubting nothing!"

On the way downstairs (the symbolic "valley" of my vision) I learned that Brother Belanger's stomach was riddled with ulcers. He was scheduled to undergo surgery the following Tuesday to remove a large portion of his stomach. His pain was so intense that he could not stand upright. Upon entering the room I observed the slightly built, balding man in the olive green suit, exactly as I had seen in my vision. He was kneeling over a chair at a 45-degree angle to me, praying and weeping heavily.

He looked up at me through tear-filled eyes as I described the details of my vision to him. I explained that in the vision I was simply an onlooker—that is, I was not *personally* involved with his healing. I said, "In the vision, when you stood upright in the river and raised your hands in praise to the Lord, you were healed. When you are in the same position, doing the same thing, you will be healed. Please stand up and raise your hands in praise." An *intense* effort ensued. I had just asked a man bent over in unbearable pain, to stand upright and raise his hands above his head. I waited for what seemed an eternity (in reality, probably no more than a minute or two) as with great difficulty he got to his feet, still slightly bent over. I said, "Now raise your hands and praise the Lord. Then you will be exactly as I saw you in the vision, and you will be healed." After another great struggle he slowly straightened up and inched his hands upward. When they were above his head, the power of God fell on him. He began shouting and jumping as he danced around the room—perfectly healed!

On Tuesday, the surgeon became agitated when his patient refused to be prepped for surgery without further x-rays. The doctor displayed his prior x-rays and pointed out the many dark spots, each one of which represented an ulcer. When Brother Belanger could not be dissuaded, the doctor appeased him by ordering *one* new x-ray, then a second, then a third, and a fourth, and *none* of them revealed even a single ulcer! The doctor scratched his head in disbelief and discharged him as healed. That miracle happened more than 25 years ago, yet a recent contact with his relatives disclosed that he has never again suffered with ulcers. Praise the Lord!

Hasten the day when our ministries extend beyond the fragmentary gifts of the Spirit, and we walk in ultimate sensitivity to the Holy Spirit. Then we will perceive the dimension of the Spirit as easily as we currently see the three-dimensional world. O, sublime moment, when our flesh becomes dominated by our spirits—as one with the Holy Spirit—and we will be consumed in our Father's will. The shock wave generated by Jesus of Nazareth, 2,000 years ago, will be multiplied through myriads of believers worldwide! (Perhaps we don't *do* what Jesus did, because we don't do *what* Jesus did!)

Beware of the Spooky Spirituals

I would understand if some of my readers are sounding the alarm to beware of the spooky spirituals (*i.e.,* Granola Christians, nuts, fruits, and flakes) and Charis*maniacs*. Sadly, the above-named weirdos *claim* to be led by the Spirit, but their elevators don't go all the way up to the top floor—their lights are on, but there's no one home. The Church in every generation has been plagued by these eccentric, glassy-eyed people who hang around the fringes, but I adamantly refuse to discard my birthright because of them. We don't burn all our 20-dollar bills because there's a rash of counterfeit 20-dollar bills in circulation, do we? Yet, that is the approach taken by many church leaders when dealing with spiritual gifts. Perhaps the real indictment lies not so much with the spooky spirituals, but with Full Gospel churches that refuse to provide a forum where sincere believers manifest genuine giftedness. Having abdicated by neglect their right to be constantly led by the Spirit, they have allowed the spooky spirituals to practice the counterfeit without challenge.

Chapter Twenty-eight

Another Peek Into the Mirror

I sometimes shake my head in disbelief when I see Christians wallow in their shallow denominational wading pools when the vastness of God's pure spiritual ocean is available to them. Some of them have obviously made their choice. But for the most part, many Christians languish in their muddied puddles because no one has ever pointed them to the ocean. They wander about in ankle-deep water, oblivious to the fact that not far from them is water to swim in. These poor souls echo the early Ephesian converts, "...we have not even heard whether there is a Holy Spirit" (Acts 19:2b). But now someone *has* told you and you need never be the same. But you have also now become responsible for the knowledge imparted to you (see Lk. 12:48b).

James wrote that the Word of God is like a mirror (see Jas. 1:22-25), and explained that some look into the mirror, go on their way, and forget what they saw there. Because the mirror of the Word is painfully truthful, not everyone can endure its revelations. We often think of ourselves as more righteous than we really are, but an honest look into the mirror quickly dispels that notion. Often, the first look frightens us by revealing something we would rather not see; so, like the man in James 1:24, we walk away from the mirror and immediately dismiss its reflected image.

"For now we see in a mirror dimly, but then face to face; now I know in part, *but then I shall know fully* just as I also have been fully known" (1 Cor. 13:12). The mirror of the Word is multidimensional, revealing not only what we *are*, but as we continue gazing, it reveals what we *shall* be. Paul wrote, "For now we see in a mirror dimly...." The Greek word translated "dimly" literally means, "in an enigma—a dark saying; obscureness."[1] W.E. Vine says: "*Ainigma* is akin to the verb *ainissomai* 'to *hint* obscurely.' The allusion is to Num. 12:8 (Septuagint), 'not in (*dia*, "by means of") dark speeches (literally, *enigmas*)' [emph. mine]. The literal Greek text reads, "we see for yet through a mirror *in a riddle*."[2] Implicit in Paul's statement is that he had composed a riddle containing a *hidden meaning*.

Paul wrote, "If there is knowledge, it will be done away" (1 Cor. 13:8). No serious examiner of that verse would believe that knowledge will cease to exist. The word used for "knowledge" is *gnosis*: "knowing (the act), *ie.* (by impl.) knowledge...science."[3] Scientific knowledge is that which is obtained by *investigation, searching, and trial and error*, and because it is fragmentary, continues to grow—*that* knowledge will cease to exist. Paul contrasted this carnal knowledge with the "full knowledge" (strongly implied in verse 12), where the word for "know fully" and "fully known," is *epignosis*: "recognition, *ie.* (by impl.) *full discernment...knowledge*."[4] Most would agree that someday supernatural knowledge—full knowledge—will replace carnal, fragmentary knowledge. Evangelicals believe that this knowledge is imparted to believers after death or the rapture, but I am firmly convinced that God wants His people to recognize that "...we [presently] have the mind of Christ" (1 Cor. 2:16).

Many have assumed that the phrase "face to face" in First Corinthians 13:12 refers to our encounter with Christ at His second coming. Building on that erroneous assumption, they conclude that verses 10-12 must *also* refer to that same event. However, any conclusion based upon incorrect information can only be likewise *incorrect*! (Even if those verses did have something to do with Christ's coming, Paul makes it very clear that there is an *enigma*—that he has also concealed a further hidden meaning, hint, something obscure to be

---

1. *Strong's* #135.
2. *The Interlinear Greek New Testament*—Marshall's literal English translation with the Nestle Greek text (Grand Rapids, MI: Zondervan Pub. House, 1974), emph. mine.
3. *Strong's* #1108.
4. *Strong's* #1922.

discovered there. God's communication with Moses was "face to face" (Ex. 33:11, which literally translated means "mouth to ear"), yet Moses was forbidden to see the face of God (see Ex. 33:20,23). As I will discuss in a later chapter, in Exodus 35:13 we find that the word *face* also means "Presence." The Greek word for *face* as used by Paul in the phrase, "face to face," is also used in the New Testament to denote "Presence."[5]

Let's read First Corinthians 13:12 in the light of what we've just discussed: "For now we see in a mirror dimly [in a riddle], but then face to face [Presence to presence; Person to person, God's mouth to my ear]; now I know in part, but then I shall know fully just as I also have been fully known." Having been in the Presence of God, Moses' face radiated His glory. The people feared the radiance of God's Presence—so much so that Moses placed a veil over his face to conceal the glory (see Ex. 34:29-35). Isaiah prophesied concerning a glorious day when God would remove the veil forever: "And on this mountain He will swallow up the covering which is over all peoples, even the veil which is stretched over all nations" (Is. 25:7). That same glory remained hidden from the people until it began to be revealed again in the Person of Jesus Christ:

> ...*the same veil remains unlifted,* **because it is removed in Christ,** but to this day whenever Moses is read, a veil lies over their heart; **but whenever a man turns to the Lord, the veil is taken away.** Now the Lord is the Spirit; and where the Spirit of the Lord is, there is liberty. But we all, **with unveiled face beholding as in a mirror the glory of the Lord, are being transformed into the same image from glory to glory,** *just as from the Lord, the Spirit* (2 Corinthians 3:14-18).

God currently desires to speak with His children "mouth to ear," and now that the veil (which concealed God's glory) has been removed in Christ, we should be able to behold His glory even as Moses did. The enigma referred to earlier is the mirror *itself,* which reflects not only the present (what we *are*) but the future (what we can and *should* become). Paul said that now we look into a mirror "with unveiled faces," that is, with nothing to obscure the reflection. The Word of God is a mystically wonderful mirror. It not only reflects our sins

---

5.   Acts 3:13,19; 5:41; 2 Cor. 10:1; 1 Thess. 2:17; 2 Thess. 1:9; Heb. 9:24.

and failures, it reflects that which we have the capacity to become—
the image of Christ, implanted in every believer. In its reflection the
mirror says, "On the one hand, here is what you *are* now; on the other
hand, (reflecting Jesus, and the way God views you in Him) here is
what God will *make* of you!"

Our preaching desperately needs to reflect a healthy balance. So
often ministers harp only on the sins of the people, and neglect to reflect the latent image of Christ that God sees in them. Constantly
hearing only about our sin leads to discouragement, and often precipi-
tates a cycle of even more sinful living. We who preach must be careful to inspire believers by unveiling the holy image within them,
giving them something high and noble to which they can aspire.

How often I've heard the lament, "At my church it seems that all
they preach about is sin, but instead of conviction, I feel condemna-
tion. What should I do?" Don't walk—**run** for your (spiritual) life!
Find a church where they will instill in you what God's Word says
about you. I've found that people will attempt to rise to the level set
before them. There is often much sin in churches where evil is constantly emphasized—because that's the level of expectancy pastors
have set before the people. There's nothing wrong with pointing out
sin. After all, the Bible certainly does, but it also clearly paints a picture of saints on higher ground, calling to those in the valley, "Come!
Join us!"

The holy image is there in the mirror. Having once caught a
glimpse of it we can no longer be the same. Paul said as we behold the
glory of the Lord we "are *being transformed into the same image* from
glory to glory" (2 Cor. 3:18b). The Greek word for "transformed" is the
same word used in Romans 12:2, and has to do with a gradual process. Once we truly behold the holy image, our journey will cease being from defeat to defeat, or from failure to failure. From that grand
moment of revelation our journey will be from *glory to glory*.

Perhaps deep inside your spirit you already knew there was a
much higher plane in Christ to be attained. This book has confirmed
that for you, but no one has ever told you how to get there. Instead of
going from glory to glory, you've been going from frustration to frustration. But there *is* a path that will lead you into the Holy of
Holies—and higher ground. I would like to be your guide as you journey on into the very heart of God.

Chapter Twenty-nine

Into the Holy of Holies

Most of Chapter Twenty-nine had already been completed when I took a break from writing in order to attend a Leadership Conference. The (previously unannounced) theme of the entire conference was "Entering Into the Holy of Holies—Into the Very Presence of God." The preaching contained many truths that I had already written in the chapter I had entitled, "Into the Holy of Holies."

Following the last service of the conference, I experienced one of the most powerful Holy Spirit encounters of my entire life. I lay on my face, sobbing before God for nearly two hours, overcome with the beauty of His Presence. When I arose to leave the sanctuary, I asked God to please not let anyone speak to me. I just wanted to be alone with my reflections of our time together in the Spirit. A lady immediately approached me requesting "just a couple of minutes of your time." I was about to say "no" when the Holy Spirit instructed me to say "yes." What she said overwhelmed me:

"While you were on your face before God," she said, "the Holy Spirit began giving me words for you. He said to tell you that what you have seen and heard here at the conference will be the next chapter, entitled 'Into the Holy of Holies', in your new book."

Not only did that sister (a layperson) know in the Spirit that I was writing a new book (of which she had no personal *knowledge), she even knew the exact title of the chapter about which she was prophesying, and that it was the **next**! (That's almost enough to make one believe in the gift of prophecy!) She went on to tell me explicit details of several other things about which God had been speaking to me. She explained that the major emphasis in my future ministry would be to prepare the Bride for the Bridegroom. That excited me, as God had been indicating this to me for some time. (Her pastor has since told me that she is a genuine, trusted, and respected prophetess in her home church.)*

*By themselves, the truths outlined in this book can be dangerous. We have talked about a shock wave of power—power beyond anything the world has ever witnessed to date! Accompanying this shock wave will be mighty enduements of power, gifts of the Holy Spirit, signs, wonders, miracles, and a Church that is a supernaturally equipped army—**and that's only the beginning**! There are few Christians (in the Church's present state of development) who could handle such power without slipping into delusions of grandeur, mingled with a large dose of egotistical megalomania.*

*This chapter lends the balance needed to bring doctrinal stability and unity of structure to the overall picture. If some readers have missed the **central** theme of this book—it is **Christ in you** doing His works. It is **He** who reigns, **He** who performs His supernatural feats—**not we**!*

*If after reading this chapter you are unwilling to make a commitment to implement its concepts in your life, please reread it. If you then remain unwilling to commit to seeking only His Presence before all and above all else, then please disregard the first 29 chapters—they are not meant for you. "Seekest thou great things for thyself? **Seek them not**!" (Jer. 45:5 KJV)*

I'm deeply convinced that the truths that follow will be the major theme in the next great Holy Spirit shock wave. I'm pleased to have seen this revelation and to have already received the approval of the Holy Spirit upon this written witness. May God bless you as you enter...

* * *

"But the people that do *know* their God shall be strong, *and do exploits*" (Dan. 11:32b KJV). Most Christians don't *know* the Lord Jesus Christ! I can almost hear the indignant rebuttal of my readers, "Oh yes I do! I'm saved, so of course I know the Lord!" Please understand where I'm coming from here. I'm not disputing their salvation, but the depth of their *relationship*. When describing the most intimate union between the first man and woman God said, "And Adam *knew* Eve his wife; and she conceived" (Gen. 4:1a KJV). You don't come to know someone intimately by simply meeting him; those kinds of relationships are cultivated over years, through much quality time spent together. I've met many political leaders: mayors, governors, senators, and congressmen. I've spent long hours in conversation with some of them, and others have even done political favors for me—but there isn't one whom I would say I *know*. I've met them, but I don't *know* them. Likewise, for some Christians, whatever knowledge of Him they have gained, has come from reading *about* Him, or from hearing sermons *about* Him. Thus, some may know volumes *about* Him, yet barely *know* Him at all.

Do you see now why I said most Christians don't know the Lord? They have met Him at the cross, left their sins and their burdens with Him and, for the most part, after a brief period of spiritual fervor, have gone their own ways. They have *met* Him, but they don't *know* Him. For many of these infant Christians He is no more than their heavenly babysitter.

Statistics tell us that a large percentage of people who claim to be Christians don't pray at all; and the average prayer time of those who do is five minutes a day! These same people attend church on the average of only once a week. During their hour and a half in church they will sing and worship (?) for approximately 20-25 minutes, which is the sum total of the time they will personally spend participating in the service. The rest of the service will consist of someone else ministering to them. This is hardly the way to develop a meaningful intimacy with someone—neither can deep, true love be nurtured in this cursory fashion. Is it any wonder then that the Church is so spiritually anemic? Much of the fault lies with those who minister, for simply introducing new believers to Jesus Christ but then failing to guide them into cultivating and nurturing a passionate *relationship* with Him.

"We do new Christians the gravest of injustices when we teach them how to 'play the part' of a Christian without giving them the inward reality of Jesus Christ. We teach them how to 'act holy', how to live 'righteously', and how to 'talk faith,' and then require it all of them. But unless we have in truth actually led them to Jesus Christ who will be the source of all these fruits, we have only succeeded in teaching them how to imitate the Christian life, and have not at all helped them to become real Christians.

"We must stop teaching unholy people how to act holy, and instead take them by the hand and lead them by the way of the altars of abandonment and surrender into the Holiest of all— into the very Presence of the Almighty, around whose throne seraphs eternally cry, 'Holy, Holy, Holy'.

"The real sin of unbelief is to perpetuate the spawning of 'imitation' Christians who have never given themselves to Jesus, who have known very little encounter with God, who have never really 'tasted' of the Lord, and whose Christianity consists solely in religious duties and an outward identification with a church and a set of beliefs, ethics and doctrines."[1]

Holiness has absolutely nothing to do with rules, regulations, rites, or rituals, while it has *everything* to do with our relationship with Jesus Christ. Rev. David Cartledge, who was then the general superintendent of the Assemblies of God in Australia, once prophesied to me. One of the prophetic words was, "Seek My face." I'm embarrassed to say that I didn't fully know what that meant. Oh, I could have given a theological answer, but I knew inwardly that there was a far deeper meaning that I was determined to uncover. A few weeks after receiving the prophecy, while reading Exodus 35:13, the phrase, "bread of the Presence," caught my attention. Looking up the meaning of the word "Presence," I found that it also meant "Face." There, as simple as that, was my answer. Whenever God exhorts us to "seek His Face," He is in reality encouraging us to "seek His Presence" which is, above all else, what is most needed in each of our lives. The Bread of

---

1. Malcolm Webber, *To Enjoy Him Forever* (Kimmell, IN: Pioneer Books, 1990), 47,50,54. I highly recommend this book.

the Presence was for the priests alone—and they *feasted* on it. We the Church, as a royal priesthood, have unrestricted access to the holy Bread of the Presence—yet we often content ourselves to eat at McDonald's. Because you must hunger before you can feast (see Mt. 5:6), perhaps we are too often in the mood only for spiritual fast food. "Come and dine," the Bridegroom calls to His bride (see Song 2:4), yet we rush to fill our stomachs with the pigs' husks (see Lk. 15:16) of temporal gratifications, while His banqueting table, spread with every good thing, *contains many vacant places.*

The truth is we seek His *hand* far more than we seek His *Face.* We seek *His* instead of seeking *Him!* Our desire is to receive from His hand those things of which we have need (or greed), when our longing should be directed toward Him who is the fountainhead of every blessing. How could one have *Him* and not have all that the human heart could by any means desire? If ever we could find Him in all His glory, majesty, and splendor, then all that is of earth would so pale by comparison that we would gladly go naked and hungry (not that He would allow that) and never care. If we were ever to behold His beauty and comprehend that He calls us His beloved, everything of this earth that we deem so necessary would become vain (see Phil. 3:8). The wedding song of the ages fills the atmosphere when we eagerly seek His Presence—our only request then is to know Him who is altogether lovely. "Let me see your form, let me hear your voice; for your voice is sweet, and your form is lovely" (Song 2:14).

Why do we fill our church services with so much that is not His Presence, when the *only* thing of any true consequence *is* His Presence? After church we often hear remarks such as, "That was such a nice service," or "Pastor, that was a nice sermon," or "The choir sang such a nice song." Actually, none of those nice things truly matters after all. As ministers, our primary (perhaps our *only*) function is to usher people into the Presence of God—nothing more, *nothing* less. If we fail to do this, then we have totally failed! People (especially sinners) ought to leave church with the awesome sense of having been in the Presence of Almighty God.

Preachers harp on sin in order to convict people of their sins. They compose long lists of things church members can't do and places they can't go, in the vain hope of making them holy. Preachers and congregations alike struggle year after heartrending year to keep the list, only to find that, after painstakingly adhering to all of the "thou shalt nots" of their church or denomination, they still are not *holy*! Why do we struggle so to produce holiness, when only the Presence of God in our lives can accomplish this? Note how simply a few minutes in the Presence of the Almighty altered Isaiah's life forever:

> *In the year of King Uzziah's death,* **I saw the Lord** sitting on a throne, lofty and exalted, with the train of His robe filling the temple. ... And one [seraphim] *called out to another and said, "Holy, Holy, Holy, is the Lord of hosts, the whole earth is full of His glory." ...* **Then I said, "Woe is me, for I am ruined! Because I am a man of unclean lips, and I live among a people of unclean lips;** *for my eyes have seen the King, the Lord of hosts"* (Isaiah 6:1,3,5).

In those few minutes he *saw*—he *heard*—he *knew*. He *saw* the Lord sitting enthroned; he *heard* seraphim crying "Holy, Holy, Holy, is the Lord of hosts"; and immediately, without any earthly persuasion, without choirs singing, without a masterfully preached three-point sermon, he *knew* he was unholy—and that brief encounter transformed the rest of his life! What was there about that fleeting moment in time that brought about such change in Isaiah? He had genuinely encountered the Presence of Almighty God for himself. As we behold Him, our desire is directed toward Him and Him alone. To be like Him will become our all-consuming passion.

When we realize that holiness is the very nature of God, we will understand that self cannot reproduce Him. Only He can do that. With what pity He must view our paltry human efforts, which can never generate His holiness. The institutional church attempts (in vain) to legislate a "clothesline holiness," dictating what Christians can or cannot wear, how short it may be or how long it must be, where they can or cannot go, what they can or cannot see, and what they can or cannot do. They end up comparing themselves with others as the measure of their holiness (see 2 Cor. 10:12). By contrast, when we spend time in His Presence, *He* becomes our only comparison. The sorry part of all this is that they actually believe that the keeping of all these laws makes one holy (see Heb. 7:18-19; Is. 64:6). Yet all they have succeeded in doing is to create a counterfeit holiness that deceives people into believing that they are *holy* for all the wrong reasons. Often Christians choose not to violate the code of holiness as set forth by their church/denomination because they don't want to offend their pastor, their church, or their denomination. These are all poor substitutes for the only reason not to commit sin: we ought not to sin against Him simply because we don't want to offend our Lover, our Lord! We must fall too passionately in love with Him to offend Him by sinning. But that depth of love can only be produced by spending much quality time in His Presence. If the institutional, brand X, commercial-strength holiness will not suffice to satisfy God's require-ments, then *how* and *where* can God's genuine formula be found? The answer is much simpler than you might imagine.

Transmitted Holiness

I often wondered what prompted the apostle Paul to send out pieces of cloth taken from his clothing to heal the sick and deliver de-moniacs (see Acts 19:11-12). The Jews had a belief that holy people transmitted virtue even into their clothing, evidenced in the account of the woman with the issue of blood who thought, "If I just touch His garments, I shall get well" (Mk. 5:28; see also 5:25-34).

This belief must have originated from the passage in Ezekiel 42:14, where it says that the garments of the priests who ministered before God were holy. Ezekiel 44:19 explains this even further:

> *And when they go out into the outer court...to the people, they shall put off their garments in which they have been ministering and lay them in the holy chambers; then they shall put on other garments **that they might not transmit holiness to the people with their garments**"* (Ezekiel 44:19).

This same thought of transmitting holiness to the people is repeated in Ezekiel 46:20. The act of having ministered before God in His sanc-tuary was sufficient for their garments to have become impregnated with the Holy Presence, which was somehow transmittable to the people.

Isaiah tells us that God's name is Holy (see Is. 57:15). That doesn't simply mean that God's name is special (although it *is*); it means far more than that. It states that one of the names attributed to God is "Holy," which immediately reveals that He is intrinsically (by nature) *Holy*. Anything placed in His Presence will, to some de-gree, absorb that Presence—thus, *holiness*!

The institutional church has spent centuries instructing followers that the path to holiness was to be followed by going to church and
keeping certain rules and regulations, when in fact that's not true at
all. If we could produce our own holiness, then we wouldn't need God;
we would just be able to pull ourselves up by our own bootstraps. The
only way to *true* holiness is to spend much quality time in the Presence of Almighty God. No one, having been in that Presence, can continue to love the flesh or the pleasures of this world. An inspired
writer once penned these words:

> Turn your eyes upon Jesus,
> Look full in His wonderful face.
> And the things of earth will grow strangely dim,
> In the light of His glory and grace.[2]

The brilliance of His Presence, brighter than the most powerful
laser beam, will cause the scales of worldliness to fall away, and we
will see Jesus only. To spend time in His Presence is to die to self and
live to Christ (see Gal. 2:20). Upon returning to the earth plane after
visiting the Holy of Holies and having experienced the heavenly side,
we will forever be aware that this earth is not our home and that we
are but pilgrims here.

Why do we seek so much that is not Him, when He is *all* that we
need—the source of life itself (see Acts 17:28), the Giver of every good
and perfect gift (see Jas. 1:17)? Scripture tells us that "He is a rewarder of them that diligently seek Him" (Heb. 11:6b KJV). Perhaps
you have understood that verse to mean, "He is a rewarder of them
who diligently seek Him for things—seek Him for *blessing*—seek Him
for *healing*—seek him for *finances*—seek him *for...*etc., etc." If this is
your concept, then you have completely misunderstood the intent of
the verse. He rewards those who diligently seek *Him*, and nothing
else! So often we approach God concerned only with our shopping lists
that we call prayers. (I wonder if some Christians even bring their favorite catalogue with them when they pray.) While it is not wrong to
pray for things (Scripture encourages us to "ask, seek, and knock,"
even to the point of persistence), what many don't understand is that
when the Bible enjoins us to pray, there is a scriptural presumption

---

2. Used by permission.

that we have already sought the Presence of the Giver *first!* Matthew 6:19-34 will help you to understand what God considers proper precedence. He doesn't rebuke His children because they seek things that are needful, "...for your heavenly Father *knows that you need all these things*," but God has established His order of priorities: "But seek *first* His kingdom and His righteousness; *and all these things shall be added to you.*" All too often we put the cart before the horse by first seeking after things and second after God. Sadly, many Christians seek *only* for things, and *never* for God.

For some of God's people their seeking takes on what they consider to be a spiritual form, as they pursue spiritual gifts, ministries, and large churches. But have they first (or at all) sought His Face, His Presence? (Nothing we do or accomplish, no matter how great, is truly spiritual without His Presence as an integral part of it.) You can attend a thousand church growth conferences, learn how each pastor built his great congregation, have your head filled with all the "how to's," and still come away with an empty heart. Has there ever been a church growth conference where the speakers have exhorted the attending ministers simply to "seek the Face (Presence) of God until He tells you what to do"? (Men have the tendency to *do* something, and then ask God to *bless* it, instead of finding out what God is *blessing,* and then doing *that*.) "The cause of our difficulties is that we seek His gifts, His works and His ways, while ignoring Him."[3] When will we ever learn that Jesus spoke the truth when He said, "...for apart from Me you can do *nothing*" (Jn. 15:5). Truly great ministries arise out of intimate relationships within the veil. The fact is that there are no truly great ministries apart from frequent worship seasons in the Holy of Holies—no matter how large the church, or successful the program. If I could communicate only one thought to every minister, it would be the following excerpt from a letter to John G. Lake from Elder Brooks:

> "I did just wish to hold up Jesus and make you look at Him from every angle and see how transportingly beautiful He is; how all sufficient He is; how He fills all; meets every requirement; satisfies every longing; is *Himself* the equipment for every service.

---

3.   Webber, *To Enjoy Him Forever,* 57.

"Oh, John Lake [insert *your* name here], there is no other need of ours in this world or that to come, but Jesus…Oh, my Brother John, I once looked for power; wanted equipment; sought usefulness; saw gifts in the distance; knew that dominion was somewhere in the future, but, glory to God! One by one these faded, and as they faded there was a form, a figure emerged from the shadows which became clearer and more distinct as these other things faded, and when they had all passed I saw *Jesus only*."

Open to All Who *Desire* to Enter

I marvel that the very throne room of God is open to all who desire to enter there. The veil of Jesus' flesh has been rent, and the way has been prepared (see Heb. 10:19-20). The Holy of Holies is far more than simply the throne room of Heaven—it is the marriage chamber, the inner sanctum where the heavenly Bridegroom and His redeemed Bride will take up eternal residence. Please read the Song of Solomon slowly and prayerfully and gain spiritual insights into the profound intimacy shared between the Holy Lovers. Many read the Song of Songs and make jest with it, thinking it to be merely a sensual description of married love. For that gross lack of spiritual perception it was almost excluded from inclusion into Scripture. The fact is that its acceptance into biblical canon was due in large part to Rabbi Akiva, a father of rabbinic Judaism, who at the Council of Jabneh of A.D. 90 declared that, "All of the Writings are holy, *but the Song of Songs is the Holy of Holies.*"[4]

When desiring to illustrate the depth of passionate intimacy with which our love and desire for Jesus should consume us, the closest humanly understandable approximation at God's disposal was the marriage relationship. Throughout life we interrelate with thousands of people. Suddenly, one day out of those masses there emerges one special person. Your heart skips beats; your temperature rises; your hands tremble. It must be that thing called love. The hours cannot pass swiftly enough to bring you into your lover's presence and time spent with that precious one is never enough. You soon realize that no

---

4.   *Mysteries of the Bible* (Pleasantville, NY: Reader's Digest Association, 1987), 227.

one else in the whole world matters to you like that special someone. The rest of your life is not sufficient time to spend with him or her, so you plan to marry. After the vows are made and congratulations are received, you and your lover are finally alone. As you close the door behind you, you know that tonight will be different from any other night thus far. From this moment on you will never have to say farewell and go your separate ways—you belong to each other. Soon the "two will become one flesh" as (God-given) passions, born out of deep love, are shared (see Mk. 10:6-8; 1 Cor. 6:17; Eph. 5:22-33).

Thereafter, throughout life you will openly and publicly show affection for your lover—a word, a touch, a glance that says, "I love you." "This is my beloved and this is my friend" (Song 5:16). But when you desire to express the true depths of your love and passion, you will retire to the seclusion of your bed chamber. With the door closed and prying eyes forbidden, lovers communicate their love and desire for each other in a manner far transcending mere sexual contact. Herein actually is a union of *spirits* inadequately attempting to convey, with frail human bodies, the immensity of love, passion, and commitment that they have for one another. Yet this intimate relationship of man and wife is precisely what God chose to illustrate the intensity of the love and passion that should also be shared between the heavenly Lover and His Bride (see Eph. 5:22-32). Because of the exquisitely intimate depths of God's relationship with His people, when Israel went after strange gods, the Lord said they had "played the harlot" (Jer. 3:1-10).

For the most part God's people fail to understand the vast extent to which their love for Jesus can and will grow. In His High Priestly prayer, Jesus requested of the Father, "That the love wherewith Thou didst love Me may be in them" (Jn. 17:26). Jesus asked the Father to cause *the same love* (same depth, same intensity, same desire, same passion, etc.) with which He (the Father) loved Jesus, to reside in His followers also. That means that we now have the same capacity to love Jesus as the Father does. Some regard that request as no more than a rhetorical statement or a simple prayer request which doesn't have to be fulfilled. I disagree. The Father inspired the prayer (see Jn. 14:10,24), the Holy Spirit energized it, and Jesus prayed it. It *will* come to pass!

Jesus, Our Heavenly Forerunner

Although He despised the shame of it, Jesus endured the cross, because He knew the joy that was to follow (see Heb. 12:2). From the cross onward He became the heavenly Bridegroom, espoused to believers who would someday become His Bride. He entered behind the veil in the heavenly tabernacle and became our hope of eternal redemption. His position behind the veil is so secure Scripture refers to Him as our "anchor" (see Heb. 6:18-20). Jesus became our forerunner, which in the Greek is, *"prodromos,* a runner ahead—precursor."[5] Webster's Dictionary defines *precursor* as: "One who...precedes—one who...goes before *and indicates the approach of someone else."*

Imagine what Heaven must have been like in that moment when Jesus returned from His victory over sin, death, hell, and the grave, with the keys to Satan's house (death and hell) in His possession. Angels could not contain their praises and the 24 Elders around the throne leaped for joy. The jubilation of Heaven must have spilled over until the universe echoed the praises of the conquering King. Perhaps Jesus called for a moment of silence—He had an announcement to make. Every eye in Heaven fastened itself on the glory of Him who was about to speak. "They're coming! They're coming! They're coming!" He shouted. I can almost hear an archangel asking, *"Who* is coming, Lord?" "The redeemed, my Church, my beloved, my bride—will soon be here with me behind the veil. I will embrace her in arms of love, and speak of the passion that drove Me to endure the cross, making a way into the Holy of Holies for her. Yes, she will soon be here!" Sadly, only a *few* entered into this most wonderfully intimate relationship—although the chamber had been prepared for *all* of the redeemed.

So many Christians have believed that our entering behind the veil is an event that will take place after death or rapture, yet Hebrews 10:19-23 makes it clear that we have immediate present access to the Holy of Holies. Our Forerunner invites us, eagerly anticipating our arrival. How can we keep our heavenly Lover waiting? Why would anyone refuse His invitation? Most Christians do so out of ignorance,

---

5.   *Strong's* #4274.

having little or no knowledge of their positions in Christ and of the rapturous joys awaiting their entrance into His Presence.

A Glimpse Into the Holy of Holies and How to Enter There

"Enter His gates with thanksgiving, and His courts with praise. Give thanks to Him; bless His name" (Ps. 100:4). Nothing could be plainer or simpler. The Bible alludes to many mysteries, but how to enter into the Presence of God is certainly not one of them. Thanksgiving and praise will open the gates and usher you inside—because thanksgiving and praise continually reside in the Holy of Holies.

Years ago I read an article in a Chicago newspaper that gripped my interest. It was written about a leading experimental physicist who had a novel theory concerning space travel. (The writer of the article said that although there was presently no absolute proof for the physicist's theory, he had been correct on several other occasions when his contemporaries had strongly disagreed with him.) He had proven that there were several places in the universe that resonate at certain frequencies. His current hypothesis was that if we were able to cause people or things to resonate at the exact frequency of some remote place light years away, they would be transported there—not in years, but in a twinkling of an eye. Is his theory credible? Who knows? However, some similar divine law of the universe seems to be at work here in Psalm 100:4: when we praise and worship, we are transported through time and space—beyond the bounds of the most far-flung galaxies never seen by man—into the Holy of Holies, into the very Presence of God!

When we praise and worship, we are replicating (resonating to that frequency) that which is continually taking place in the Presence of God.

And the four living creatures, each one of them having six wings, are full of eyes around and within; and day and night they do not cease to say, "Holy, Holy, Holy, is the Lord God, the Almighty, who was and who is and who is to come." And when the living creatures give glory and honor and thanks to Him who sits on the throne, to Him who lives forever and ever, the twenty-four elders will fall down before Him who sits on the throne, and will worship Him who lives forever and ever, and will cast their crowns before the throne, saying, "Worthy art Thou, our Lord and our God, to receive glory and honor and power; for Thou didst create all things, and because of Thy will they existed, and were created" (Rev. 4:8-11; see also Rev. 5:11-14; 7:9-12; 19:4-7).

The entire universe resounds with His praises. This fact was forcefully brought home to me several years ago when I was caught away in a powerful vision. The Holy Spirit transported me to what seemed to be the center of the universe where I was immersed in a sea of black velvet studded everywhere with stars that sparkled like diamonds. All at once, from somewhere behind me I heard a majestic choir singing: "Hail, Hail, Lion of Judah! How wonderful you are!" I turned to see who was singing, but no one was visible. Then, suddenly, from the opposite direction another choir joined in the round of the same song. Again, there was no one visible. Then off to my right the third choir joined and soon, to my left, a fourth. As all four groups of the heavenly host sang the rounds in harmony (a harmony such as I had never heard on earth), everything in the universe seemed to reverberate with His praises. I was surrounded on all sides with pure worship! I stood there in a mixture of awe and rapture as I heard angelic choirs sing an anthem of praise to my wonderful Lord. There are no words to adequately describe the glorious music that filled the heavens and echoed within my own spirit. After having witnessed that vision, Psalm 19:1 took on a whole new meaning for me: "The heavens are telling of the glory of God; and their expanse is declaring the works of His hands."

Is God a Megalomaniac?

I've been asked by skeptics whether God suffers from megalomania.[6] "After all," they quip, "He wants everyone to repeatedly tell Him how great He is." I asked God for an answer with which to refute the skeptics' charges, and here's what I believe He said to me:

"I don't need anyone to praise Me for My sake. I know who I Am! If I needed praise, how do the skeptics think I managed before I created the angels? I didn't create the angels in order to receive worship, but as soon as they came into existence they worshiped **spontaneously***, because they witnessed My*

---

6. A psychopathological condition in which delusional fantasies of wealth, power, or *omnipotence* predominate."—Webster.

glory and splendor. When a man praises Me it is mainly for ***his*** *own sake that he does so. As he proclaims My greatness and My awesome power, and enumerates My mighty deeds,* ***he becomes convinced that I Am who I say I Am.*** *As he worships, he begins to recognize the strength of My right arm and gains assurance that I am able to be his God and to deliver him from all his enemies."*

In Psalm 34:3, David enjoined us: "O *magnify the Lord* with me, and let us exalt His name together." *Magnify* means to "make larger." It is an impossibility to "make larger" He who fills the fathomless universe: "Him who fills all in all" (Eph. 1:23); "...the high and lofty One that inhabiteth eternity..." (Is. 57:15 KJV). How then can the *finite* magnify the *Infinite*? By doing as David encouraged us to do: make God bigger *in our own sight*! One of Israel's besetting sins was that they continually limited God (see Ps. 78:40-41). For countless centuries Christianity has also lived with the concept of a pygmy God, because they have not truly realized who He is and what He can do. With David of old, I exhort you, "O magnify the Lord with me, and let us exalt His name together."

Disciple = *Discipline*

In the following chapter I will instruct you how to praise and worship effectively. Be advised in advance. There are no shortcuts. There is no back door to the Holy of Holies. In the Word, Christians are referred to as disciples, a word that has its roots in the word *discipline*. If we are to grow in the things of the Spirit and become the fulfillment of God's dream for the Church, we *must* discipline ourselves. You must diligently apply yourself. Nothing will happen if you don't take the time and make the sacrifice of self to make it happen. To the extent that you thirst after God (see Ps. 42:1-2) to that same extent you will be compelled to discipline your mind to praise and worship Him. Discipline is never easy. Like the Marine slogan, God could rightfully say to us, "I never promised you a rose garden!" But if you are willing to apply yourself to follow God's Word, then a whole new world of glorious relationship with the Almighty lies within your reach!

Throughout this book we've taken a hard look at the Church and the awesome supernatural shock wave that will be manifested through God's people—because that is the major emphasis of this volume. I would be remiss in my obligation to my readers if I did not give an overview of the greater effect ultimately produced when Christians successfully renew their minds and enter into the fullness of His Presence.

As "Christ in you, the hope of glory" becomes a reality in believers, we will embrace certain laws of the kingdom, which in the past were foreign to us because of fleshly rebellion. The following is an encapsulated list of some neglected kingdom laws:

1. The greatest must become least.

2. The meek shall inherit the earth.

3. The first shall be last.

4. It is more blessed to give than to receive, etc.

We will also come to understand that:

1. Reward for service is not retirement, but *more* service.

2. Authority is given to serve.

3. We must obey those in authority to help them to serve.

4. Victories are achieved by surrender.

5. We are safest when weaponless.

6. We attain perfect liberty by total submission.

7. We gain our lives when by grace we begin to lose them.[7]

The above list is simply an introduction. As "Children of light" (Eph. 5:8), we will begin to live out the light within us. May it be recorded of us, "*This* is the generation of those who seek Him, who seek Thy face" (Ps. 24:6).

---

7. E.W. Kenyon—selected.

Chapter Thirty

Worship—Key to the Holy of Holies

Have you ever noticed that sometimes the answers to extremely complex questions are embarrassingly simple? Some things are like that. For instance, Karl Barth, the world-renowned Swiss theologian and prolific author of more than 90 books on systematic theology, was asked to give a synopsis of his belief structure. He replied by simply quoting a child's Sunday school song: "Jesus loves me, this I know, for the Bible tells me so." That's like fitting an ocean into a thimble. He was able to take the combined study and copious writings of several decades and condense it all into the essence of one simple yet profound sentence. (Would that this chapter could be so succinct.)

One of my mother's favorite sayings was, "Sometimes you can't see the forest for the trees." The implication is that we often overlook the obvious, searching for something else—when, in fact, that "something else" is the trees themselves.

The nature of man is to search for difficult solutions to otherwise simple problems, as is reflected in the following narrative. Naaman, captain over the Syrian king's army, had contracted leprosy, an incurably fatal disease in those days (see 2 Kings 5:1-14). He had traveled to Israel to visit the prophet Elisha in search of a cure. The prophet's prescription was, "Dip seven times in the River Jordan, and be healed of your leprosy." Naaman became furious and drove his chariot away in a rage. After all, weren't the Syrian rivers, Abanah and Pharpar better than all the waters of Israel (v. 12)? Now there was a man who truly "could not see the forest for the trees." His servant (who obviously didn't share his master's nearsightedness) shared this simple yet profound insight: "Had the prophet told you to do some great thing, would you not have done it? How much more then, when he says to you, 'Wash and be clean'?" (2 Kings 5:13). Naaman turned his chariot around, dipped seven times in the Jordan, and was healed.

Many believers live in a state of constant discouragement; others vacillate between victory and defeat; and most content themselves with living mediocre spiritual lives. All of them share one common denominator: they all live far beneath their scriptural station and privileges in Christ! A few, like cream, rise to the top and become radiant examples of the Christ-life within them. As we view the sorry state of the current Church, we are confronted with the realization that some key ingredient must be lacking in their formula for greatness. This chapter will address this missing ingredient.

We've discussed deeply profound revelations from Scripture that unveil the awesome destiny of the Church. But what will ultimately bring about their metamorphosis into the "glorious Church, without spot or wrinkle"? Prayer? Fasting? Bible study? Better church services? A combination of some, or all of the above? Actually, every one of the above will play a role in the development of believers into the image of Christ. But the major role will be played by another spiritual exercise—praise and worship. We learned in an earlier chapter that the priestly turban (which speaks of our position as worshipers) must be in place before we are permitted to don the kingly crown (which signifies our position of power and authority in Christ).

How Do I Praise And Worship?

If you have ever asked that question (or been afraid to ask it) you need not feel embarrassed—you are not by any means alone. (Perhaps the subtitle above should have been, "Everything You Ever Wanted to Know About Praise and Worship—But Were Afraid to Ask.") The question of how to praise and worship also plagued me for many years before I found a satisfying answer, which I would like to pass along to you.

First of all, a distinction must be made between praise and worship. It may be a fine line (and sometimes we may cross back and forth over it), but there is a difference. Praise seems to have more to do with thanking God for what He *does* (miracles, signs, wonders, provision, blessings, etc.). The word "worship," derived from an old English word, "*worth*ship," meaning "to ascribe worth (weightiness) to," seems to have more to do with who He *is* (King of kings, Lord of lords, eternal Father, Lamb of God, etc.) and His attributes (love, mercy, kindness, generosity, *et al*). Purely and simply put, the ultimate goal of worship is to express passionate, fervent love to Jesus. Praise is often loud and exuberant, whereas worship is usually more subdued, softer, and gentler. (It would seem out of place to *yell*, "**I LOVE YOU**" at someone, wouldn't it?)

Praise, whether spoken, sung, shouted, or danced is a great way to get started. I often open my personal worship sessions by praying or singing in the Spirit (see 1 Cor. 14:15; Jude 20). Some people have a problem articulating (speaking out) their praise. If you do (as I once did), begin at the mental level and think your praise—but think it *fervently*. You might begin by thanking Him for some of the many things He's done for you (healings provision, a good job, wonderful family, etc.) and/or beautiful things He's created (blue sky, birds, water, green trees, etc.). That could be a long list, but you don't have to thank Him for *everything* at once—you just might want to leave some things for next time.

At first, you may experience a problem common to most people. You have to think so much about what to say that your praise seems mechanical.[1] This may temporarily be the case, but it won't continue for long. Remember how you faltered over every other word the first few times you tried to tell that special someone how wonderful you thought he was? At times you might even have said something stupid (of course, not *you*). But did it stop you? Absolutely not, because it was of utmost importance for your beloved to know how you felt! Perhaps you even went on to marry that person. (Husband, I hope you *continue* to tell her how much she means to you.) The least fulfilling marriages are those in which one partner (usually the man) refuses to

---

1. To help you, I've composed a booklet entitled "Praises Phrases," ® © filled with phrases of praise and worship. Write: Burton W. Seavey, 10350 Royal Oak Court, Osceola, IN 46561 for pricing.

talk, just talk to the other, and they share no meaningful communication. Those relationships are doomed to failure before they begin. In the Song of Solomon, the Bride said, "This is my beloved and *this is my friend*" (5:16). Friends talk—they talk a lot. Because Jesus is our friend, we ought to spend much time talking to (and praising) Him.

When offering praise, any posture is acceptable to God. Scripture speaks of standing, kneeling, leaping, clapping, dancing, lying down on one's bed, and prostrating oneself (to lie with the face on the ground). When I'm leading public praise and worship, I enjoy walking back and forth across the platform. During praise or worship, your posture is not important to God, but it is quite important to *you*. Try to avoid physical discomfort, because that is always a distraction that Satan will exploit.

Some readers may call attention to the account where, after having been beaten, Paul and Silas sang praises in prison despite great pain. True, point well taken. However, they were not novices when it came to praise and worship—they were leaders! Our goal is to learn to praise, so that when unpleasant situations arise, we will be able to overcome them as Paul and Silas did. We will then praise God in *spite* of the physical, mental, or emotional distractions that beset us.

When learning to praise, discomfort or pain can pose a needless distraction that will prevent you from freely worshiping your Lord and King. Sometimes older people or those with physical restrictions cannot stand throughout a lengthy worship service. Perhaps your work load was excessive that week, and you're simply too tired to stand. Whatever the circumstances, select a posture that will enhance your ability to worship. (Just be careful you don't become too relaxed and fall asleep!) If I'm not leading a service, I sometimes sit down during the praise even though others are standing.

Praise and Worship at Home

Yes, *at home*! Too many Christians restrict themselves to the 20-25 minute song service that many churches call a worship service. Others enjoy great worship at church, but never indulge at home. Both groups wonder why they're so often down and out of victory. The diagnosis is "spiritual anemia," due in large part to limited praise and worship. No, the prescription is not, "Take two aspirins, and if you're no better in the morning, call me." The remedy for your spiritual pains and general weakness is a large dose of praise and worship—several times every day.

One great problem plaguing worship leaders is that people arrive at church all worn out, simply unprepared to worship. Helping to guide them into praise is akin to priming an old rusty pump, and just about as rewarding. Just when the people begin to feel like praising the Lord, the worship part of the service is over. That can easily be remedied if you will praise and worship at home, and then in the car while on the way to service. When you arrive at church you won't have any major mental gear shifting to go through before entering into praise and worship. Obviously, if you love the Lord only on Sunday, then you will praise and worship Him only on Sunday. If you truly *love* the Lord all week long, you will praise and worship Him all week long! Then, what you do at church will simply be an extension of what you've been doing throughout the week. Perhaps the frequency and intensity of your praise and worship are true barometers of the depth and intensity of your love for Him

Paul admonished the Thessalonians to, "Pray *without ceasing*" (1 Thess. 5:17). The phrase "without ceasing" originates from a Greek word meaning "incessantly." Given the average church member's interpretation of prayer (that we present God with our shopping list of wants, desires, "greeds," and "gimmees"), praying incessantly would be virtually impossible to do and still function in the physical world and provide for our families, etc. Fortunately, prayer is *far* more than asking—it is primarily communion and fellowship. We are told to be in *incessant fellowship and communion with the Lord*! In much the same way, praise should fill your every waking moment, not be simply a mechanical exercise or ritual performed at church once a week. You can even praise God mentally in public places. (I do.) You can discipline your mind (I have) so that it will automatically shift into praise and worship, even speaking and singing in the Spirit, when not engaged in some otherwise necessary function. It works. Try it—you'll like it! When you accomplish this, it will be the beginning of a new life of victory for you.

Upon taking an honest mental inventory you might discover that instead of a mind filled with God, you've got the stinkin' thinkin' we mentioned in a previous chapter. A great deal of our time is often spent mentally griping, finding fault, complaining, etc. Often mingled with those unpleasantries (and sometimes prompted by them) are darker thoughts—impure thoughts. Some Christians even harbor thoughts of hatred, jealousy, lust, and envy, to name but a few. Enlarging the list would be impressive but needless—you know what constitutes a dark thought. Whatever God does, or has, Satan emulates, impersonates, or counterfeits in one fashion or another. As God inhabits the praises of His people, Satan similarly inhabits the *dark thoughts*. They are his fortresses—the strongholds from which he wages war against us. But he becomes entrenched there only when that position is yielded to him. Psalm 22:3 tells us that God inhabits (lives in) the praises of His people; thus when you fill your mind with praise, you are filling it with God. Since God inhabits praise, perhaps we should move in with Him, and *live* in praise!

The enemy cannot endure hearing the praises of God. It was not by chance that the first fortified city encountered in Canaan (Jericho) was conquered as Israel shouted praise to God. In yet another passage (see 2 Chron. 20:14-24) we read how the armies of Moab, Ammon, and Mount Seir came to fight against Judah ("Judah" means *praise*). Satan hates praise, unless it's directed toward him. In verse 21, God instructed King Jehoshaphat to set those who sang and praised out in front of the army—an unheard-of tactic in any military situation. As the people praised the Lord, God set their enemies against one another; so that those who had originally come out against God's people, now destroyed each other. God grant us the wisdom to learn from that illustration. If you will diligently praise God, no matter how you feel, or what the circumstances may be, the weapon of praise will destroy longstanding mental strongholds. By consistently filling your mind, heart, home, car, workplace, etc. with His praises, you will notice a marked improvement in your mental attitude almost immediately. As your mind becomes totally absorbed in praise and worship (see Phil. 4:7-8), it gradually crowds out all negative (dark) thoughts, and collapses those formidable walls behind which Satan has concealed himself for so long.

Music—A Doorway Into Spirit

Music is an extremely important facet of the diamond of worship that often opens the door to the dimension of Spirit. The narrative in Second Kings 3:15 lends some insight into the role that music plays to aid our entry into His Presence. This Scripture records that when the prophet Elisha desired to hear a word from God he said, " 'But now bring me a minstrel.' And it came about, when the minstrel played, that the hand of the Lord came upon him." Elisha was a man well acquainted with the power of God, having performed twice the number of miracles of his predecessor Elijah. Yet, Holy Spirit-anointed music was the *instrument* (no pun intended) he relied upon to usher him into the very Presence of God.

King Saul was troubled by an evil spirit (demon), and nothing he tried brought him any relief until David played anointed music. The scriptural narrative explains that, "So it came about whenever the evil spirit from God came to Saul, David would take the harp and play it with his hand; and Saul would be refreshed and be well, and the evil spirit would depart from him" (1 Sam. 16:23; see also 16:14-23). From the foregoing record it's obvious that demons recognize anointed music as a direct threat to their kingdom and power—they fled when David played his harp.

At Philippi, after being severely beaten with rods, Paul and Silas found themselves imprisoned in the inner dungeon (a most unusual place to conduct a praise and worship service). "But about midnight Paul and Silas were praying and *singing hymns of praise to God...*and suddenly there came a great earthquake...and immediately all the doors were opened, and everyone's chains were unfastened" (Acts 16:25-26; see also 16:22-30). These scriptural records show that the Holy Spirit, demon spirits, nature (earthquake), stocks, chains, and prison doors all respond to holy, anointed music. Perhaps we ought to investigate more closely what role anointed music should play in our lives.[2]

Choose anointed Christian music that *ministers* to you, not necessarily songs that get your feet to tapping (although they might). Don't select some trite Christian jingle, but music that truly exalts and glorifies God. It should be music that reaches inside, grips your heart and spirit, and moves you toward a desire to worship God. (I'm fortunate to have discovered many examples of such music. In fact,

---

2. For more information on music as it relates to the supernatural, see my book, *Christian Meditation: Doorway to the Spirit,* chapter 17, "Learning to Hear the Voice of God."

I've listened to one particular CD for hours on end for a total of hundreds of hours, and never grow weary of it.[3] No, I don't earn a commission!) If lyrics are a distraction, play music without words. Most of the time I fill my office, home, and car with Christian music, because I've discovered that it helps cultivate an atmosphere of continual praise and worship. Background music (both Christian and secular) is absorbed into your subconscious mind and becomes a part of your personality.

My favorite (although not my only) positions when worshiping God at home are sitting in a comfortable recliner, lying down on the sofa, or prostrate on my face before Him. With music at a low volume, I relax and attempt to block out all mental distractions (see 2 Cor. 10:5). Then I meditate by simply relaxing my mind and body and, as much as is possible, by laying aside all earthly distractions, problems, business, etc.

Visualization

Some Christians enhance the practice of His Presence by using visualization. This can be a valuable tool in clearing your mind of other thoughts. At times I visualize Jesus standing before me, and I gaze upon His radiant beauty. At other times I see the throne room of Heaven, with the brilliance of His Presence emanating from His Majesty. If you desire to use visualization to enhance your praise and worship, allow your imagination to direct what form your mental pictures will take. Often, in deep worship, actual spiritual visions will replace your own visualization.

Easy Does It!

The literal translation of Psalm 46:10 is, *"Let go, relax and know that I am God"* (emph. mine), so I take Him at His word. I never struggle to think of key worship phrases. I often begin by praying in the Spirit for a brief period, then continue by saying things like, "I praise you, Lord. I love you so much; I desire to love you even more. Hallelujah, glory to God," etc. At the outset, these worship thoughts come from my mind and seem to originate in the front of my brain. These praises are generated consciously, but with as little mental

---

3.   The Brooklyn Tabernacle Choir, "Live With Friends."

effort as possible (after all, God is not impressed by our originality, but by our desire to be in His Presence). As I continue, a mental shift occurs, at which time the praises seem to generate from *all* parts of my brain.

With further relaxation, the area of my worshiping shifts to the solar plexus (the stomach area just below the ribs). How often have you heard someone say (while indicating their solar plexus area), "I just feel it in my spirit"? When the praise seems to be originating from that area, another shift occurs and I begin to truly *worship* the Lamb of God, my Savior and my Friend. I'm convinced that at these moments all my conscious efforts cease, and my spirit begins to lead worship with a freedom that I cannot explain. Gradually, I become increasingly aware of His Presence filling the room and my entire being. Words fail me to define the overwhelming glory that often sweeps over me as I welcome His Presence. There have been numerous occasions when I've been so completely engulfed in His radiance that I have lost all conscious awareness of my physical surroundings (see Acts 10:10; 11:5; 22:17). Often, when carried away in His sweet companionship, He has shared visions of things to come—the details of which were subsequently all minutely fulfilled. On other occasions, the sweet fragrance of the Rose of Sharon has wafted into my prayer closet; and twice the distinctive aroma of incense penetrated my season of worship. Somehow, at those moments in time, I knew I had crossed over the threshold and entered the Holy of Holies. After experiencing these times of intense worship and communication, I've found that a special sense of His Presence lingers for hours—sometimes for days afterward. I've discovered that the more frequently and passionately I worship and adore Him, the longer His Presence follows after. Continually living in an attitude of praise and worship is one way for believers to learn to walk in the Spirit. I'm anticipating the day when I will no longer be distracted by this world or my flesh—attracted *only* by the awareness of His Presence.

We often speak of the Presence of God as alternately coming or leaving when in reality these terms are misleading. God's Presence doesn't come and go with the capriciousness of the wind—He is *always* present! We are simply not *aware* of (or *sensitive to*) His *being* there. We have been instructed that God is in Heaven. Thus, we have come to believe that He is not always present here. But He desires that we become sensitive to His continual Presence in our lives, aware that He is always with us. Praise and worship will do just that for you. It will enable you to discern His Presence, *i.e.*, what it *feels* like to sense (be aware of) Him. As with everything in life, there are three things that make for success: (1) practice, (2) practice, and (3) *more* practice. (Remember, the word is *discipline*.) Diligently practicing His Presence on a daily basis will cause you to become more and more sensitive to Him. Ultimately, your spiritual metamorphosis will be complete and every waking hour will bring an acute awareness of His Presence. It was this same sensitivity that enabled Jesus to be constantly aware of the Father's Presence and activity. A ministry of spectacular miracles was the result. Jesus' desire for His Church is that we come to know and experience Him in the same way He knew and experienced the Father. As your awareness of His Presence grows, so also will personal holiness. Like Isaiah, you will see Him in His radiant holiness and recognize your own shortcomings. But you will also come to another life-changing realization: His Presence imparts cleansing, healing, overcoming power, and His very own holiness. With that realization, sin will lose its grip as you become "partakers of the divine nature" (2 Pet. 1:4) "until Christ is formed in you" (Gal. 4:19) and "we *all* attain to the unity of the faith, and of the knowledge of the Son of God, to a mature man, to the measure of the stature which belongs to the fulness of Christ" (Eph. 4:13).

"The Beginning"